Human Rights and UN Peace Operations: Yugoslavia

Human Rights and UN Peace Operations: Yugoslavia

By

Bertrand G. Ramcharan

MARTINUS NIJHOFF PUBLISHERS

LEIDEN • BOSTON
2011

This book is printed on acid-free paper.

Library of Congress Cataloging-in-Publication Data

Ramcharan, B. G.
Human rights and UN peace operations : Yugoslavia / By Bertrand G. Ramcharan.
p. cm.
Includes bibliographical references and index.
ISBN 978-90-04-20296-2 (hardback : alk. paper) 1. Human rights--Yugoslavia. 2. Civil rights--Yugoslavia. 3. United Nations--Peacekeeping forces. 4. United Nations Protection Force. I. Title.
KKZ2460.R36 2011
341.4'809497--dc23

2011022313

ISBN 978 90 04 20296 2

The Security Council strongly condemns
these acts of unspeakable brutality

Security Council resolution 798 (1992)

Give us bombs for peace.
Richard Holbrook[1]

Give us the health and strength to be peacemakers
Ecumenical Prayer[2]

We welcome your decision to convene in special session to consider the serious situation of human rights in the area of the former Yugoslavia, especially in Bosnia and Herzegovina.

Regrettably, the disgraceful practice of ethnic cleansing has not ceased and violations of international norms on human rights and humanitarian law are rampant. We condemn these violations in the most categorical terms.

In our efforts to promote peace with justice in the area of the former Yugoslavia, we have placed emphasis on the provision of humanitarian assistance; the strict application of sanctions; helping to bring about a cessation of hostilities in Bosnia and Herzegovina; and the preparation of a constitution for Bosnia and Herzegovina. We have also sought to promote preventive measures to avoid the spread of the conflict. We would draw your attention to the recent report submitted by the Secretary-General to the Security Council on the activities of the International Conference. It provides detailed information on our activities.

We urge the distinguished members of the Commission on Human Rights, all Member States of the United Nations, and non-governmental organizations, to do everything possible to support and to strengthen

[1] R. Holbrooke, To End a War. New York, Random House, 1998. p.132. Holbrook was making the case to Washington and NATO for a sustained bombing campaign against the Serbs. He continued: "Give us a resumption of the bombing by morning "!

[2] Ecumenical prayer, Meeting of the Commission of the Churches on International Affairs, St. Vlash Theological Academy, Durres, Albania, 7 October, 2010.

the endeavours being undertaken in accordance with decisions of the Security Council of the United Nations.

We hope that your session will help in bringing an end to the violations of human rights and humanitarian law taking place. We also hope that you will give attention to the important question of protecting the rights of minorities. This issue is of great importance to the future stability and security in the area of the former Yugoslavia.

We wish you a successful session.

Message of the Co-Chairmen of the International Conference on the Former Yugoslavia[3] to the United Nations Commission on Human Rights, 30 November, 1992

[3] Cyrus Vance and Lord David Owen

CONTENTS

HUMANITARIAN PLEAS

1

Statement delivered by Dr. Cornelio Sommaruga, President of the International Committee of the Red Cross (ICRC) to the London Conference on the Former Yugoslavia 26 August, 1992

"The ICRC has rarely been so outspoken while active in a country affected by conflict. Following several public appeals launched since the ICRC first began work in the former Yugoslavia on 29 June, 1992… the ICRC issued a solemn appeal to the parties to the conflict on 13 August, 1992, urging them to respect civilians and prisoners and to comply with the Geneva Conventions in general.

"All these appeals were made necessary by the seriousness of the humanitarian situation in the former Yugoslavia, particularly in Bosnia-Herzegovina. They were launched following meetings held under ICRC auspices with representatives of the parties involved in this armed conflict…

"However, when bilateral steps are not sufficient to improve the plight of the victims, showing that traditional means are insufficient to restore respect for international humanitarian law, we have to move on to other measures, such as public statements and appeals to all the States party to the Geneva Conventions of 1949.

…

"Today I appeal to you again. The way in which hostilities are being conducted in Bosnia-Herzegovina leaves no room for humanity:

- The civilian population is systematically harassed: thousands of civilians are arrested in their homes, brutalized or even killed.
- Whole minority groups comprising tens of thousands of civilians are systematically transferred by force or, as is currently the case in Sanski Most, driven without any protection towards and across front lines.
- Hundreds of thousands of civilians have been besieged for several months in cities such as Bihac, Bosanski Brod, Derventa, Gorazde and Sarajevo.

- Detainees, the majority of whom are civilians, are held in conditions of extreme hardship in places of detention which are totally inadequate for the purpose. They are ill-treated and hundreds of them have been executed, either in places to which the ICRC has been denied access or in places to which the ICRC has been allowed to visit only after the executions had stopped.
- Hospitals and other public and private property are not respected, to say the least. The Red Cross emblem is totally disregarded, so humanitarian convoys have in some instances to be accompanied by armed escorts.
- The ICRC has not been allowed to monitor the situation properly in the field. Indeed, it has been denied access to several areas of Bosnia-Herzegovina for lack of necessary authorization and/or security guarantees. The ICRC has therefore not been able to bring protection and assistance in time to all civilians affected by the conflict.

"This unacceptable situation cannot go on. The humanitarian organizations have done everything within their power to bring about more humanity in this conflict, but I can only say this is not enough. The time has come for the international community of States to assume its responsibilities.

"This is now imperative....

...

"Please, behave with more humanity, respect prisoners and civilians, and envisage solutions that will permit a return to normal life.

...

"I hope that this Conference will be able to work out a peaceful settlement to this conflict, which has already gone on far too long. The most pressing needs are to ensure better protection for the civilian population and to make conditions safe and acceptable for detainees."[4]

* * * * *

[4] LC/R28. Text in the possession of the author. It bears mentioning that after this searing humanitarian appeal, the principal response of the London Conference was to call for continuous negotiations among the Bosnian parties in Geneva to find a peaceful settlement to the conflict. Thus it was that the late Cyrus Vance and Lord David Owen began the process of negotiations a week later in Geneva. The arms embargo was maintained; and no one contemplated peace enforcement at this stage.

2

International Conference on the Former Yugoslavia
press statement, 24 September, 1992

"The Co-Chairmen[5] are deeply concerned about reports which have just reached them from the Banja Luka region indicating a build-up of tension, bomb incidents, and intimidation with the potential threat of violence and the development of an ethnic-cleansing campaign.

"This morning the Co-Chairmen called in Ambassador Pavicevic of the Federal Republic of Yugoslavia, and Dr. Koljevic, the Bosnian Serb representative, and urged that immediate steps be taken to reduce tensions in the area.

"In view of the urgency of the situation, the Co-Chairmen have decided to fly to Banja Luka tomorrow. There they will assess the situation on the ground, and speak to representatives of the local communities and humanitarian agencies."[6]

* * * * *

3

International Conference on the Former Yugoslavia
"Notes of a meeting with delegation of Bosnian Serbs,
Thursday 8 October, 1992, 2—3pm"

"Attendance: Mr. Vance, Lord Owen, Mr. Ahtisaari, Mr. Szasz (ICFY) Dr. Karadzic, Mr. Buha (Bosnian Serbs).

"Mr. Vance: First of all, ethnic cleansing is getting worse.

"Dr. Karadzic: Need details.

"Mr. Vance: We know that yesterday there had been a meeting of the BH Serb Parliament in Banja Luka at which the local administration had come under heavy attack because ethnic cleansing was not going fast enough; that was a totally unacceptable reaction to the Co-Chairmen's visit the previous week. Furthermore, the Muslim leaders who had talked to the Co-Chairmen during that visit had been called to the Serbian party headquarters for questioning; that too was

[5] Cyrus Vance and Lord David Owen.
[6] Press Release in the possession of the author.

entirely unacceptable. Finally, reports had reached us that in Kator Varos the entire Muslim population had been arrested.

“Dr. Karadzic: The radicals, i.e. the extreme rightists, in Parliament were not representative of the whole; it was they who had conducted the attack. My party was more moderate.

“Mr. Vance: Did the moderates speak up?

“Dr. Karadzic: The majority in Parliament is opposed to the extreme rightists; however, the radicals are getting more and more influential. I guarantee that the Muslim leaders would be protected. In any event, what is happening to the Serbs in Sarajevo is much worse than anything in Banja Luka. The Muslims had just announced that they had just killed some 250 Serbs.

“Mr. Vance: This cannot justify what is happening in Banja Luka. It was not acceptable to harass those who had spoken to the Co-Chairmen.

“Dr. Karadzic: Mr. Vance is right. If something like that should happen again, Dr. Karadzic would replace the local party leader. But his moderates were losing influence to the radicals.

“Mr. Vance: It wasn't apparent that Mr. Karadzic was losing influence.

“Dr. Karadzic: Showed pictures from a local magazine of foreign Muslims holding heads of slain Serbs.

…

“Lord Owen: Majority of EEC Foreign Ministers are for a War Crimes Tribunal. What about the reported arrest of Muslims in Kator Varos.

“Dr. Karadzic: There is fighting going on around there.

“Mr. Vance/Lord Owen: The horror there is unacceptable to the world community.

“Dr. Karadzic: The world doesn't quite understand what is going on… The European Union shares responsibility for what has happened, for everyone knew the consequences of recognizing Bosnia and Herzegovina prematurely. It must not be forgotten that 50 years ago, 750,000 Serbs were killed. Now his party was preparing a White Book on Muslim war crimes; there are already hundreds of names.

“Lord Owen: History is not the point—the issue is what is happening at present. Right now there is an opportunity to negotiate.

"Dr. Karadzic: I have never committed a war crime. I have publicly condemned those (Serbs) who have committed any; we will try them ourselves.

...

"Mr. Vance: Who are the snipers in Sarajevo?

Dr. Karadzic: The Serbs have no snipers. Those are the 'green berets', who are commanded by criminals.

...

"Mr. Ahtisaari: Important that the time be used before people start dying in the winter. The political leaders will be blamed. ...."[7]

* * * * *

4

International Conference on the Former Yugoslavia press statement, 23 October, 1992 "Vance and Owen warn that carve-up of Bosnia and Herzegovina will not be tolerated"

"The international community will not tolerate the taking of territory by force, nor acquiesce in ethnic cleansing, Lord Owen and Cyrus Vance said at a press conference today. Responding to reports that B-H in fact had been carved up by Serbian and Croatian forces, the two Co-Chairmen of the International Conference on the Former Yugoslavia said that the status quo on the ground was not acceptable, and that international recognition and the lifting of sanctions would not take place until a political solution had been found.

"This is not going to be settled by people who have taken up arms, and have abandoned humanitarian principles, and trampled on international law.," Lord Owen told the assembled correspondents. "We do not accept this status quo as permanent", he added, "and we intend to see that it is changed." While some advocated the use of force, he went on, the Geneva Conference would use other methods that in the end would triumph. Mr. Vance agreed, saying, "That is the way we will act;

[7] Excerpted from a Note on the Meeting by Paul C. Szasz, PCS, 09/10/92. Text in the possession of the author. Spellings are as in the Note.

that is what we expect to happen; and we will not be turned back in our determination to see that happen."[8]

*****

5

Statement by Mrs Sadako Ogata, UN High Commissioner for Refugees and Chairperson of the Humanitarian Issues Working Group of ICFY 27 October, 1992

"You should rest assured that I shall continue to expose the persistent practice of ethnic cleansing, especially in North-West Bosnia. During both the September and October meetings I have reminded all parties of their London commitments to respect international humanitarian law and human rights. The freedom of movement is an important human right, which should be respected on all sides, but it should not be used to facilitate the abhorrent practice of ethnic cleansing, as part of a cruel strategy to compartmentalise Bosnia and Herzegovina. In my Working Group, and elsewhere, I shall continue to insist on the right to stay, in conditions of security, and on the responsibility of everyone to ensure respect for this right. I have asked the Serbian side (Dr. Karadzic) in particular to take measures to prevent the outbreak of ethnic cleansing in Banja Luka town, where the harassment of non-Serbs has thus far been less violent than in many surrounding towns and villages.

"Despite the commitments of the parties the situation on the ground remains critical. The very day I talked to the parties here in Geneva, a UNHCR convoy on its way to Sarajevo was shelled near Mostar. Last week fighting broke out between the Croatian side and governmental forces in Central Bosnia, a region which accommodates under very difficult conditions a large and ever rising number of displaced persons. As a result I havc been compelled to suspend all land deliveries, from Split to Sarajevo and Central Bosnia, whereas my staff in Vitez had to be evacuated."[9]

*****

[8] Press Release of the International Conference on the Former Yugoslavia, 23 October, 1992. Text in the possession of the author.

[9] Statement by Mrs Sadako Ogata, UN High Commissioner for Refugees and Chairperson of the ICFY Working Group on Humanitarian Issues to the ICFY Steering Committee, Geneva, 27 October, 1992.

6

Secretary-General expresses indignation at inexcusable assault on civilians in Srebrenica, calls on Bosnian Serb forces to halt unjustifiable attacks, 15 April, 1993

The following statement was issued today by Secretary-General Boutros Boutros-Chali:

"Over the last two days, I have received reports on the situation in the town of Srebrenica in Bosnia and Herzegovina. I wish to express my indignation at the inexcusable assault on civilians in that town. I condemn the shelling of Srebrenica by Bosnian Serb forces, which has inflicted further casualties and destruction upon its suffering residents and upon the displaced people who have sought refuge there.

"I urgently call upon the Bosnian Serb forces in the area to halt their unjustifiable attacks, which have occurred despite explicit assurances to the contrary from their military and political leaders. I also renew my appeal to all concerned to cooperate with the efforts of the Force Commander of the United Nations Protection Force (UNPROFOR) to restore a cease-fire and to allow free passage and the unimpeded delivery of humanitarian assistance."[10]

* * * * *

7

Security Council Resolution 761 (1992)

"10. Reaffirms that all parties are bound to comply with the obligations under international humanitarian law and in particular the Geneva Conventions of 12 August 1949 and that persons who commit or order the commission of grave breaches of the Conventions are individually responsible in respect of such breaches."

Security Council Resolution 787 (1992)

"2. Reaffirms that any taking of territory by force or any practice of 'ethnic cleansing' is unlawful and unacceptable and will not be

[10] UN Press Release, SG/SM/4978, 15 April, 1993.

permitted to affect the outcome of the negotiations on constitutional arrangements for the Republic of Bosnia and Herzegovina and insists that all displaced persons be enabled to return in peace to their former homes.

"7. Condemns all violations of international humanitarian law in particular the practice of 'ethnic cleansing' and the deliberate impeding of the delivery of food and medical supplies to the civilian population of the Republic of Bosnia and Herzegovina, and reaffirms that those that commit or order the commission of such acts will be held individually responsible in respect of such acts."

Security Council Resolution 798 (1992)

"Strongly condemns these acts of unspeakable brutality".

*****

8

Secretary-General warns that emergency food supplies in former Yugoslavia will run out in days; appeals to donors to ensure adequate food

The following statement was issued by the Spokesman for Secretary-General Boutros Boutros-Ghali on 12 April, 1993:

"Secretary-General Boutros Boutros-Ghali today warned that emergency food supplies for refugees and displaced people in parts of former Yugoslavia, particularly Bosnia and Herzegovina, will run out within days. He called on the international donor community to act with speed to provide the food needed to prevent high rates of deaths from starvation.

"The Secretary-General said the United Nations has already reached the point in the former Yugoslavia where the most severely affected have only a few days of food supplies and trucks are standing idle because there is no food to transport.

"Despite several conferences and many appeals that have been issued by the United Nations and the two agencies directly involved in providing relief supplies to former Yugoslavia, the United Nations High Commissioner for Refugees (UNHCR) and the World Food Programme (WFP), neither food nor the necessary funds have been forthcoming in sufficient quantity.

"The Secretary-General said that despite all efforts by the United Nations agencies involved to find more food supplies for former Yugoslavia, a breakdown in the food supply pipeline for the remainder of April is inevitable. He appealed to the donor community to do everything possible to ensure adequate food for the affected population in former Yugoslavia in the months to come."

*****

9

Report of the UN Secretary-General to the Security Council 13 November, 1993[11]

Report on the attack on two United Nations convoys near Novi Travnik on 25 October 1993

"1. The attack upon two humanitarian convoys…begain at approximately 0830 local time on 25 October, 1993…

"2. As a result of the attack, the Danish Refugee Council convoy sustained one fatality and one casualty and the UNPROFOR convoy sustained nine casualties.

"4. The Board of Inquiry concluded, based on the result of the joint investigation, that the convoys entered into the area unaware that a battle had just begun between HVO and Bosnian government forces. They were directly targeted… The evidence collected by the investigation indicated that the cabins of the vehicles were the principal target. The possibility that some impacts may have been the result of crossfire is considered highly improbable…The investigation concluded that the attacks upon the convoys were carried out by a few individuals, and the killing of the civilian driver was, with high probability, a deliberate act. The evidence available has led the Board to conclude that the attack on both convoys was deliberate.

"5. The investigation revealed that Bosnia and Herzegovina forces had infiltrated HVO positions in the area the night before the attack. The position from which the targeting of the convoys occurred was considered to have been held by Bosnian forces at the time of the incident. The investigation thus concluded that, with high probability, the

[11] S/26742, 13 November, 1993.

responsibility for the attack lies with soldiers of the Bosnian government forces.

"8. On 9 November, 1993, Mr. Stoltenberg met with Prime Minister Silajdzic in Sarajevo and Mr. Boban in Split to discuss the finding of the Board of Inquiry…Mr. Stoltenberg discussed the conclusion of the Board of Inquiry that the death of the driver, Mr. Bjarne Nielsen, was, with high probability, a deliberate act and that it was highly probable that the firing came from an area controlled by Bosnian government forces. Mr. Stoltenberg said that it was incumbent upon the responsible authorities to ensure that the person or persons responsible were arrested and brought to justice. It was also imperative that immediate measures be taken by all responsible authorities to prevent further attacks on humanitarian convoys and United Nations personnel and to guarantee their safety."[12]

*****

10

Thorvald Stoltenberg to the Security Council

"… Mr. President, it is important to note that—along with the constant activity of the Geneva Conference—Lord Owen and I have sought to keep certain basic principles clearly in view.

"The Council and the General Assemby have spelled out the guidelines for devising solutions to problems in the former Yugoslavia. You have called for a political settlement consistent with the principles of the Charter and of international norms on human rights. You have rightly condemned forcible expulsions, illegal detentions, and all attempts to change the demographic composition of territories. You have invoked the principles of the OSCE, in particular the inviolability of borders—both internal and external—and the non-recognition of attempts to alter such borders unilaterally.

"The General Assembly has also called for peaceful solutions in line with the Charter and the principles of international law. It has expressly mentioned respect for the sovereignty and the territorial integrity of States, non-recognition of the spoils of aggression and of the acquisition of territory by force.

[12] No one was, to the knowledge of the author, ever charged or brought to justice.

"I mention these statements of principle in order to emphasize a simple, but crucial point: the international community cannot accept non-compliance with these guidelines.

"As Co-Chairmen of the Steering Committee, our mandate requires that we maintain lines of communication with all sides, while preserving our neutrality and independence. Other United Nations bodies are looking into violations of human rights and humanitarian law. We are cooperating with them—and will continue to do so. I do, however, want to underscore my firm conviction that there can be no compromise when it comes to respect for the principles of the Charter, and of the international norms of human rights and humanitarian law."

FOREWORD

I am pleased that Bertie Ramcharan, my close partner and friend in peacemaking, peacekeeping, peace-building, humanitarian and human rights operations in the former Yugoslavia for three years has written this objective study of the role of human rights in UN peace operations in the former Yugoslavia, covering the period 1992-1996, which is the period of the International Conference on the Former Yugoslavia (ICFY) of which he was Director and Political/Legal Adviser to the Co-Chairman, first Cyrus Vance and Lord Own, then Lord Owen and myself, and in the closing phase, Carl Bildt and myself. I have much friendship for him and his family (Lily and Robin) but this does not influence the high regard I have for him for his dedication, hard work, and inventiveness during our cooperation. I have written about this elsewhere.[13]

He was at my side throughout during the three years I served as Co-Chairman (Negotiator) of the Steering Committee of ICFY and, within that period, during the year when I served simultaneously as Special Representative of the UN Secretary-General in charge of UNPROFOR and all UN operations in the former Yugoslavia. He advised, he drafted, he helped me deal with emergencies, and he helped me operate the system for the use of air power under UN Security Council resolution 836, a system that he himself helped to shape. He was the author of numerous human rights positions of ICFY and UNPROFOR that he writes about in this book.

When I joined ICFY in April/May, 1993, human rights concerns in Bosnia and elsewhere in the former Yugoslavia were everywhere in the media. My boyhood and life-long friend, the late Professor Torkel Opsahl, particularly impressed upon me the importance of putting human rights at the centre of the peace process. Torkel was at the time a member of the UN Commission of Experts looking into war crimes and crimes against humanity in the former Yugoslavia. He died at his desk in Geneva while performing this task. Bertie and I were in Istanbul attending a meeting with the Foreign Minister when I heard this distressing news.

---

[13] T. Stoltenberg, De tusen dagen: Fredsmedlere pa Balkan, 1996. (Memoirs on his efforts as a peacemaker and peacekeeper in the Balkans).

When I became, simultaneously, Special Representative of the Secretary General (SRSG) in charge of all UN operation in the former Yugoslavia in May, 1993, Torkel had urged me to make sure that UNPROFOR contribute to the protection of human rights. I asked Bertie Ramcharan, as Director of the Office of the SRSG in Zagreb, to pursue this matter with the military leadership of UNPROFOR. He did this and this initiative would lead to a change in the policy and practice of UN peacekeeping forces inasmuch as they began to share information within the UN on human rights violations. As we would see later, UN forces came to use force, in the end, for the defence of civilian populations. United Nations peacekeeping changed for ever in the former Yugoslavia.

At one stage, Bertie Ramcharan wrote for me a study on our efforts in the former Yugoslavia and gave it the title, Mission, Morality, Mediation. I had my mission from the UN Secretary-General and the UN Security Council, I tried to integrate moral considerations in the course of the mediation and peacekeeping work, and I had to deal with the political and military realities on the ground in the peacemaking, peacekeeping and humanitarian processes.

There were many wrenching situations we had to deal with, and it was not easy to advance the human rights cause in the midst of brutal military and political leaders on all sides in the conflicts in Bosnia and Croatia. I had been a former UN High Commissioner for Refugees, and I had much feeling for my successor, the hearty Sadako Ogata, and her Personal Envoy in the former Yugoslavia, my good friend Nicholas Morris. Nicholas and his colleagues submitted to me as SRSG the most heart-rending accounts of ethnic cleansing and other atrocities and I, and Lord David Owen, my partner and friend in the negotiations, spoke to the political leaders on many occasions with varying results. But at the time, few Governments, if any, were willing to see UN peacekeepers go into battle against those who violated basic norms of humanitarian and human rights law. That would come only in 1994 -1995 when Bosnian Serb atrocities brought the international community to go to war against them. The Security Council had instituted an arms embargo and had given me, as UN negotiator, a mandate to pursue negotiated solutions. At the end of the day, the way to end the atrocities was to negotiate an honourable peace.

We had many good blueprints for peace in Bosnia and Croatia but some parties, with external backing, preferred to fight on. In September, 1993, on the HMS Invincible sailing on the Adriatic Sea, the Bosnian parties accepted what has come to be known as the Owen -Stoltenberg Plan or the Invincible Peace Plan. President Alija Izetbegovic and Foreign Minister Haris Siladjzic were buoyant and are recorded as having made public comments to the media in this vein. They travelled back with us on a plane from Split in Croatia to the capital, Zagreb. They were both quite happy and looked forward to the implementation of the plan. They went back to Sarajevo and, we are advised, came under US pressure to fight on. The public records indicate that they were then receiving arms from the USA, Turkey, Iran and other countries.

After this, the European Union Foreign Ministers sought to help us clinch a deal and asked David Owen and me to arrange for the Bosniacs (Muslims) to have thirty three percent of the land of Bosnia, up from the 31 percent we had negotiated until then. At a meeting in Brussels in December 1993, the EU Foreign Ministers faced total recalcitrance from the leadership of the warring parties. German Foreign Minister Klaus Kinkel then organized a meeting in Bonn with President Izetbegovic of Bosnia and President Franjo Tudjman of Croatia to see if the outstanding territorial disagreements between Bosniacs and Croats could be settled in Central Bosnia. President Izetbegovic told President Tudjman: "Franjo, there is an ammunition factory in the town of Vitez. We shall take Vitez and seize the ammunitions factory." Tudjman replied, "Alija, you will never take Vitez but if, for purposes of discussion, you did, we would blow up the ammunitions factory long before you could put your hands on it." This is what one had to deal with in the negotiations.President Izetbegovic had been emboldened by the political and armed support he was receiving from the USA and others.

I remember another occasion, in the summer of 1994, when Secretary-General Boutros Boutros-Ghali asked me to go to Pale, the capital of the Bosnian Serbs, and to persuade them to accept the Contact Group map for a settlement of the Bosnian conflict. Bertie Ramcharan accompanied me. When I told Radovan Karadzic that, if he did not cooperate, the arms embargo could be lifted, he replied, laughing: "Let them lift the arms embargo and then we shall all buy arms from the Israelis!" This was evidence, once again, that parties with the will and the means to fight will fight.

My point in relating the above snippets is to illustrate the challenges of the negotiators and to show that the Bosnian and Croatian leaders, political and military, played to their own agendas throughout.

Admonishing them about human rights violations, which we did frequently, was on occasions like throwing water on a duck's back. But we had to persist in the negotiations. There was no other choice. In the end, NATO bombs and Dayton brought the war in Bosnia to an end and I and US Ambassador Peter Galbraith mediated a settlement for Eastern Slavonia. Bertie Ramcharan wrote the first draft of what eventually became the Erdut agreement at the passenger lounge in Frankfurt Airport.

The mediators came in for a lot of criticisms from the media and the human rights community. In this book, Bertie Ramcharan faithfully presents our efforts for the promotion and protection of human rights in UN peace operations and leaves it to the judgment of the reader to assess those efforts. I shall do likewise and let the evidence speak for itself.

In the nearly four years of the existence of ICFY it made remarkable contributions to the search for peace in the former Yugoslavia. ICFY initiated the highly successful preventive deployment of peacekeeping forces in the Former Yugoslav Republic of Macedonia—the first ever deployment of UN peacekeeping forces. Its efforts helped save many lives and helped alleviate many grievances.

ICFY established and operated an International Monitoring Mission along the Drina River for nearly three years. This key stabilization regime had a staffing of over 500 persons at its height. We raised financing and managed it without a glitch. Bertie Ramcharan, as the Director of the ICFY, watched over this closely.

ICFY negotiated the withdrawal of the Yugoslav National Army from the Prevlaka Peninsula and thus avoided further conflict between Croatia and the Federal Republic of Yugoslavia in the fall of 1992.

ICFY negotiated the demining of the Peruca Dam which, in the fall of 1992, threatened several communities in the vicinity of the Dam in Croatia.

ICFY's Working Group on Humanitarian Issues, led by Mrs Ogata, helped raise awareness and resources for dealing with humanitarian problems in the former Yugoslavia through the winters of 1992, 1993, 1994 and 1995. It helped negotiate, in September, 1992, following the shooting down of a humanitarian aircraft, an agreement on safe corridors for aircraft engaged in the humanitarian airlift.

ICFY initiated the excavation of the mass-grave site at Ovcara near Vukovar. As SRSG in charge of UNPROFOR I arranged for the site to have military guards for several months. ICFY worked assiduously for the establishment of the International Criminal Tribunal for the Former Yugoslavia, which followed up on the report of the Commission of Experts on which my friend, the late Torkel Opsahl, served.

ICFY negotiated the 29 March, 1994 ceasefire agreement in Croatia. It also negotiated the 2 December 1994 Economic Agreement in Croatia that led to the re-opening of the Zagreb-Belgrade Highway.

ICFY was a lead negotiator in the settlement of the highly dangerous problem of Sector East in Croatia (the Erdut Agreement).

ICFY did the groundwork negotiations that laid the basis for the Dayton/Paris accords on Bosnia and Herzegovina. Two earlier agreements negotiated by ICFY in 1993 were first accepted by the parties and subsequently repudiated by one or other side.

ICFY drafted the 1993 treaty that was eventually signed by Greece and the Former Yugoslav Republic of Macedonia to settle key disputes.

ICFY mediated highly dangerous inter-ethnic problems in the Former Yugoslav Republic of Macedonia, organized and help raise funds and arranged for international monitoring of the crucial national population census, provided good offices for its national elections, and generated international assistance for a multi-ethnic media to promote inter-ethnic harmony.

ICFY provided good offices for dealing with problems affecting other ethnic communities, nationalities or minorities in the whole of the former Yugoslavia.

ICFY drafted a treaty on succession issues that was eventually concluded among the successor republics. ICFY initiated studies on confidence-building measures in the former Yugoslavia. ICFY also initiated studies on future development cooperation in the former Yugoslavia.

ICFY thus contributed to conflict prevention, peacemaking, peacekeeping, peacebuilding, humanitarian and human rights efforts in the former Yugoslavia for a period of three and a half years.

UN humanitarian operations in the former Yugoslavia, which I supervised directly in 1993, saved numerous lives and brought assistance and protection to many tens of thousands of people.

UN peacekeeping forces, including Civilian Police and Civil Affairs personnel, performed with guts and valour in the former Yugoslavia, even if some do not accord them the recognition they rightly deserve. As the SRSG in charge of UNPROFOR and all UN peace operations in the former Yugoslavia, I saw their work first hand. We in Norway contributed troops to the Nordic Battalion that did so much for the people of the former Yugoslavia.

I have cited these achievements because I think that they provide the necessary background against which we must view the efforts for the promotion and protection of human rights that Bertie Ramcharan discusses in this book.

Thorvald Stoltenberg,
Oslo, 15 December, 2010

INTRODUCTION

Human Rights issues were at the core of the conflicts in Bosnia, Croatia, Serbia and Macedonia during the period 1991 to 1995. The Ottoman Empire had ruled Bosnia with an Islamic framework and Christians had been pressurized into converting to Islam or to endure inequalities if they did not, and to provide children each year for service with the Ottoman Emperor. The Christians resented these exactions deeply during the five hundred year period of Ottoman occupation. In Bosnia, converts to Islam came to enjoy privileged status and as the demise of the Ottoman Empire appeared imminent in the late 19th century they fought to retain their privileges. A century later, as Tito's Yugoslavia was disintegrating Islamic leaders in Bosnia fought hard for an Islamic State.[14]

In Croatia and in Bosnia during the Second World War, Croatian Ustashas, supported by Bosnian Muslims, had committed acts of genocide and ethnic cleansing against the Serbs, who had bitter memories of the concentration camp at Jasenovac. As Croatia asserted its independence in 1991, the Croatian Serbs, who had the status of a constituent people in Tito's Yugoslavia, wished to detach themselves from the Croatian State and to join their brethren in Serbia. In Bosnia the Bosnian Serbs were determined not to fall under what they feared would be Islamist rule.

In Kosovo, the heartland of the ancient Serb Kingdom, the Serb population had dwindled to some 10 per cent and the more than two million Kosovar Albanians felt discriminated against by the Serbian rulers in Belgrade. The Serbian President Slobodan Milosevic undoubtedly played the Serbian nationalist card when he withdrew Kosovar autonomy and use of their language in schools. Issues of autonomy, minority rights, culture, and use of language were very much human rights issues at the heart of the Kosovo situation.

Elsewhere, in the Former Yugoslavia there were issues of the rights of peoples and minorities in Macedonia, in Vojvodina and the Sandzak. Put simply, solutions to the Former Yugoslavia's numerous problems

[14] See John R. Schindler, *Unholy Terror. Bosnia, Al-Qaida and Global Jihad.* (St. Paul's Minn., Zenith Press, 2007).

could only be conceived and implemented in terms of human rights. The UN and other international peacemakers would have to wrestle with these challenges. Simultaneously, as war came to Croatia and Bosnia, issues of protection and humanitarian relief took centre stage and Cyrus Vance and Marrack Goulding would pioneer in Croatia the concept of UN protected areas, which would later be adapted and put into use in Bosnia as United Nations safe areas. The UN Security Council, however, could declare protected and safe areas but could it actually protect them, or make them safe? UN peacekeeping operations would encounter grave difficulties in meeting these challenges.

Since peacemaking and peacekeeping had to be carried out keeping human rights very much in mind, it followed that the planning and implementation of peacebuilding programs needed to do likewise. United Nations peace plans for Bosnia, in particular, envisaged strong human rights institutions. The United Nations idea of a human rights court for Bosnia would be taken forward at the Dayton Peace Conference and the Bosnia Human Rights Chamber would make a landmark contribution to the reinforcement of peace in that country.[15]

To present the matter as we have done above in terms of the centrality of human rights in peacemaking, peacekeeping and peacebuilding makes it sound simpler and more straightforward than it actually was. In fact the reality was much more complex:

- Dynamic efforts were attempted to monitor human rights while the conflict was going on. These included the insertion in Bosnian peace plans of the idea of the establishment of an international human rights monitoring mission, the establishment of human rights ombudspersons and the establishment of a human rights court. In the end the idea of the human rights court would take hold in the post-conflict stage. During the conflict itself the efforts of the United Nations Commission on Human Rights and its Special Rapporteur on the Former Yugoslavia made worthwhile contributions in the area of human rights.

[15] See, generally, G. Nystuen, Achieving Peace or Protecting Human Rights? Conflict between Norms Regarding Ethnic Discrimination in the Dayton Peace Accords. Nijhoffs, 2005.

See also Human Rights Chamber of Bosnia and Herzegovina. Digest. Decisions on Admissibility and Merits, 1996–2002. With an Introduction by Manfred Nowak. Kehl/Strasbourg, Engel Publisher, 2003.

- UN peacemakers in Bosnia, while understanding that human rights needed to be addressed, followed more classical power-based negotiating strategies and did not initially endeavour—unlike the negotiations in El Salvador—to build peace blueprints around human rights by addressing human rights issues.
- The peacemakers had to wrestle with parallel Yugoslav concepts of the rights of peoples, nationalities and minorities and with the concept of autonomy. Peacemaking based on the concept of autonomy failed in Croatia regarding the Croatian Serbs simply because the Croatian government refused to accord the Croatian Serbs the status of a constituent people with rights to autonomy.
- UN peacekeeping operations had had a little experience before Yugoslavia in the implementation of the human rights provisions of peace agreements in places like El Salvador and Cambodia but UN peacekeepers had never before been called upon to play a role in protecting human rights in the very midst of conflict. UN peacekeeping cut its teeth in addressing human rights challenges in the former Yugoslavia.

In this work, we shall endeavour to trace the place accorded to human rights—or not—in the areas of conflict prevention, peacemaking, peacekeeping and peace building. We shall submit the following:

Human rights and conflict prevention

It would be accurate to make the claim that the human rights work of the international mediators helped prevent a descent into conflict in FYR Macedonia.

Human rights and peacemaking

The peacemakers, Vance, Owen, Stoltenberg and Bildt desired very much to reverse ethnic cleansing in Bosnia. But the distribution of power on the ground was such that they lacked the means to bring this about.

Human rights and peacekeeping

While UN peacekeepers initially helped to protect the Croatian Serbs, in the end the latter would be expelled from Croatia by Croatian forces with the support of training, logistics and intelligence from the United States. The United Nations peacekeepers were never given the resources to actually protect the safe areas in Bosnia. UN peacekeepers performed heroically in supporting UN humanitarian relief operations in the former Yugoslavia. But overall the contribution of UN peacekeepers to the protection of human rights was only partial.

Human rights and peacebuilding

The blueprints for peace in Bosnia worked out by Vance and Owen and Stoltenberg and Owen, and eventually embraced at Dayton, by providing for institutions such as the Human Rights Court for Bosnia and Herzegovina made useful contributions to peacebuilding. The patient work done in the FY Macedonia on interethnic dialogue and understanding, including organizing the country's first ever census, undoubtedly helped stabilize that fragile country.

*****

There is much original materials available on the human rights violations that took place in the various crises in the Former Yugoslavia and the inability of the international community to act meaningfully in dealing with those violations. In the end it would take NATO air power to vindicate what has nowadays come to be termed the responsibility to protect. If there are any central conclusions to be drawn from an examination of human rights issues in the Former Yugoslavia it would probably be that efforts for conflict prevention are crucial if one is to have a chance at avoiding the descent into the abyss. Second, if peacemaking efforts are not supported by major powers when it really matters they may have, in the end, to resort to force for purposes of protection. In the meantime many will have died and a great deal of suffering will have been caused by the military operations. Efforts for prevention and support for international peacemakers are thus of the utmost importance.

In this book we take up the story during the period of the International Conference on the Former Yugoslavia (ICFY), from September, 1992 until the end of the conference in the spring of 1996. During this period we were Director of the ICFY and, for a year, simultaneously Director of the Office of the Special Representative of the UN Secretary-General for the Former Yugoslavia. Thorvald Stoltenberg of Norway served simultaneously as ICFY Co-Chairman and as SRSG and we assisted him in both capacities. It would not be claiming too much to say that we were at the heart of the UN peace operations in the former Yugoslavia.

At the beginning of ICFY the Co-Chairs were Cyrus Vance and Lord David Owen, the former designated by the UN and the latter by the European Union. Vance had been active on UN peacemaking and peacekeeping efforts since the previous year, when he served as Special Envoy of UN Secretary-General Javier Perez de Cuellar and negotiated, with the help of Marrack Goulding, the Vance Plan for Croatia, elaborated in 1991, the implementation of which began in the spring of 1992. The Vance Plan had built on the concept of UN Protected Areas: a United Nations peace-keeping operation as an interim arrangement to create the conditions of peace and security required for the negotiation of an overall settlement of the Yugoslav crisis. The military and police personnel required for the operation would be contributed, on a voluntary basis, by the Governments of member States of the UN approved by the Security Council. The protection arrangements were admittedly not the strongest possible but they represented the best that could be negotiated in the circumstances.[16] One would see this throughout the peace processes and operations: what could be achieved depended on what could be negotiated or, towards the end, what powerful governments were prepared to enforce.

When Vance and Owen arrived in Geneva at the beginning of September, 1992, to commence their activities as ICFY Co-Chairs, the human rights issues landed on their desk with poignancy. On 23 September, 1992, shortly after ICFY began to operate in Geneva on 2 September, UNHCR shared a paper on The Human Rights Situation in NW Bosnia and Herzegovina: How Can it be Improved, signed by W. van Hovell. The paper opened, "Human rights are violated by all parties in the Bosnian conflict.". It explained: "The drive to establish ethnic homogeneity in Serbian controlled areas continues… There are indications that the pressure on non-Serbs may soon intensify, especially in Banja Luka town…Currently, UNHCR and the ICRC form the only international presence in the region, with 5 and 15 staff members respectively based in Banja Luka town. The Muslim and Croatian

[16] Cf., Lawyers Committee for Human Rights, Refugee Project. Discussion Paper: Protection by Presence. The Limits of United Nations Safekeeping Activities in Croatia, September, 1993.

parties consider this presence in itself as a form of protection, and are highly appreciative of it. However, more international attention would be required to address the situation in a meaningful way."

The memorandum ended with the following recommendations:

(a) It is recommended that the ongoing abuses of human rights in BH, in particular in the Banja Luka region, be discussed in the framework of the follow-up to the London Conference (ICFY). This could lead to an agreement with the parties on practical measures to improve the situation.
(b) In view of their forthcoming mission to the former Yugoslavia, it is recommended to bring to the attention of the Co-Chairmen of the London Conference reports on imminent 'ethnic cleansing' in Banja Luka town. It is hoped that the deployment of the Canadian UNPROFOR battalion can be speeded up. Their presence may have a calming and, to some extent, preventive effect.
(c) In a comprehensive effort to attenuate the situation and to prevent blatant abuses of human rights, a sizable international monitoring presence should be established in BH, to start with in the Banja Luka region. The European Community Monitoring Mission, (ECMM) might be the most suitable body to perform this task, i.e. to monitor the treatment of minority groups as well as the implementation of the practical measures mentioned under (a), to expose abuses to the authorities, and to report to the London Conference and the Security Council, as appropriate. It is recommended that this be discussed with the British EC-Presidency.
(d) Failing a formally mandated agency or pending its deployment, UNHCR should, security conditions permitting, pursue its monitoring role, in close collaboration with the ICRC and in future with UNPROFOR. It is hoped that all future UNPROFOR battalions and their Civilian Affairs staff, despite the absence of a formal mandate in this regard, will register and report on human rights abuses, throughout BH.
(e) It is recommended that Special Rapporteur Mazowiecki, during his forthcoming mission to the former Yugoslavia, visit Eastern BH (largely Serbian held) and Herzegovina (Croatian held). Too little is known about the human rights situation in those areas. Monitoring in non-Serbian controlled areas will be conducive to, and might be indispensable for progress in the Serbian held areas."[17]

---

[17] Memorandum in the possession of the author.

We have cited this memorandum because it gives an idea of the anguish being felt and the ideas being considered in the lead humanitarian agency.

On 24 September, 1992, the Co-Chairmen of the ICFY, Cyrus Vance and Lord David Owen issued the following Press Statement:

"The Co-Chairmen are deeply concerned about reports which have just reached them from the Banja Luka region indicating a build-up of tension, bomb incidents, and intimidation with the potential threat of violence and the development of an ethnic-cleansing campaign.

"This morning the Co-Chairmen called in Ambassador Pavicevic of the Federal Republic of Yugoslavia, and Dr. Koljevic, the Bosnian Serb representative, and urged that immediate steps be taken to reduce tensions in the area.

"In view of the urgency of the situation, the Co-Chairmen have decided to fly to Banja Luka tomorrow. There they will assess the situation on the ground, and speak to representatives of the local communities and humanitarian agencies."[18]

On 13 October, 1992, USG for Peacekeeping, Marrack Goulding, sent the following cable to General Satish Nambiar, the Commander of UNPROFOR, based in Zagreb:

"1. At a meeting with SecGen this morning Mr. Vance expressed his grave concern about continued abuses by the Bosnian Serb authorities in and around Banja Luka. Large numbers of Muslims were being rounded up and bussed to the Travnik area and made to walk through no-man's land into Muslim-controlled territory, many being shot as they went. Mr. Vance felt that early deployment of UNPROFOR troops could help to deter such activities. This would be achieved when the new Canadian contingent was deployed for humanitarian protection duties. Meanwhile, was there any possibility of temporarily detaching some elements from Canadian battalion in Sector West to Banja Luka, ostensibly as advance party for new Canadian battalion?
"2. SecGen agreed that your views should be sought on this idea."[19]

On 27 October, 1992, Amnesty International sent to the Co-Chairmen of the ICFY an open letter on human rights issues and coordination of human rights initiatives in the former Yugoslavia, as well as a recent report on Human Rights Issues in Bosnia and Herzegovina. The Open

[18] Statement in the possession of the author.
[19] Text in the possession of the author.

Letter, sent to the Foreign Ministers of a series of concerned countries, stated that Amnesty International was gravely concerned about the human rights abuses committee by all parties to the conflict in the former Yugoslavia. Amnesty considered that leaders of parties to the conflict within Bosnia-Herzegovina, as well as the Governments of the Federal Republic of Yugoslavia and Croatia, must all bear some responsibility for human rights abuses that had occurred.

Amnesty International called for coordination among the various UN bodies dealing with the former Yugoslavia. It considered that the Special Rapporteur of the Commission on Human Rights, Tadeusz Mazowiecki, should play a central role in documenting the human rights situation and making recommendations about preventive measures. It expressed the hope that the International Conference on the Former Yugoslavia (ICFY) would contribute to the coordination of intergovernmental human rights initiatives and that the Steering Committee of the Conference as well as its six working groups would actively consider the human rights issues raised by reports from Amnesty International, other NGOs and intergovernmental fact-finding missions.

In the longer term, Amnesty International believed that any eventual political settlement of the conflict in the former Yugoslavia must include a strong human rights component. This included on-site human rights monitoring and measures to reform or strengthen institutions essential for the long-term promotion and protection of human rights. It noted that in his Agenda for Peace, UN Secretary-General Boutros Boutros-Ghali had also rightly emphasized that advancing efforts to protect human rights must be part of comprehensive post-conflict peace-building measures.[20]

On 5 November, 1992, Ambassador H. S. Okun, Special Adviser to Co-Chairman Cyrus Vance, replied to the Amnesty Interntional Representative in Geneva, Isabelle Scherer stating that Co-Chairmen Vance and Owen "agree fully that human rights issues are at the core of the current crisis in the former Yugoslavia and should be given the utmost priority. In recognition of this, the Co-Chairmen, in making proposals for the proposed constitutional structure for Bosnia and

[20] Boutros Boutros-Ghali, An Agenda for Peace. Report of the Secretary-General pursuant to the statement adopted by the Summit Meeting of the Security Council on 31 Januaqry, 1992. United Nations, New York, 1992, para. 55.

Herzegovina, have advanced far reaching ideas on human rights norms that should be included in the future constitution: the role of the Constitutional Court, the role of a Special Human Rights Court, the need for an International Commission on Human Rights for Bosnia and Herzegovina, the need for Ombudsmen; the need for the protection of minorities; and the importance of the ratification of international human rights treaties."

The letter provided instances and copies of statements by the Co-Chairmen on pressing humanitarian and human rights issues and continued: "The Co-Chairmen agree fully with the view that the Special Rapporteur of the Commission on Human Rights, Mr. Mazowiecki, 'should play a central role in documenting the human rights situation and making recommendations about preventive measures'. Indeed, the day after their arrival in Geneva—on September 4—the Co-Chairmen had an extensive meeting, lasting over two hours, with the Special Rapporteur. They had discussed a broad range of issues. The Co-Chairmen had met with the Special Rapporteur again on October 8 to review developments and to coordinate their efforts."

The letter concluded: "The Co-Chairmen are very much of the view that human rights concerns should be given the highest priority. They have been doing precisely that and will continue to do so."[21]

On 21 January, 1993, Mr. G. Mautner-Markhov, of the UN Centre for Human Rights (now the Office of the UN High Commissioner for Human Rights), wrote to this author as Director of the ICFY, a memorandum titled, "Petitions concerning killings of civilians, rape and torture in the Former Yugoslavia". It read as follows:

> "The Centre for Human Rights has received from Amnesty International a small selection of 500,000 petitions and letters from people around the world urging the delegates of the International Conference on the former Yugoslavia to ensure that international human rights agreements are fully respected.
>
> "Amnesty International requested that the selection of these letters, which I enclose, be passed on to the Secretariat of the International Conference on the former Yugoslavia."[22]

---

[21] Letter in the possession of the author.

[22] Memorandum in the possession of the author. It will be noticed that Amnesty International was requesting ICFY to 'ensure that international human rights agreements are fully respected'. But it was one of the tragedies of the situation that nobody could ensure anything at the time.

In the opening pages of this book we cited some of the fervent pleas for justice from the ICRC, the negotiators, from the UN High Commissioner for Refugees, from the UN Secretary-General, and from the UN Security Council. We saw the UN Secretary-General, Boutros Boutros-Ghali, on 15 April, 1993, expressing his indignation over reports of the situation in the town of Srebrenica in Bosnia and Herzegovina and in particular the inexcusable assault on civilians in that town. He unequivocally condemned the shelling of Srebrenica by Bosnian Serb forces, which had inflicted further casualties and destruction upon its suffering residents and upon the displaced people who had sought refuge there. He urgently called upon the Bosnian Serb forces in the area to halt their unjustifiable attacks, which had occurred despite explicit assurances to the contrary from their military and political leaders. He renewed his appeal to all concerned to cooperate with the efforts of the Force Commander of the United Nations Protection Force (UNPROFOR) to restore a cease-fire and to allow free passage and the unimpeded delivery of humanitarian assistance.[23]

We saw the Security Council reaffirming that all parties were bound to comply with their obligations under international humanitarian law and in particular the Geneva Conventions of 12 August 1949 and that persons who committed or ordered the commission of grave breaches of the Conventions were individually responsible in respect of such breaches. We saw the Security Council reaffirming that any taking of territory by force or any practice of 'ethnic cleansing' was unlawful and unacceptable and would not be permitted to affect the outcome of the negotiations on constitutional arrangements for the Republic of Bosnia and Herzegovina, and insisting that all displaced persons be enabled to return in peace to their former homes.

We saw the Security Council condemning all violations of international humanitarian law, in particular the practice of 'ethnic cleansing' and the deliberate impeding of the delivery of food and medical supplies to the civilian population of the Republic of Bosnia and Herzegovina, and reaffirming that those who committed or ordered the commission of such acts would be held individually responsible in respect of them. We saw the Security Council strongly condemning acts of unspeakable brutality.

---

[23] UN Press Release, SG/SM/4978, 15 April, 1993.

From the foregoing one could see that verbal condemnations of gross violations of human rights and humanitarian law were numerous. But what impact did they have? Did they influence the behaviour of the combating parties or their leaders? The evidence would suggest that, for the most part, the combatants paid little heed to them. In Bosnia-Herzegovina and in Croatia there were parties with the means and the will to fight and very few countervailing forces able or willing to stop them. A Discussion Paper published by the Refugee Project of the Lawyers Committee for Human Rights in September, 1993[24] which was authored by a highly qualified team of seasoned scholar/practitioners,[25] assessed that. there were no U.N.-imposed guarantors of respect for human rights, the rule of law, or protection for the displaced population.[26] This was an understandable comment, but who could have provided "U.N.- imposed guarantors"? This is a fundamental issue when it comes to assessing efforts, or lack thereof, for the protection of human rights in the former Yugoslavia.

If a powerful Government, or set of Governments, is ready to call upon their assets to move against a human rights violator, as the Coalition Forces did against Serbia-Montenegro in the case of Kosovo in 1999, then it might be possible to 'impose guarantees'. Serious issues of legality arose in that case, in the absence of express Security Council authorisation. The same issue of legality would arise when another Coalition decided to act against Saddam Hussain in 2003.

In the case of the Former Yugoslavia, the Security Council did act. It established UNPROFOR, the largest peacekeeping operation in the history of the world organization. It instituted an arms embargo on all parts of the former Yugoslavia. It encouraged negotiated solutions and it adopted numerous resolutions condemning violations of humanitarian and human rights norms. But condemnation proved not to be anough. And when the Security Council declared safe areas and gave rise to expectations in the international community that the people of the safe areas would be protected, leading members of the Security

---

[24] Lawyers Committee for Human Rights, Refugee Project. Discussion Paper: Protection by Presence. The Limits of United Nations Safekeeping Activities in Croatia, September, 1993.

[25] The late Arthur Helton, Guy Goodwin-Gill, Walter Kalin, Michel Moussali, and Deborah Blatt.

[26] Ibid, p. 5.

Council were unwilling to back up the Council's writ by providing the means necessary for the protection of the safe areas.

In its famous or infamous resolution 836 (1993) on the protection of the safe areas, the Security Council, acting under Chapter VII of the UN Charter, reaffirmed the unacceptability of the acquisition of territory by the use of force. It decided to extend the mandate of UNPROFOR in order to enable it, in the declared safe areas, to deter attacks against those safe areas, to monitor the cease-fire, to promote the withdrawal of military or paramilitary units other than those of the Government of the Republic of Bosnia and Herzegovina and to occupy some key points on the ground, in addition to participating in the delivery of humanitarian relief to the population. The Security Council affirmed that the primary objective in the safe areas remained to reverse the consequences of the use of force and to allow all persons displaced from their homes in the Republic of Bosnia and Herzegovina to return to their homes in peace.

But after these lofty statements of objectives, what did the Security Council actually authorise UNPROFOR to do? It authorised UNPROFOR, in carrying out its mandate, and when acting in self defence, to take the necessary measures, including the use of force, in reply to bombardments against the safe areas by any of the parties or to armed incursion into them or in the event of any deliberate obstruction in or around those areas to the freedom of movement of UNPROFOR or of protected humanitarian convoys.

The key condition in the preceding authorisation was 'when acting in self-defence'. After resolution 836 was passed, Secretary-General Boutros-Ghali convened a high-level meeting to discuss the modalities of its implementation. This writer, then performing the functions of Director in the Office of SRSG Thorvald Stoltenberg, joined with the Military Advisor to the SRSG, Brigadier-General John Wilson of Australia, in writing a detailed paper for Stoltenberg in preparation for the meeting with the Secretary-General. The restricted scope of resolution 836 jumped off the paper on which it was written.

The Security Council decided that Member States, acting nationally or through regional organizations or arrangements, may take, under the authority of the Security Council and subject to close coordination with the Secretary-General and UNPROFOR, all necessary measures, through the use of air power, in and around the safe areas in the Republic of Bosnia and Herzegovina, to support UNPROFOR in the performance of its mandate. But the fundamental condition remained, namely, that support must be to UNPROFOR when acting in self-defence.

When all is said and done, this was not a resolution providing for *protection* of the people in the safe areas. It was a resolution providing for assistance to UNPROFOR when it needed such assistance for self-defence purposes. This became quite clear when SRSG Stoltenberg and, under his authority, Force Commander Jean Cot, came to work out the modalities for the application of resolution 836. This writer, as Director of the Office of the SRSG, worked on the modalities with Brigadier-General John Wilson and Finnish Colonel Pasi Koronen and has vivid recollections of the convoluted provisions of resolution 836 that had to be kept in mind when proceeding with its implementation.

The scheme we worked out with the Force Commander and his staff provided that a request from the Force Commander for the use of air assets would be referred to the SRSG and that the SRSG would decide within one hour whether to recommend the use of aerial assets to the UN Secretary-General.[27] The final decision would be made by the UN Secretary-General. From this author's perspective, as senior adviser to the SRSG, any recommendation he made to the Secretary-General had to respect the express requirement in resolution 836 that aerial force could only be used in a situation wherein UNPROFOR was acting in self-defence.

The then Force Commander, French General Jean Cot, initiated a number of simulations to trial-run the system. These were almost real-life situations. In one instance, Stoltenberg and Lord Owen had the Bosnian leaders in negotiations in a conference room in the Palais des Nations, Geneva. General Cot initiated a simulation exercise: Fifteen UNPROFOR soldiers were pinned down by hostile Bosnian Serb forces and would surely be killed unless he could call in NATO air support for the defence of the UNPROFOR soldiers. General Wilson and

[27] This meant that wherever in the world the SRSG was, since he was also the lead UN negotiator as Chairman of ICFY, he would have to have communications equipment through which he could be contacted and could respond to a request by the Force Commander. We arranged for the SRSG to be accompanied wherever he went by a military attaché with the communications equipment. It also meant that this writer and Military Adviser John Wilson had to be ready to consider any request from the Force Commander and to make a recommendation to the SRSG so that he could reply within an hour of the request being made. These were dramatic developments in the history of the UN.

this writer left the negotiating room, huddled together and called Stoltenberg out of the negotiations with a recommendation that he authorise calling in the air assets. Stoltenberg, a wise statesman and former Defence Minister of Norway, told us: "In the room next door I have the Bosnian parties in negotiations. If I authorise the use of air power against the Bosnian Serb forces, the Bosnian Serb party will in all likelihood leave the negotiations and could well stay away for some time. During this period the fighting would continue and dozens, hundreds of people will lose their lives. I am sorry, I cannot authorise calling in the planes. I must give priority to the search for a negotiated solution".

As a career professional in the United Nations it was hard for me to accept that we would not come to the aid of 15 UN peacekeepers who would in all likelihood be killed. I swallowed hard, and we replied to Cot why the SRSG considered that he could not authorise calling in air power. Fortunately, it was only a simulation!

There is another point we would wish to make about the implementation of Security Council resolution 836. After the resolution was adopted, the then Force Commander, Swedish General Lars-Eric Wahlgren estimated that its implementation would require an additional 34,000 forces. In the event that the Security Council would consider this too many he provided an alternative 'light option' that would require 7,000 forces. I have always regretted that he put up this alternative option. If, in his professional assessment, he considered that he needed 34,000 additional forces he should have held to his professional assessment. He probably provided the light option because of what was said to him by leading members of the Security Council.

Whatever the reasons for his providing the light option, powerful members of the Security Council made it clear that it was a non-starter to pursue his request for an additional 34,000 forces. There is a cable from USG Annan to General Lars-Eric Wahlgren, reporting on urgent representations by the British Permanent Representative, Sir David Hannay, who insisted that in no circumstances would the major powers agree to the additional 34,000 forces.

The significance of this cable is that it confirmed that although the Security Council had adopted the pretentious and misleading provisions of resolution 836, the Members had no intention of providing the means for its implementation. This is what it came down to when one came to 'protecting' human rights in the former Yugoslavia in the face of unscrupulous and criminal political and military leaders, of whom Lord Carrington had 'unprintable' views!

At the end of the day, one is compelled to recognize, that human rights 'protection' in the former Yugoslavia was limited to what could be done in the circumstances. Many actors were striving for protection and some protection did undoubtedly take place. UNHCR, ICRC, and UNPROFOR were on the ground and did what they could against great odds. The Special Rapporteur of the Commission on Human Rights, Tadeusz Mazowiecki, did much to publicise the violations taking place and this might have had a mitigatory role, although this is not to be taken for granted. The UN Secretary-General and the peace negotiators sought to put pressure on the parties and this might have had some effect, but here also it is not to be taken for granted. The Secretary-General's decision to establish the Commission of Experts to inquire into war crimes and crimes against humanity was an important building block. It laid the foundation for the eventual establishment by the Security Council of the International Criminal Tribunal for the Former Yugoslavia, which has done much to serve the cause of justice.

In this book on human rights in UN peace operations in the former Yugoslavia we shall try to relate a story of what was essentially striving for the promotion and protection of human rights in the former Yugoslavia. We make no claim more than that it was a story of striving. We shall content ourself with presenting the evidence of the striving and let the reader make his or her own assessments of the efforts that were made. We deliberately do not consider the academic literature on human rights in peace operations because we wish the record to speak for itself.

In the first chapter we shall relate the UN efforts in the UN Protected Areas (UNPAs) in Croatia. In the second chapter we shall follow the humanitarian operations under the UN High Commissioner for Refugees and see how she tried, conceptually, to situate the problems in lack of protection of human rights. In the third chapter we shall present the efforts of the Special Rapporteur of the UN Commission on Human Rights.

In the fourth chapter we shall look at efforts to negotiate peace on the foundation of human rights principles. In the fifth chapter we shall discuss preventive strategies closely related to the avoidance of human rights violations. In the sixth chapter we shall relate how the negotiators sought to integrate human rights in their peacemaking strategies. In the seventh chapter we shall discuss how peacekeepers sought to uphold and advance human rights.

In the eighth chapter we shall discuss human rights initiatives meant to build the foundations of peace. In chapter nine we shall review human rights monitoring and fact-finding initiatives. In the tenth and final chapter, we shall examine efforts to advance the cause of justice in the former Yugoslavia.

Finally, we shall suggest some conclusions that might be drawn from the materials presented in the preceding chapters. It was, as we indicated above, very much a story of striving, and of doing what could be done in the circumstances, in the face of great odds and in the face of criminal military and political leaders who were largely impervious to international pressure. Striving for the promotion and protection of human rights is the insight that emerges from this book. There was some measure of protection but, faced with the magnitude of the violations, it must be recognized that it was limited. Another insight that probably comes out of the book is that, at the end of the day, the Commission of Experts into war crimes and crimes against humanity, and the International Criminal Tribunal for the Former Yugoslavia were of the greatest significance from the point of view of the actual protection of human rights. Their efforts, however, fall into the category of remedial protection—protection after the fact. The other actors whose efforts we discuss in this book sought to bring their influence to bear on preventive, mitigatory, and curative protection. We leave it to the reader to judge whether the efforts were meaningful and to consider what lessons might be learned from the human rights efforts recounted.

CHAPTER 1

UN PROTECTED AREAS

Introduction

The United Nations Protected Areas (UNPAs) in Croatia were, despite the name, more of a peace-stabilization than a human rights concept. They were meant to dampen the fighting and provide an international presence while peacemaking efforts continued to bring the conflict between Croats and Serbs to an end. Nevertheless, there were shades of protection in the concept and in the implementation given to it by United Nations forces. Some people were protected while others were not—inside, and on the perimeters of the UNPAs. Some ethnic cleansing took place under the very nose of the UN peacekeepers. But they did what they could to protect those they could, in difficult circumstances. They practised the art of the possible, which is a hallmark of United Nations peace and humanitarian operations. In this chapter we shall look at the concept, protection efforts on the ground, and the limitations of the operation.

By way of background, it will be recalled that on 27 November, 1991, the UN Security Council had adopted resolution 721 endorsing efforts for the deployment of a UN peacekeeping operation in Croatia, then still a part of the Socialist Federal Republic of Yugoslavia. An implementing Accord was signed in Sarajevo on 2 January, 1992. Six weeks later, on 15 February, 1992, the Security Council confirmed acceptance by all parties of what became known as the Vance Plan and agreed to establish UNPROFOR.

The Vance plan had been the result of a six month negotiation process. The plan's aims were as follows: the cessation of hostilities; the withdrawal of the Yugoslav National Army (JNA) from Croatia; the demilitarisation of areas designated as UN Protected Areas to protect the Serbs and other populations within the UNPAs; and facilitation of the return of displaced persons to the UNPAs.

UNPROFOR was initially deployed in Croatia, with its Headquarters in Sarajevo which, at the time, early 1992, before the recognition of its independence, was peaceful. Subsequently, with the spread of civil war in Bosnia and Herzegovina, UNPROFOR's mandate was extended to Bosnia and later, as a preventive deployment, to the Former Yugoslav Republic of Macedonia. In addition, UNPROFOR had an operational mandate in Serbia and Montenegro and a liaison presence in Slovenia.

1. The concept of UN Protected Areas

The concept for a United Nations peace-keeping operation in Yugoslavia, which was discussed with Yugoslav leaders by Cyrus Vance, Personal Envoy of the UN Secretary-General and Marrack Goulding, USG for Special Political Affairs (Peacekeeping) in November/December, 1991, envisaged an interim arrangement to create the conditions of peace and security required for the negotiation of an overall settlement of the Yugoslav crisis. The military and police personnel required for the operation would be contributed, on a voluntary basis, by the Government of Member States of the UN approved by the Security Council.[28]

All members of the peace-keeping operation would be under the operational command of the UN Secretary-General. They would be required to be completely impartial between the various parties to the conflict. Those personnel who were armed would have standing instructions to use force to the minimum extent necessary and normally only in self-defence.

United Nations troops and police monitors would be deployed in certain areas in Croatia, designated as "United Nations Protected Areas". These areas would be demilitarized; all armed forces in them would be either withdrawn or disbanded. The role of the United Nations troops would be to ensure that the areas remained demilitarized and that all persons residing in them were protected from fear of armed attack.

The role of United Nations police monitors would be to ensure that the local police forces carried out their duties without discrimination against persons of any nationality or abusing anyone's human rights. As the United Nations Force assumed its responsibilities in the United Nations Protected Areas (UNPAS), all Yugoslav National Army (JNA) forces deployed elsewhere in Croatia would be relocated outside that republic.

[28] See UN doc.S/23592.

The United Nations Force would also, as appropriate, assist the humanitarian agencies of the United Nations in the return of all displaced persons who so desired to their homes in the UNPAs.

The UNPAs would be areas in Croatia in which the Secretary-General judged that special arrangements were required during an interim period to ensure that a lasting ceasefire was maintained. They would be areas in which Serbs constituted the majority or a substantial minority of the population and where inter-communal tensions had led to armed conflict in the recent past. The special arrangements in these areas would be of an interim nature and would not prejudge the outcome of political negotiations for a comprehensive settlement of the Yugoslav crisis. There would be three UNPAs: Eastern Slavonia, Western Slavonia and Krajina. The districts contained in each of them were enumerated.

The functions of protecting the inhabitants of the UNPAs would be shared between the United Nations Force's infantry units and its civilian police monitors. The infantry would ensure that the UNPAs remained demilitarized. The police monitors would ensure that the local police carried out their duties without discrimination against any nationality and with full respect for the human rights of all residents of the UNPAs.

The infantry units would be deployed throughout the UNPAs. They would be lightly armed but would use armoured personnel carriers and helicopters. They would control access to the UNPAs by establishing check-points on all roads and principal tracks leading into them and at important junctions inside them. At these check-points they would stop and, if necessary, search vehicles and individuals to ensure that no military formations or armed groups entered the UNPAs and that no weapons, ammunition, explosives or other military equipment were brought into them. They would patrol extensively inside the UNPAs on foot, and by vehicle and helicopter. They would also investigate any complaints made to them about violations of the demilitarized status of the UNPAs. Any confirmed violations would be taken up with the offending party and would, if necessary, be reported by the Secretary-General to the Security Council. If serious tension were to develop between nationalities in a UNPA, the United Nations Force would interpose itself between the two sides in order to prevent hostilities.

The civilian police monitors would also be deployed throughout the UNPAs. They would be unarmed. They would have no executive responsibility for the maintenance of public order but they would closely monitor the work of the local police forces. To this end, they would be located with police headquarters in each region and opstina (district) and would accompany the local police on their patrols and in their performance of their other duties. They would investigate any complaints of discrimination or other abuse of human rights and would report to the Chief of the United Nations Force any confirmed cases of discrimination or abuses. They would require free and immediate access to all premises and facilities of, or under the control of, the local police forces.

The United Nations Force would also include a group of military observers. They would be unarmed, in accordance with normal UN practice. They would initially be deployed in the UNPAs to verify the demilitarization of those areas. As soon as demilitarization had been effected, the military observers would be transferred to parts of Bosnia and Herzegovina adjacent to Croatia. Their functions there would be to patrol extensively, to liaise with the local authorities and to warn the Chief of the United Nations Force if inter-communal tension threatened to disturb the peace and tranquillity established by the Force in the UNPAs. Their good offices would be available to help to resolve local difficulties and to investigate allegations of inter-communal tension or aggression.

In accordance with established international principles, the United Nations policy would be to facilitate the return to their homes of all persons displaced by the recent hostilities who so desired. The lead in that matter would be taken by the humanitarian agencies of the United Nations. United Nations forces would provide all appropriate support to this effort in the UNPAs. The United Nations police monitors would have an especially important role in this regard.

2. The Practice of Protection

In the preceding section we saw the concept of protection. How did it operate in practice? A few illustrative cases will help to show how it fared on the ground.

2.1. *The challenges of protecting the areas*

The challenges of protecting the areas, and the valiant performance of UNPROFOR personnel, could be seen in the following illustrative report from Sector West on 5 November, 1993. On the political front, the Civil Affairs Officers reported that the situation in Sector West remained calm but tense. The Croatian Government had repeated its warning to UNPROFOR that it might attack the Serb-controlled part of the Sector. The Serb side was protesting against the presence of around 150 heavily armed Croatian Special Police inside the Sector.

Civil Affairs had nearly succeeded in arranging a further face-to-face meeting between the Croatian and Serb political and police leaders on 3 November but the Serb side had cancelled at the last moment. Civil Affairs would keep trying. Meanwhile, the Sector Commander was contacting the military leaders of both sides, trying to arrange a face-to-face meeting aimed at concluding a ceasefire agreement.

On human rights issues, Civil Affairs and CIVPOL had continued their activities aimed at the protection of human rights of ethnic minorities on both sides of the Sector. On the Croatian side, Civil Affairs had been approached by local Serb citizens who had requested assistance in obtaining citizenship papers and other official documents. In Daruvar, Civil Affairs had started working on the case of discriminatory job dismissal of a Serb woman. In Grubisno Polje, Civil Affairs had visited people requesting humanitarian assistance and old people who wanted to be reunited with their children living in Bosnia. Steps had been taken, in cooperation with UNHCR, to arrange for their medical evacuation through the channels of the ICRC. On the Serb side, Civil Affairs had been taking up the cases of Croats prevented by local authorities from leaving or, in one instance, from coming back, to join families. In each of these two cases the applicants had been waiting for two to six months.

CIVPOL had also continued their involvement in the protection of human rights prisoners, both within the Sector, and prisoners taken from the sector to prisons outside the UNPA. This had been accomplished by making periodic prison visits on both sides and interviewing POWs. CIVPOL continued monitoring a wide variety of human rights related investigations in the Sector ranging from murders, sexual assaults, missing persons, harassment, and in cooperation with Civil Affairs, eviction from residences and wrongful dismissal from employment. CIVPOL had also been liaising with UN officials on the excavation of mass grave sites in Sector West.

On both sides of the Sector, the number of local citizens requesting UNPROFOR's assistance in obtaining documents required for crossing the cease-fire line had increased. Civil Affairs and UNHCR had continued to provide humanitarian assistance for old and sick people on both sides of the Sector.[29] UNPROFOR was doing what it could in the circumstances.

2.2. *Alleged war crime at Marino Selo*

On 26 October, 1992, A UN Civilian Police Officer submitted to the Civil Affair Officer for Sector West, one of the UNPAs, a report on alleged war crimes at Marino Selo. Based on reports and on their observations, he and another colleague had gone to Belgrade on 23 September to take a statement from a witness to alleged war crimes committed by Croatian military against Serb civilians. The statement provided a harrowing account of the abuse and killing of Serb civilians in Marino Selo. The CIVPOL Officers sent up an English translation of the statement with a note saying that the witness and his son were afraid for their life because of the statement. However, they were willing to point out the graves where the victims had been buried and the place where they were tortured.

Based on the statement of the witness and a sketch that the two CIVPOL officers had drawn up based on what they were told, they had gone to the location and thought that they had located the graves. The area was just outside the UNPA. They advised that if measures were not taken to guard the graves there was a possibility that the police or the military would move the bodies. The families of the persons killed had on several occasions asked CIVPOL to help them locate the bodies. They wanted their family members buried in a proper way. Because of the rain and winter coming, time was running out, the CIVPOL officers advised. The river next to the grave sites was getting higher every day. The CIVPOL officers provided the name of the Croatian commanding officer in Marino Selo at the time the alleged killing took place. They asked for advice on "what further action is recommended, in order that their families concerned may be advised."

On 30 October, 1992, the Civil Affairs Officer for Sector West wrote to the Civil Affairs Division of UNPROFOR in Zagreb transmitting the information above, together with a copy of the witness statement, a harrowing account of the wilful killing of Serb civilians. He stated that he had discussed the possibility of guarding the site of the alleged crime on a 24-hour basis with a Major in the Sector West

[29] Document in the possession of the author.

military component. The most difficult aspect of such an exercise was likely to be the fact that the grave site was located outside of the UNPA, although in clear visibility (200 meters) from the sector boundary. In the Major's opinion, the military component could provide a two-man observation team that would ensure that no remains of the victims were moved until the appropriate international body could exhume and identify them.

However, the Major was cautious about such an undertaking unless some basic conditions were met. An observation post might attract the attention of the perpetrators of the alleged crime who might try to remove the bodies and destroy traces of the graves. Furthermore, establishing a guard post would place an undue burden on the military unit concerned in terms of manpower and logistics, which could not continue indefinitely. The military component could establish the observation/guard post provided that the War Crimes Commission or other appropriate body started preparatory work promptly for exhumation, identification and forensic examination of the remains and also if such an operation were contemplated within a definite time frame, within a week or two, with minimum disruption of the operational schedule of the military unit concerned. The Civil Affairs Officer requested the direction of the Civil Affairs Division in Zagreb to "urgently bring this information to the attention of all parties concerned in order to advise us accordingly."

On 31 October, the Director of Civil Affairs, in the name of the UNPROFOR Commander, sent a communication to the UN peacekeeping department "for onward transmission to the appropriate quarter, a statement relative to alleged war crimes" and requesting "appropriate guidance" in respect of the request of the Civil Affairs Officer in Sector West for the site to be guarded.[30] Again, UN personnel were doing what they could in circumstances.

3. Limitations of the UN operation

From the evidence cited above, a fair-minded observer would probably grant that UNPROFOR did contribute in some measure to the protection of people in the UNPAs. At the same time, there were limitations

[30] The communications in question are all in the possession of the author.

to the UN operations and some of these were brought out in a Discussion Paper published by the Refugee Project of the Lawyers Committee for Human Rights in September, 1993.[31] This discussion paper, authored by a highly qualified team of seasoned scholar/practitioners,[32] concluded that a basic underlying assumption to the humanitarian response—that human rights and refugee protection can be provided through the presence of international personnel—was suspect in the situation of the former Yugoslavia. Dedicated UN field personnel had helped many individuals but severe restrictions on access to the concerned populations had rendered many protection activities illusory. "There are no U.N.-imposed guarantors of respect for human rights, the rule of law, or protection for the displaced population."[33] This begs the question, could there be but very rarely "U.N.- imposed guarantors"?

The authors of the report concluded that the original rationale for the United Nations Protected Areas (UNPAs) had been largely frustrated and that political considerations and objections to disturbing the demographic composition in the UNPAs had caused UN forces at times to neglect human rights and refugee protection principles by rejecting and restricting the movements of asylum seekers at borders. This conflict of interests, they felt, should have been addressed by promulgating explicitly in the mandate of UNPROFOR and other concerned agencies and entities the primacy of human rights and refugee protection.[34] Again, this was an admirable recommendation, but could it have been negotiated in the UN Security Council and who would have enforced it? In the end, it took the air forces of NATO to bring the Bosnian Serbs to heel in 1995. In 1992–93 hardly any Government would have been willing to join in an enforcement operation.

Conclusion

The significance of the UN Protected Areas lies in the precedent they provided and in the very name: the idea that UN forces would act for

---

[31] Lawyers Committee for Human Rights, Refugee Project. Discussion Paper : Protection by Presence. The Limits of United Nations Safekeeping Activities in Croatia, September, 1993.

[32] The late Arthur Helton, Guy Goodwin-Gill, Walter Kalin, Michel Moussali, and Deborah Blatt.

[33] Ibid, p. 5.

[34] Ibid, p. 6.

the protection of those at risk. For the first time in the history of the United Nations, peacekeeping personnel were given an explicit protection mandate and could be seen performing protection and justice-related functions as best as they could in the circumstances. This is of some importance when considering the role of human rights in UN peace operations.

Human rights protection can be put into the categories of preventive protection, mitigatory and curative protection, and remedial and compensatory protection. UN forces certainly contributed to preventive protection from 1992 to 1994, when the political and military circumstances changed and Croatian military forces moved against three of the four safe areas. Croatia received explicit backing from powerful governments such as the USA and there was little that UN forces could do in the circumstances.

UN forces also contributed from 1992 to 1994 to mitigatory protection. Some human rights violations were prevented or curtailed while some were not. One could not expect the forces to do more than they had the means or the mandate to do. Protection in UN peacekeeping is practising the art of the possible. No one, in the circumstances, could provide absolute human rights protection, or human rights guarantees.

To the extent that UN personnel investigated reports of war crimes and crimes against humanity, they contributed to remedial protection. Their task was to submit the evidence to the war crimes investigators—which they did in some instances.

So, all in all, one cannot say that the level of protection was spectacularly high. But, and this is what is significant about the experience, UN forces experimented with the practice of protection in the UNPAs. Should the occasion arise in the future when UN forces are given an explicit protection mandate, there are lessons that might be learned from the concept of UNPAs and from the practice and limitations of protection on the ground. The first lesson is that protection cannot be achieved by UN forces in the midst of criminal warring factions determined to pursue their war aims. If one is seeking such protection then it must be done by a coalition of forces with overwhelming military power over the combatants.

The second lesson is that words create expectations. The concept of a UN protected area raised more expectations than the UN could live up to. The same experience would be repeated when, in Bosnia, the UN Security Council declared safe areas that it could not protect or was not ready to protect.

The third, and most important lesson, is that UN forces can help mitigate human rights violations to some extent. It is important that this be understood by Governments, NGOs, and the public at large. UN forces cannot stop all atrocities, but they might be able to stop some, and report on violations to international criminal tribunals.

The fourth lesson is that UN forces must be ready to provide ample reporting on criminal violations and to cooperate with international war crimes investigators and tribunals. Warring parties in theatres where UN forces are present must know that they are under the watchful eyes of UN forces and might have to answer before international criminal tribunals for their war crimes or crimes against humanity.

CHAPTER 2

HUMANITARIAN OPERATIONS

Introduction

Human rights were at the heart of the situations that humanitarian actors had to deal with in the former Yugoslavia. The lead humanitarian UN agency, designated as such by the UN Secretary-General, was the Office of the UN High Commissioner for Refugees. Under the inspired leadership of Mrs Sadako Ogata, it sought valiantly to address the challenges of protection and assistance. Mrs Ogata and UNHCR kept drawing attention to the human rights root causes of the problems in the former Yugoslavia, calling on the warring parties to stop their violations, and calling on the international community and the designated peacemakers in the ICFY to work out political solutions to the conflicts. Mrs Ogata and her colleagues pointed out that humanitarian operations were being used by the international community as a 'fig leaf' to cover their failure to stop the conflict. I have among my papers submissions from UNHCR to me as Director of the ICFY pleading that the Co-Chairmen should take action to bring violations to an end and should see to it that there were political solutions.

Unfortunately, in this conflict the point was registered forcefully that parties with the will to fight and the means to fight will fight. Yugoslavia had broken apart and the three communities in Bosnia and Herzegovina wanted to have their share of the land of the country. On top of that, for whatever historical or other reasons, universal standards of human rights had no influence on the Serbs, who kept pointing to their treatment under the Ottomans and the fascist Ustashas and vowing never to live under Muslims again. The Croats wanted to take areas of Central and Western Bosnia into Croatia and were quite brutal themselves. And the Muslims wanted to avenge injustices at the hands of the Serbs and the Croats and committed their share of inhuman actions. No one was willing to abide by civilized standards of conduct.

UNHCR was thus left to cry in the wind as it sought to assist and protect people as best it could. I cannot honestly say that the international community, or we in ICFY, responded in a timely manner or fittingly to Mrs Ogata's calls for effective action to stop human rights violations or to devise political solutions as she sought. Mrs Ogata would conclude in her Memoirs:

> "Operating in war-torn countries in the Balkans for nearly a decade, we saved innumerable lives and mitigated human suffering. We strove and came up with new approaches and new hypotheses to address constantly evolving situations. We often had to deal with problems that were beyond what we could achieve. The humanitarian 'fig leaf' filled the gap that political and military action failed for so long to address."[35]

Still, she presented the human rights dimensions of the situation with clarity and forthrightness. In this chapter we shall present UNHCR's analysis of the situation, the place it accorded to human rights in its analysis, and how it thought human rights approaches could be used to help protect people at risk. The significance of UNHCR's analysis is that it stands historically as an attempt to rally the international community to human rights ground and provided ideas that might be considered on a future occasion.

1. The Centrality of Human Rights in a Comprehensive Response to the Humanitarian Crises in the Former Yugoslavia

As United Nations involvement in the former Yugoslavia intensified in 1991-1992, the UN Secretary-General designated the United Nations High Commissioner for Refugees as the lead agency for assistance to 1.8 million refugees and displaced persons as well as some 850,000 persons affected by the ongoing conflict in Bosnia-Herzegovina. Following the deployment of the United Nations Protection Force (UNPROFOR), and in accordance with the UN peacekeeping plan, UNHCR was entrusted with the design and implementation of a scheme to facilitate the voluntary return of the displaced to their homes in the UN Protected Areas in Croatia.[36] UNHCR undertook its activities in close cooperation with UNICEF and WHO, and in close cooperation with UNPROFOR as well as with the ICRC.

[35] S. Ogata, The Turbulent Decade, Confronting the Refugee Crises of the 1990s. New York, W.W. Norton (2005), p. 171.

[36] See UN doc. S/23592.

Against the background of a large-scale and complicated refugee situation, the High Commissioner, following consultations with the UN Secretary-General and a number of governments, convened in Geneva on 29 July, 1992, an informal international meeting at the Ministerial level, with the objective of launching an initiative to address the immediate humanitarian needs of the victims and receiving States, and to intensify action in search of lasting solutions to the plight of the victims of the conflict. In a note that the High Commissioner submitted to the meeting, she urged concerted and coherent action towards a comprehensive approach that would serve to (1) enhance respect for human rights and humanitarian law (2) strengthen efforts to prevent or contain displacement; (3) provide refuge and material assistance for those in need of international protection; and (4) initiate action to create conditions, including for the socio-economic rehabilitation of affected areas, in order to encourage refugees and displaced persons to return home.[37]

The presentation of the High Commissioner focused on the centrality of human rights in the comprehensive humanitarian strategy of UNHCR.

1.1. *Respect for human rights and humanitarian law*

The High Commissioner noted that the situation in the former Yugoslavia had been "characterized by widespread atrocities, disregard for humanitarian law and massive violations of human rights, particularly targeted against civilians on grounds of national, ethnic or religious origin. Some of the most preoccupying features includes systematic expulsions, forcible relocations, assassinations and occupation or destruction of homes, particularly in Bosnia and Herzegovina and parts of Croatia. International relief workers have also been subjected to attacks" The High Commissioner underlined in her report that:

> "The reaffirmation of basic human rights and humanitarian law principles must be an essential element of a comprehensive humanitarian approach, and demands for their respect should be pursued vigorously at the highest political levels. The commendable efforts of the ICRC to negotiate agreements respective of the provisions of the 1949 Geneva Conventions and their Additional Protocols must be supported. The States emerging from the former Yugoslavia should be strongly encouraged to

[37] UN doc. HCR/IMFY/1992/2, 24 July, 1992.

develop legislation and build institutions for the protection of human rights, particularly those of minorities."[38]

1.2. *Preventive protection*

The High Commissioner thought that an important objective of humanitarian action in the former Yugoslavia had been, and should continue to be, to prevent and contain displacement, to the extent possible, by providing protection and assistance to victims of the conflict who might otherwise feel compelled to move. However, preventive protection should not prejudice the right to seek asylum. In her assessment, a preventive strategy appeared to have had some effect in containing the problem in the former Yugoslavia. "Therefore it is incumbent on the international community to pursue every opportunity for preventive action in order to reduce the factors which compel displacement and ease the way for early resolution of the problem."[39]

Preventive protection, aimed both at areas where conflict had broken out and also where tensions were mounting, could, in the assessment of the High Commissioner, be undertaken through such activities as monitoring of the treatment of ethnic minority groups, mediation between parties, exposure of the practice of forced relocation and other measures to improve respect for human rights and humanitarian law. Such action was being carried out by UNHCR in cooperation with other organizations but required greater support and encouragement of the international community as well as the parties concerned, both politically and financially. The presence of international organizations and NGOs for the purpose of providing relief could help to build confidence in fragile security situations. "International presence to provide relief to affected population should be increased to enhance preventive protection, in addition to addressing humanitarian needs."[40]

1.3. *Humanitarian access*

The High Commissioner stressed that humanitarian access at all times to those in need of protection and assistance, whether in conflict or non-conflict areas, must be upheld by all parties and the international

[38] Ibid, para. 6.
[39] Ibid, para. 7.
[40] Ibid, paras. 8–9.

community, as must respect for the freedom of movement of the individuals and their right to seek protection and assistance. Principles must be established to ensure respect for the safety of relief workers and staff of international humanitarian organizations as an important aspect of humanitarian access.[41]

1.4. *Special humanitarian needs*

The High Commissioner noted that concern had been voiced by a number of Governments, NGOs and others about the evacuation of critical medical cases, notably children from Bosnia and Herzegovina. Given the limited resources and extremely precarious security conditions, she thought that the utmost efforts should continue to be made to reduce the need for evacuation by providing adequate medical supplies and equipment for local treatment.[42]

1.5. *Temporary protection*

The High Commissioner stressed that, since the outbreak of the Yugoslav conflict, it had been the position of her Office that persons fleeing from the former Yugoslavia who were in need of international protection should be able to receive it on a temporary basis. Because of the large numbers involved, UNHCR believed that it was not practical to use individual asylum procedures, although persons who had a valid claim under the 1951 Convention relating to the Status of Refugees should not be precluded from applying for it if they wished. The concept of temporary protection would require further elaboration in the light of national legislation and procedures. It should include, as a minimum, admission to the country where such protection was being sought, respect for the principle of non-refoulement and basic human rights (the elements of which had been outlined in Conclusion 22 (XXXII) of the Executive Committee of the High Commissioner's Programme), and repatriation when conditions so allowed in the country of origin. The determination of the duration of temporary protection would require an ongoing assessment of the situation in the country of origin on the basis of reliable and up-to-date information. Appropriate mechanisms should be established for the collection,

[41] Ibid, para. 10.
[42] Ibid, para. 11.

analysis and dissemination of such information, and for consultations among concerned Governments and UNHCR.[43]

1.6. *Material assistance*

Because of the dramatic daily increase in the number of refugees, recently some 10,000 per day, and the constantly evolving situation on the ground, the High Commissioner pointed out that the magnitude of the needs went far beyond the target of the appeal of the previous May, as well as the capacity of UNHCR and a few agencies. It would require the massive mobilization of the entire United Nations humanitarian system and the international community at large.[44]

1.7. *Return and rehabilitation*

Temporary protection and international assistance, the High Commissioner explained, could not be allowed to become protracted and must be linked clearly to the pursuit of lasting solutions, which, in turn, must respect the rights of the individuals concerned, including their right to return home in safety and dignity. A mechanism should be developed for regular and reliable information exchange on conditions prevailing in the areas to which persons could return, dialogue, including through Tripartite Commissions involving the parties and UNHCR, to create conditions conducive to return, and promotion of guidelines and arrangements for return in keeping with internationally recognized safeguards.[45]

1.8. *Modalities for a comprehensive approach*

The High Commissioner recommended that a comprehensive approach should be accompanied by the creation of an international coordinating mechanism at the political and technical level that would allow regular exchange of information, dialogue and consideration of options for concerted action in relation to prevention, protection and return, as well as for the mobilization of international assistance and support for humanitarian action. Such a coordinating mechanism should comprise a core group of States directly concerned with the

---

[43] Ibid, paras. 12–13.
[44] Ibid, para. 17.
[45] Ibid., paras. 18–20.

problem, including both receiving States and donor governments, as well as interested organizations, and could be convened under the auspices of UNHCR.[46]

1.9. *Inter-agency cooperation*

The High Commissioner considered that the coordination mechanism established by UNHCR as the lead agency with UNICEF, WHO, IOM, ICRC, and the International Council of Voluntary Agencies (ICVA), and the cooperation established with ICRC to meet the requirements of the relief operation, should be reinforced. The Inter-Agency Standing Committee established pursuant to General Assembly Resolution 46/182, under the auspice of the UN Department of Humanitarian Affairs, should be utilized to mobilize the enormous material and financial resources necessary for the short-term assistance, as well as the longer-term rehabilitation needs which might call for the involvement of lending and development-oriented agencies.[47]

* * * * *

In her Memoirs, *The Turbulent Decade*, Mrs Ogata provided a dramatic account of her efforts to promote protection and assistance for refugees, displaced persons, and threatened civilian populations in the former Yugoslavia. The following points may be singled out:

1.10. *Protection through presence*

Addressing the problems of internally displaced persons, Mrs Ogata wrote:

> "In the absence of adequate legal principles or effective enforcement mechanisms that covered internally displaced persons, international presence proved to be the only available tool for their protection. UNHCR's presence would also respond to the concerns of those who had not yet moved from their homes but feared they might be removed. UNHCR had to place colleagues in conflict zones instead of evacuating them out from insecure situations. We posted large contingents of field protection officers throughout Bosnia and Herzegovina and opened as many as twenty seven suboffices. Their functions ranged from responding to the safety and assistance needs of the fleeing people to negotiating

[46] Ibid, para. 21.
[47] Ibid, para. 22.

> with the local authorities to counteract displacement and to publicly denouncing abuses as a last resort."[48]

1.11. *Protection for people where they lived*

Mrs Ogata recapitulated the origins of the idea of establishing safe areas in Bosnia-Herzegovina and UNHCR's response to the concept. A UNHCR Working Group on International Protection had examined the organization's basic position on safe areas and concluded that "the overriding principle in Bosnia and Herzegovina should be to bring safety to the people rather than to bring people to safety". She explained:

> "In other words, the first policy priority was to improve the level of safety and to provide assistance in the place where people were. Since suffering and displacement were caused by armed conflict, a genuine and durable cessation of hostilities should be the goal. UNHCR would be against the establishment of safe areas that might distract from the necessity to bring all fighting to an end. Where displacement in Bosnia and Herzegovina was caused by ethnic persecution, special measures should be taken to improve the conditions of the remaining minority groups through three means: deployment of peacekeeping forces, human rights monitoring, and humanitarian assistance. Failing the cessation of hostilities so that admission to safety became necessary, UNHCR's priority was to seek entry to neighbouring countries or to relatively secure regions of Bosnia and Herzegovina. To UNHCR, the establishment of one or more clearly delineated safe areas under military protection should be only a last option."[49]

1.12. *Release of prisoners and detainees*

Because the ICRC had suspended its presence in Bosnia and Herzegovina at one point due to attacks on its personnel, UNHCR had been called upon to help ameliorate the situation of peope detained in the conflict and to help dismantle the detention centres that had become infamous.[50] The ICFY Humanitarian Issues Working Group that Mrs Ogata chaired had dealt with the dismantling of the detention centres, with representatives of ICRC joining the negotiating meetings in Geneva. Within this framework, the ICRC was able to reach agreement for the simultaneous release of five thousand detainees by all

48 The Turbulent Decade, op.cit., p. 55.
49 Ibid, pp. 90–91.
50 Ibid, p. 70.

three sides from ten different locations. "Some thousand detained persons were released on October 19" (1992).[51]

1.13. *Pressing for political solutions*

Mrs Ogata wrote:

> "I had been long convinced that the humanitarian problems would not be solved without an overall political settlement for Yugoslavia. The ICFY came as a challenge to seek and promote solutions to the conflict."[52]

Unfortunately, she "recognized more than ever the limits of the Security Council. Its concern was primarily political, with limited heed to humanitarian consequences."[53] She "noted an increasing gap between the Security Council and the Secretary-General in New York, and UNHCR in the field, on the understanding of the needs of these 'safe' areas. The reality was that we could carry on humanitarian action only within the range allowed by the war situation."[54]

The peacemakers did what they could. Cyrus Vance told a meeting on the 'Comprehensive Response to the Humanitarian Crisis in Ex-Yugoslavia, on 4 September, 1992 :

> "Let us all work together to bring the day nearer when we may never more hear expressions such as 'ethnic cleansing', or see the daily suffering of hundreds of thousands of displaced persons."

Exhortations, however, did not suffice, and Mrs Ogata was left to fend for the victims as best she could, with remarkable innovativeness, courage, and perseverance.

Conclusion

Without a doubt, UNHCR carried a heavy burden during the Yugoslav conflicts. It had to raise funds for assisting such large numbers of people and its operatives had to work in the most difficult of conditions. I have in my mind's eye a twenty-eight year old Japanese colleague who moved in and out of dangerous areas, interacting with the leaders of warring parties, pleading with them to help alleviate the suffering of

---

51 Ibid, pp. 73–74.
52 Ibid, p. 71.
53 Ibid, p. 89.
54 Ibid, p. 93.

the people, and sending to Headquarters the most moving of reports about the plight of the civilian victims.

Nicholas Morris, the Special Envoy of the High Commissioner, Mrs Ogata, spoke to me on different occasions, as Director in the Office of the SRSG and as Director of the ICFY, that humanitarian personnel were operating in the most unsafe conditions of any UN humanitarian operation to date. I asked him to document this and included this in a report from the ICFY Co-Chairmen to the UN Security Council. Nicholas also made strong representations to me that humanitarian assistance was being diverted for military purposes on all sides of the Bosnian conflict. It was harder to make a case about this in a report to the Security Council and, eventually, we did not.

Later in this book we shall see poignant representations that Nicholas made to Dr. Radovan Karadzic to bring ethnic cleansing to an end. So did the SRSG in Zagreb, all to no avail. UNHCR had to operate in the most difficult environment, doing what it could to protect people in distress while pleading for political solutions and for effective action on the part of the international community to protect the human rights of people at risk.

We shall see in subsequent chapters the efforts of the UN Special Rapporteur on human rights in the former Yugoslavia, as well as efforts by the peacemakers and the peacekeepers to help protect human rights. Unfortunately, we have to recognize that though they did what they could in the circumstances, it was not enough. In fact, only negotiated solutions could bring an end to the suffering of the people. The Vance-Owen plan might have stopped the conflict in Bosnia and Herzegovina in the spring of 1993, two and a half years earlier than the Dayton peace accords. The USA, however, wanted to, and did arm, the Bosnian government so that it could continue fighting and take back territories lost to the Bosnian Serbs.

Whatever the moral rationale for this US policy, the fact of the matter is that countless people died or suffered in the conflict from the spring of 1993 to November, 1995. While UNHCR was calling for political settlements, the most powerful country in the world was arming the Bosnians to fight. We also had peace agreements such as the Invincible package a full two years before Dayton. President Izetbegovic and Foreign Minister Haris Silajdzic accepted this agreement on the HMS Invincible and then repudiated it a week later under US pressure. History will judge the Invincible package a more stable one than that concluded at Dayton. Again, the question arises, why did so many people have to die and to suffer in the two years between September, 1993 and November 22, 1995, when the Dayton accords were signed?

There was a moment in August, 1993, when President Izetbegovic asked for, and obtained, six concessions from Dr. Karadzic. Lord Owen and Thorvald Stoltenberg secured these concessions but Izetbegovic would still not sign. One of his close aides, in a private moment, wept on my shoulder and asked, "Why does he not sign? Does he not know how much we are suffering?"

I relate the above not to be accusatory, or judgmental. Rather, it is to address UNHCR's plea that everything be done to bring about a political solution, and to protect the rights of the victims. The sad fact of the matter is that a solution to the Bosnian conflict could not be achieved until the US government was ready. And it was only in the summer of 1995 that the US was ready to bring about a solution. And, in the meantime, in the words of the song by Elvis Presley, singing about the plight of the victims in the slums of Chicago, "And his Momma cried."

By a strange quirk of circumstances, I was present at Dayton when the accords were negotiated and signed. The US team, under criticism in the media, kept briefing journalists that what was being worked out was the best that could be attained in the circumstances. When Vance, Owen, Ahtisaari and Stoltenberg did this a full two and half years earlier, the US Government and the media pundits all came down hard on them.Well, in fact, there were better peace agreements long before Dayton, negotiated by the ICFY negotiators. Uncle Sam chose to let the conflict continue. And the victims cried. And UNHCR cried. And we cried. And Mommas cried!

UNHCR's analysis on the centrality of human rights, on protection through presence, all depended on a negotiated solution to the conflict. Without an end to the conflict human rights solutions were hardly possible. Uncle Sam had ordained that the fighting must continue until it was ready to ordain peace. What, then, did the Special Rapporteur of the UN Commission on Human Rights try to achieve in these circumstances? This is the question we address in the next chapter.

CHAPTER 3

THE UN SPECIAL RAPPORTEUR

Introduction

The Special Rapporteur initially appointed by the UN Commission on Human Rights to investigate the situation of human rights in the territory of the former Yugoslavia, Mr. Tadeusz Mazowiecki, former Solidarity Prime Minister of Poland, was undoubtedly a stirring voice of conscience on behalf of the victims of abuses in the former Yugoslavia. His successors continued in the path he had mapped out in highlighting the plight of the victims. In this chapter we review the endeavours of the Special Rapporteur and discuss his relations with the peacemakers and peacekeepers.

By way of background, it is useful to recall the message Cyrus Vance and Lord Owen sent on 30 November, 1992 to the second special session of the Commission on Human Rights. Vance and Owen welcomed the Commission's decision to convene a second special session to consider the serious situation of human rights in the area of the former Yugoslavia, especially in Bosnia and Herzegovina and declared:

> "Regrettably, the disgraceful practice of ethnic cleansing has not ceased and violations of international norms on human rights and humanitarian law are rampant. We condemn these violations in the most categorical terms."

They added that in their efforts to promote peace with justice in the area of the former Yugoslavia, they had placed emphasis on the provision of humanitarian assistance; the strict application of sanctions; helping to bring about a cessation of hostilities in Bosnia and Herzegovina; and the preparation of a constitution for Bosnia and Herzegovina. They had also sought to promote preventive measures to avoid the spread of the conflict. They continued:

> "We urge the distinguished members of the Commission on Human Rights, all Member States of the United Nations, and non-governmental organizations, to do everything possible to support and to strengthen the endeavours being undertaken in accordance with decisions of the Security Council of the United Nations.

"We hope that your session will help in bringing an end to the violations of human rights and humanitarian law taking place. We also hope that you will give attention to the important question of protecting the rights of minorities. This issue is of great importance to the future stability and security in the area of the former Yugoslavia."

1. Mandate of the Special Rapporteur

At its first special session on the former Yugoslavia, the Commission on Human Rights adopted resolution 1992/S-1/1 on 14 August 1992 in which it requested its Chairman to appoint a special rapporteur to investigate first hand the human rights situation in the territory of the former Yugoslavia, in particular within Bosnia and Herzegovina, and to receive relevant, credible information on the human rights situation there from Governments, individuals, intergovernmental and non-governmental organizations, on a continuing basis, and to avail himself or herself of the assistance of existing mechanisms of the Commission on Human Rights. The Chairman of the Commission appointed Mr. Tadeusz Mazowiecki, former Prime Minister of Poland, as Special Rapporteur.[55]

2. Initial report

The Special Rapporteur visited the region from 21- 26 August and, in his first report to the Commission,[56] submitted the following conclusions to the Commission based on the information that he marshalled in his report: Massive and grave violations of human rights were occurring throughout the territory of Bosnia and Herzegovina. Human Rights violations were being perpetrated by all parties to the conflicts. There were also victims on all sides. However, the situation of the Muslim population was particularly tragic. They felt that they were threatened with extermination.

Acts of violence, he continued, were tolerated and often even encouraged by responsible authorities. Consequently, the rule of law

[55] Amnesty International's Conception of the Role of the Special Rapporteur was as follows: The Special Rapporteur 'should play a central role in documenting the human rights situation and making recommendations about preventive measures'—Amnesty International, Open Letter, 27 October, 1992.

[56] The UN Secretary-General circulated the report to the UN General Assembly and the Security Council on 3 September, 1992 : UN doc. A/47/418; S/24516.

did not exist. The situation of people being detained in camps and staying in refugee centres was particularly dramatic. The indoctrination of a large part of the population that was taking place encouraged national and religious hatred. In spite of the high level of commitment of the United Nations personnel—UNPROFOR and UNHCR—they were unable adequately to protect the affected population and in many circumstances were helpless to prevent violations of human rights. There was urgent need for immediate concerted action. Even when peace was achieved, serious violations of human rights were likely to continue due to the intensity of mutual distrust and hatred.[57]

The Special Rapporteur made a number of ground-breaking recommendations that would influence UN policy and lead to innovative developments. He recommended that the United Nations, without delay, issue a peremptory warning to the authorities controlling the different parts of the territory of Bosnia and Herzegovina that, with respect to their duty to safeguard the security of the civilian population, they may, in accordance with the norms and standards of international law, be brought to justice not only for the direct perpetration but also for the toleration of acts of atrocity, violence and other violations of human rights. The United Nations, he wrote, should continue firmly to call upon the competent authorities to abandon the policy of ethnic cleansing in all its forms. Every victim of this policy should be guaranteed the possibility of claiming his/her rights under international supervision.

The Special Rapporteur considered that it was indispensable not only to increase the size of UNPROFOR but also to expand its mandate in three areas: First, the mandate should cover the whole territory of Bosnia and Herzegovina; second, UNPROFOR personnel should have the right to react directly to the human rights violations committed in their presence and to assist the victims; third, UNPROFOR personnel should be given the mandate to collect information and receive complaints concerning human rights violations occurring also on the territories which at the time were not covered by UNPROFOR's mandate. This should include access by the UNPROFOR civilian police to places of detention. Their findings should be communicated not only to the local police but also to the competent juridical authorities.

---

[57] Ibid, paras. 51–57.

The Special Rapporteur considered that there was an urgent need to establish an investigative commission, under the auspices and in cooperation with the competent United Nations bodies, vested with the task of determining the fate of the thousands of persons who had disappeared after the seizure of Vukovar as well as of other persons who had disappeared during the conflicts in the former Yugoslavia.

The Special Rapporteur emphasized that the need to prosecute those responsible for mass and flagrant human rights violations and for breaches of international humanitarian law and to deter future violators required the systematic collection of documentation on such crimes and of personal data concerning those responsible. He recommended that a Commission be created to assess and further investigate specific cases in which prosecution might be warranted. This information should include date already collected by various entities within the UN system, by other intergovernmental organizations and by non-governmental organizations.[58]

The Special Rapporteur considered that further implementation of his mandate required the appointment of staff based in the territories of the former Yugoslavia in order to coordinate the monitoring of human rights violations together with the other UN bodies. He recommended the creation of an adequate professional and logistical infrastructure within the Centre for Human Rights (now the OHCHR). It also required the establishment of a working relationship with other multilateral initiatives, in particular the Co-Chairmen of the International Conference on the Former Yugoslavia.[59]

These were innovative recommendations of the Special Rapporteur, all of which would come to be implemented in the subsequent months. The Special Rapporteur thus made a major contribution to UN and international policy in the former Yugoslavia, particularly the pursuit of justice in respect of war crimes and crimes against humanity.

3. The Special Rapporteur and the Peacemakers

The Co-Chairmen saw Mr. Mazowiecki on Friday 4 September, within days of their arrival in Geneva. On that occasion he indicated that he saw his mission as an integral part of their efforts. Subsequently

58 Ibid, paras. 58–70.
59 Ibid, paras. 72–73.

he submitted a detailed memorandum to the UN Secretary-General, which he copied to the Co-Chairmen, concerning his mandate. Among other things, he advocated putting human rights monitors on the ground.

In a letter to the Co-Chairmen he proposed the designation of contact persons. He designed Professor Roman Wieruszewski. In their reply the Co-Chairmen designated Mrs Ogata and Ambassador Geert Ahrens.

On 22 September, 1992, the Office of the UN Secretary-General consulted Cyrus Vance on the following policy proposals, which Vance endorsed. In his reply to the Secretary-General, Vance explained that they had already been implemented:

- Mr. Vance would bring to the attention of the Steering Committee of ICFY the recommendations which the Special Rapporteur might make for their consideration, as part of the effort to address the crisis in the former Yugoslavia in all its aspects.
- Similarly, Mr. Vance would encourage Mr. Mazowiecki's participation in the Working Group on Humanitarian Questions chaired by the UN High Commissioner for Refugees.
- Provision was being made for making available to the Centre for Human Rights five professional posts so as to assist the Special Rapporteur. While it was not the usual practice for support personnel of Special Rapporteurs to be posted in the field, allowance could be made in this case having regard to the high priority given by the Commission on Human Rights to the mission entrusted to Mr. Mazowiecki.
- The Special Rapporteur was answerable to the Human Rights Commission. His reports were also being published as Security Council documents. Provision would be made for Mr. Mazowiecki to report in person to the General Assembly when the item came up in the Third Committee of the General Assembly.[60]

The Office of the Secretary-General also suggested that the attendance of Mr. Mazowiecki in the periodic meetings of the Steering Committee of ICFY as an observer, an idea which Mr. Vance supported, should be put to the members of the Committee when they met next. Some

---

[60] Commuication from De Soto to Vance dated 22 September, 1992, in the possession of the author.

senior officers in ICFY did not support this recommendation on the ground that there were no observers on the Steering Committee. This was an unfortunate position. Giving Mr. Mazowiecki the opportunity to brief the Steering Committee would have been a way of highlighting the human rights issues in the Steering Committee.

In a briefing paper that a senior advisor wrote for the Co-Chairmen for their second meeting with Mr. Mazowiecki on 8 October 1992, he suggested that, in the future, their relationship with Mr. Mazowiecki could be placed on the following basis:

(a) "If he has information on specific events that he feels would be useful to you, he could send specific briefing notes to you.
(b) If he has specific issues he would like to consult you on, he may indicate them to a member of your staff and you would try, if possible, to get back to him.
(c) He should understand that the Co-Chairmen, as peace-makers, have to maintain a discreet posture and, therefore, the roles of the Co-Chairmen on the one hand, and the Special Rapporteur on the other hand, would need to be kept distinct."[61]

The briefing paper continued:

"It might be a good idea for you to indicate, from your vantage point, some issues that Mr. Mazowiecki might look into. The following come to mind:

- What are his perceptions about any forms of cooperation that could be pursued by the Republics of the former Yugoslavia to promote and protect human rights in the area?
- Does he have any thoughts to offer on a mechanism or mechanisms that could be developed to ensure protection for human rights in BH?
- Would he see a role for an International Verification Commission on Human Rights in the region or in BH, for, say, a five year period?
- Could he provide the Co-Chairmen with his reflections on issues of group rights that would need to be addressed in the area of the former Yugoslavia in the future, and what are his recommendations."[62]

---

[61] Background Notes for the Co-Chairmen's Meeting with Mazowiecki, 8 October 1992, 10 a.m. Document in the possession of the author.

[62] Ibid.

In the actual meeting on 8 October, which lasted forty-five minutes, Mr. Mazowiecki informed the Co-Chairmen that he would be undertaking a mission to the area of the former Yugoslavia in the coming week and he wished to have an exchange of views with them. He raised the following issues: information on gross violations of human rights; the latest situation in Bosanski Brod and Sarajevo; developments regarding the proposal for a no-fly-zone over Bosnia and Herzegovina; developments in relations between the Bosnian Croats and the Bosnian Serbs.

Lord Owen suggested that it might be helpful if the Special Rapporteur could get in to Kosovo and help bring a wide international presence to that area. Mr. Vance followed up on his request for assistance during his forthcoming field mission.[63]

The Special Rapporteur operated in the Polish language. Conversations were therefore through an interpreter. As a former Prime Minister he saw himself operating on this plane. He had little practical experience on human rights matters and therefore could not engage in a discussion on issues such as minority and group rights. One had the impression that there was never really a substantive dialogue between the Special Rapporteur and the Co-Chairmen.

4. The Special Rapporteur and the peacekeepers

As we saw earlier, the Special Rapporteur, in his first report, considered that it was indispensable not only to increase the size of UNPROFOR but also to expand its mandate in three areas: First, the mandate should cover the whole territory of Bosnia and Herzegovina; second, UNPROFOR personnel should have the right to react directly to the human rights violations committed in their presence and to assist the victims; third, UNPROFOR personnel should be given the mandate to collect information and receive complaints concerning human rights violations occurring also on the territories which at the time were not covered by UNPROFOR's mandate. This should include access by the UNPROFOR civilian police to places of detention. Their findings should be communicated not only to the local police but also to the competent juridical authorities.

---

[63] Note on the Meeting in the possession of the author.

5. The Special Rapporteur leads a campaign to expose ethnic cleansing

Counting interim reports, including reports to the General Assembly and the Security Council, Mr. Mazowiecki submitted sixteen reports.[64] One of his major contributions was his campaign to alert the international community to the practice of ethnic cleansing in the former Yugoslavia, especially Bosnia and Herzegovina. He highlighted this theme in report after report submitted to the Commission on Human Rights and the General Assembly. In his report of 17 November, 1992, Mr. Mazowiecki defined the practice as follows:

> "The term ethnic cleansing refers to the elimination by the ethnic group exerting control over a given territory of members of other ethnic groups."[65]

In his second periodic report, Mr. Mazowiecki stated "that the principal objective of the military conflict in Bosnia and Herzegovina is the establishment of ethnically homogenous regions. Ethnic cleansing

---

[64] On 27 July, 1995, following the Bosnian Serb attacks upon and occupation of United Nations safe areas of Srebrenica and Zepa, Mr Mazowiecki resigned his mandate with an emotional appeal to the international commuity. See the International Herald Tribune, 28 July, 1995, p.1.

[65] A/47/666-S24809. In the first interim report submitted by the Commission Experts established pursuant to Security Council resolution 780 of 6 October, 1992 to investigate grave breaches of the Geneva Conventions and other violations of international law committed in the territory of the former Yugoslavia, the Commission stated: "The expression 'ethnic cleansing' is relatively new. Considered in the context of the conflicts in the former Yugoslavia, 'ethnic cleansing' means rendering an area ethnically homogenous by using force or intimidation to remove persons of given groups from the area. 'Ethnic cleansing' is contrary to international law.

"Based on the many reports describing the policy and practices conducted in the former Yugoslavia, 'ethnic cleansing' has been carried out by means of murder, torture, arbitrary arrest and detention, extra-judicial executions, rape and sexual assaults, confinement of civilian population in ghetto areas, forcible removal, displacement and deportation of civilian population, deliberate military attacks or threats of attacks on civilians and civilian areas, and wanton destruction of property. Those practices constitute crimes against humanity and can be assimilated to specific war crimes. Furthermore, such acts could also fall within the meaning of the Genocide Convention": S/25274.

In its final report to the Security Council, the Commission of experts concluded that it was a deliberate policy to instill terror so as to induce persons to leave. Among the coercive means used to remove the civilian population were: "mass murder, torture, rape and other forms of sexual assault; severe physical injury to civilians; mistreatment of civilian prisoners and prisoners of war; use of civilians as human shields; destruction of personal, public and cultural property; forced expropriation of real property; forceful displacement of civilian population; and attacks on hospitals, medical personnel and locations marked with the Red Cross/Red Crescent emblem.": S/1994/674.

does not appear to be the consequence of the war but rather its goal."[66] In his third report he elaborated that "the continuation of ethnic cleansing is a deliberate effort to create a *fait accompli* in flagrant disregard of international commitments entered into by those who carry out and benefit from ethnic cleansing."[67]

In his sixth report, submitted on 21 February 1994, Mr. Mazowiecki referred to the various manifestations of 'ethnic cleansing' and population transfers, in particular the terrorization of Muslims and Bosnian Croats in Serb-held territory. He reiterated his outright condemnation of such practices "which violate fundamental human rights including the right to life, integrity of the person, property, privacy and family life, freedom of thought, conscience, religion and of movement, to earn one's livelihood, to nationality, and rights as a member of an ethnic or cultural group."[68]

He deplored the escalation in the rate of 'ethnic cleansing' in Banja Luka, where there had been a sharp rise in repossessions of apartments, whereby Muslim and Croat tenants were summarily evicted. Almost all non-Serbs had lost their jobs in Banja Luka and he estimated that only 3 per cent of non-Serbs continued to hold employment within the territories administered by the Bosnian Serbs. The authorities in Banja Luka had removed all physical traces of the presence of a Muslim community through the demolition of all of the municipalities' 202 mosques and four other mosques/mausoleums had been razed. On 15 December 1993 the remains of a 16th century Ferhadpasina mosque and four other mosques/mausoleums had been razed. The site had since been turned into a car park.[69]

In the same report, Mazowiecki drew attention to the terrorization of Muslims and Bosnian Serbs in Bosnian Croat held territory, in particular in Mostar: "A result of the 'ethnic cleansing' of Serbs is that their population in Mostar has been reduced from a pre-war figure of 30,000 to just 400"[70] He also deplored the killing in Mostar on 18 October, 1993, of a well known Muslim doctor and members of her family, apparently by members of the Bosnian Croat Defence Forces.[71]

---

[66] E/CN.4/1994 of 19 May, 1993, para. 6.
[67] E/CN.4/1994 of 26 August 1993, para. 135.
[68] E/CN.4/1994/110, paras 7 ff.
[69] Ibid, 8–13.
[70] Ibid, paras 15–19.
[71] Ibid,para. 17.

Mr. Mazowiecki continued that displacements of populations had been effected by three means: involuntary population exchanges between municipalities under the control of opposing belligerents; private arrangements for emigration to the territory of another of the belligerents; and the forced and immediate expulsion of communities from their places of residence. The various forms of displacement were often accompanied by extortion and theft. Displaced persons leaving Serb held territory were routinely subjected to strip searches at the frontier and to the confiscation of all valuables.[72]

In his seventh report, Mr. Mazowiecki reported on the destruction of Gorazde by Bosnian Serb forces, including a deliberate "scorched earth policy".[73]

6. Documenting the Violations

Following horrible massacres of Muslims in Bosnia and Herzegovina, Mr. Mazowiecki resigned as Special Rapporteur during 1995 because he felt that the international community had not done enough to protect human rights in Bosnia and Herzegovina. He sought, by his resignation, to draw attention to the plight of the victims in Bosnia and Herzegovina. He was succeeded, in turn, by Elizebeth Rehn of Finland, Jiri Dinstbeir of the Czech Republic, and Jose Cutileiro of Portugal. All of these special rapporteurs, through their reports to the Commission on Human Rights, the General Assembly, and the Security Council, documented as best they could the criminal violations of human rights that had taken place in the former Yugoslavia. They therefore made historic contributions in alerting the international community to what had taken place.

Conclusion

However, as we stated in the conclusion to the previous chapter on humanitarian operations, there could really be no serious possibility of stopping the violations without stopping the conflicts through negotiations. Whatever the Special Rapporteurs documented and reported on, and whatever they recommended, the violations and atrocities

[72] Ibid, paras. 40–48.
[73] E/CN.4/1995, para. 15.

would continue once the conflicts continued. That was the nature of the conflicts. One was not dealing with political or military leaders who were mindful of international human rights and humanitarian law. In the absence of countervailing force, only negotiated solutions could hope to alleviate the plight of innocent civilians. This is why it was so terribly wrong for the USA to support the continuation of the conflict between 1993 and 1995 while people died or were ethnically cleansed in large numbers.

There were those who said that the peace negotiators should not negotiate with the leaders of the warring factions but with leaders of civil society supportive of peace. No one could explain how these leaders of civil society would overwhelm the fighting forces or their military or political leadership. At the end of the day, peace has to be made through those with fighting forces on the ground.

The Special Rapporteurs of the Commission on Human Rights served an important function inasmuch as they acted as the voice of conscience and justice. This was their greatest contribution. At the end of the day, however, it was the peace negotiators who had to try to stop the conflicts, provided that major powers, notably the USA, would let them do their job. The Americans never gave the ICFY negotiators on Bosnia a chance because they blocked peace agreements and armed the Bosnian Muslims and the Croatian government.

The ICFY negotiators persisted nevertheless, and endeavoured to negotiate on the basis of the principles laid down at the London Conference in August, 1992. How they did this we shall see in the next chapter.

CHAPTER 4

EFFORTS TO NEGOTIATE ON THE FOUNDATION OF PRINCIPLES

Introduction

The preceding chapters will have shown how haunting were the problems of human rights violations in the former Yugoslavia. The Vance Plan had helped to bring a measure of respite to the UNPAs in Croatia. But then conflict had spread to Bosnia and Herzegovina and widespread ethnic cleansing was underway in that unfortunate country. For almost a year, a European Community Conference led by Lord Peter Carrington had sought to negotiate among the constituent republics of the former Yugoslavia a treaty providing for a loose confederation anchored in respect for human and minority rights. Lord Carrington's efforts were scuttled by Germany's pressure within the EC to recognize the constituent republics as independent countries. The Cutileiro plan which was being negotiated for the political future of Bosnia and Herzegovina had envisaged Bosnia and Herzegovina being a confederation of three constituent entities, Bosniac, Croat and Serb. The Serbs and the Croats sought to 'ethnically cleanse' the areas being envisaged for them of Muslims. The situation was desperate, and UN Secretary-General Boutros Boutros-Ghali was pressing for the Europeans to deal with a European problem in the Balkans. In the end result, the British Presidency of the European Community and the UN Secretary-General agreed to hold an international conference at the end of August, 1992, the London Conference, to map new strategies for peacemaking and peacekeeping in the former Yugoslavia.

Marrack Goulding, the UN Under-Secretary-General in charge of peacekeeping attended the London Conference with Secretary-General Boutros-Ghali. In his book, Memoirs of a Peacemonger, he writes that the UN had very few staff members at the London Conference to work on the different issues over the two days of the conference. Most of the drafting had been done by the host country, the British, and the UN Secretary-General and himself were left to fend for themselves as best they could. One of the documents adopted at the London Conference contained a set of principles for future peace efforts. The London

Conference decided on the establishment of the International Conference on the Former Yugoslavia, with the EC Presidency and the UN Secretary-General as the political heads, and Lord David Owen and Cyrus Vance as the lead negotiators, with the title of Co-Chairmen of the Steering Committee of ICFY.

How would they seek to implement the human rights Principles of the London Conference? At the outset of the negotiations among the Bosnian parties, Martti Ahtisaari, the Head of ICFY's Working Group on Bosnia and Herzegovina, began by discussing the Principles of the London Conference with them. He invited them to give their views on the elements of a constitutional structure that they wished to be taken into account. He then spent several sessions with their delegations going through with them, painstakingly (with the assistance of Legal Advisers Paul Szasz and this author) the principal international instruments on human rights that should be taken into account in establishing a constitutional structure for Bosnia and Herzegovina.[74]

In this chapter we shall first look at the human rights framework of the treaty being negotiated by Lord Carrington in the EC conference. Then we shall summarise the Principles of the London Conference. We shall proceed thereafter to see how Ahtisaari and his colleagues sought to build the peace negotiations on the Principles of the London Conference and on the principal international human rights instruments. We shall finally discuss some of the difficulties experienced in implementing general principles in the course of complex and tortuous negotiations.

1. The human rights approach of the EC Conference

Lord Carrington, in his efforts for the formation of a loose confederation among the Yugoslav Republics put on the table draft "Treaty

[74] See, generally, DPI Note, "Press Briefing on Human Rights Aspects of Vance-Owen Plan for Bosnia and Herzegovina", 17 March, 1993. (5 pages). The Note, in the possession of the author, summarized the content of a Press Briefing given by this writer. On page 5 of the Note one reads the following: "A correspondent said there seemed to be no provisions to enforce the decisions of the (human rights) court. 'One is trying to stitch a country together', Mr. Ramcharan replied, 'one is trying to take a country from war into peace. The Co-Chairmen's plan was to devise a fabric of institutions that would be respected in good faith in the future. The Co-Chairmen's scheme was to 'walk the parties to the conflict down a path leading to human rights institutions, in the hopes that they would respect their commitments."

Provisions for the Convention" which would place the new relations between the Republics on comprehensive arrangements, including supervisory mechanisms for the protection of human rights and special status for certain groups and States.[75] Chapter 2 of the draft treaty dealt with human rights.

Article 2 envisaged that the Republics would guarantee enumerated human rights grounded in instruments such as the Universal Declaration of Human Rights, the International Covenants, the Final Act of the Helsinki Conference, the European Convention for the Protection of Human Rights and Fundamental Freedoms and other international and European instruments. It also envisaged that the Republics would guarantee human rights as applied to national or ethnic groups as embodied in a number of international and European instruments including the International Convention on the Elimination of Racial Discrimination and the Convention on the Prevention of the Crime of Genocide.

Furthermore, the Republics would undertake to guarantee enumerated rights of persons belonging to a national or ethnic group. These included the principle of non-discrimination, the right to be protected against any activity capable of threatening their existence, and the guarantee that no disadvantage shall arise from a person's choice to belong or not to belong to a national or ethnic group.

Areas in which persons belonging to a national or ethnic group formed a majority would enjoy a special status of autonomy. Such a status would provide for the right to have and show the national emblem of that area; an administrative structure, including a regional police force and a judiciary responsible for matters concerning the area, which reflected the composition of the population of the area. There would also be appropriate provisions for international monitoring.

The Republics would provide for international monitoring of the implementation of the special status of autonomy. To this end, they would conclude agreements that would provide for a permanent international body to monitor the implementation of the special status of autonomy.

The draft convention envisaged the establishment of a Court of Human Rights that would have jurisdiction within the republics to consider appeals from courts in the republics involving questions of

[75] The text of the draft convention is reproduced in UN doc. S/23169.

human rights. It also envisaged the establishment of Mixed Commissions where such mixed commissions might assist in avoiding or dealing with disputes concerning human rights and the rights of ethnic or national groups and areas having special status.

Lord Carrington's draft convention was accepted by all the Yugoslav leaders except President Slobodan Milosevic, who was not willing to subscribe to the provisions on autonomy and minority rights. Lord Carrington felt that he could overcome this difficulty but German insistence on recognition of the Yugoslav republics cut the ground from under his efforts and brought his efforts to an end. As was widely expected, recognition of Bosnia and Herzegovina brought war to that country and, by August, 1992, the situation was acute. The British Government, which then held the presidency of the European Community, convened a conference in London at the end of August to discuss the way forward. The London Conference decided on the establishment of the International Conference on the Former Yugoslavia and put down a set of principles to guide the negotiations.

2. The Principles of the London Conference

At the start of the negotiations with the Bosnian parties, the lead negotiator on Bosnia and Herzegovina, Martti Ahtisaari, gave them the following "Checklist of London Principles in Relation to the future constitution of BH":

(1) The guarantee of the highest standards of human rights, including individual rights and fundamental freedoms in a democratic society, as set out in a series of important human rights instruments of the United Nations, the Council of Europe, and the Conference on Security and Cooperation in Europe;
(2) The special guarantee of the rights of ethnic and national communities, as well as of minorities;
(3) Constitutional and legal structures that can assure democratic governance and the protection of the above-mentioned rights;
(4) Respect for international treaties and agreements.[76]

Ahtisaari reminded the Bosnian leaders that they were meant to negotiate an agreement to end the conflict on the basis of these principles.

---

[76] Document given by Martti Ahtisaari to the Bosnian delegations on 18 September, 1992. Document in the possession of the author.

It was not evident that this had any significant impact on them. Nevertheless, Ahtisaari and his colleagues persisted along this route, as we shall see next.

3. Negotiating on the foundations of international and European human rights norms

From the very outset of the work of ICFY, as the Bosnian delegations advanced claims in respect of the rights of the constituent peoples of Bosnia and Herzegovina, ICFY personnel raised fundamental issues of principle regarding the human rights foundations of a future peace agreement. Thus, on 21 September, 1991, the late Paul Szasz, Legal Adviser of ICFY, wrote a memorandum titled "Problems in Basing Political Institutions on National or Ethnic Status."[77] Szasz wrote:

> "This note will discuss some of the technical difficulties that might be anticipated in including any provisions relating to ethnic or national or similar groupings in the institutional provisions of the proposed BiH constitution (as distinguished from those relating to human rights—though even there, general principles on minority rights would be much easier than any that refer to specific groupings). These considerations are aside from any related anomaly of introducing such provisions into an internationally brokered instruments in the last decade of the 20th century, against the entire trend of international human rights developments of the past several decades (e.g., in particular, the firm rejection of apartheid).
>
> "If any institutional political rights are to be based on any group (national, ethnic or other) identification (i.e. in BiH: Muslim, Serb, Croat), for example, if one of the houses of the legislature is to be composed of a particular number of members of each group and/or if the executive is to have a multi-group composition, it will be necessary to define in some way how the group representatives in the legislature/executive are to be chosen, i..e. how they are to be elected. For this, there would seem to be two possible approaches:...(a) geographic—based on the assumption that identifiable regions have a pure enough group composition that representatives elected from those regions are, in effect, representatives of that group; (b) personal—which would require classifying citizens to determine which of them may vote for which group representatives.

In discussing these two possible approaches Szasz cautioned that one or both could be the pretext for resorting to or allowing the continuation,

[77] Memorandum in the possession of the author.

and accepting the results of "ethnic cleansing." He clearly favoured an approach that based itself on international human rights norms.

4. Guiding the Delegations on International Human Rights Law

When discussions began with the three Bosnian parties in Geneva in the second half of September, 1992, Martti Ahtisaari, in addition to giving them a document recaputaling the key principles of the London Conference on human rights, invited each delegation to submit in writing its views on the future constitutional structure of Bosnia and Herzegovina, gave them checklists of issues for discussion based on the provisions of international and European human rights instruments, and requested Paul Szasz and this writer to brief each delegation, step by step, on the provisions of key international and European human rights instruments. Paul Szasz took each delegation separately through the main human rights instruments, explaining them, and answering questions from members of the delegations. This author took detailed notes on these briefings which are in the archives of the ICFY at the United Nations Office in Geneva and copies of which are also in the possession of the author.

The checklists provided to the delegations included the following:

- Checklist of principles related to the Constituton,18 September, 1992.
- Checklist of International Human Rights Instruments Relevant to a Constitution for Bosnia and Herzegovina, 22 September, 1992, revised on 25 September.
- List of human rights that might be considered for inclusion in or other protection under the BiH Constitution, 25 September, 1992.
- Preliminary thoughts for discussion on implementation, enforcement and guarantees of human rights provisions of BiH Constitution, 25 September, 1992.
- Distribution of Governmental Responsibilities between Central Government and other Constituent Instruments (Request for indication of preferences), 29 September, 1992.

We provide below some excerpts from the Notes written by this author of the guidance sessions with each delegation. Mr. Szasz first met with the Bosnian (Muslim) delegation on 25 September, 1992: Dr. Haris

Siladzic, Foreign Minister, Mr. Pejanovic, Mr. Ljubic, Mr. Brkic, Mr. Filipovic and Mr. Lazovic. Mr. Szasz began by introducing the checklists enumerated above. Foreign Minister Silajdzic said that his delegation's human rights expert had had to go back to Zagreb. The delegation would ask him to study the human rights documents provided. The note on the meeting reads:

> "Foreign Minister Silajdzic stated that, while his delegation appreciated the work that had gone into preparing the documents, it was very difficult to discuss detailed questions on the human rights contents of the future constitution while aggression was continuing on the ground in Bosnia and Herzegovina. He stressed the urgency of implementing the agreements concluded in London."[78]

On Monday 28 September, 1992, Mr. Szasz and this author met again with Mr. Pejanovic, Mr. Ljubic, Mr. Filipovic, and Mr. Lazovic of the Bosnian (Muslim) delegation. The note on the meeting reads:

> "Mr. Ljubic commented on one of the papers that the delegation had received…containing Preliminary thoughts for discussion on implementation, enforcement and guarantees of human rights in a future constitution of Bosnia and Herzegovina…He stated that he and his colleagues had studied these materials and would like to see the wholly domestic and partially international arrangements all incorporated into the future constitutions. If implemented faithfully they would provide full guarantee of human rights. He added that this paper had been well prepared. The proposals were good proposals and he and his colleagues would like all the parties to accept them.
>
> …
>
> "Professor Pejanovic…fully agreed with Mr. Ljubic about the importance of accepting international instruments as well as international supervision. He added that gross violations of human rights had appeared in Bosnia and Herzegovina only after the appearance on the scene of authorities beyond the control of the Government…."[79]

On Monday, 28 November, Mr. Szasz and this author met with Dr. Koljevic and Mr. Buha of the Bosnian Serb delegation. Mr. Szasz began by introducing the checklists enumerated above. The note on the meeting reads:

> "Dr. Koljevic asked whether the idea was that the international human rights instruments being discussed would be listed in the future

[78] ICFY/BH/MTG. 11.
[79] ICFY/BH/MTG. 12.

> constitution, would be quoted from, or whether their essence would be included. Mr. Szasz replied that perhaps the best method would be to list the rights, define them concisely, and provide that legislation would spell them out. It could also be provided that the rights included should be interpreted in accordance with, or in the spirit of, the international instruments…
>
> …
>
> "Dr. Koljevic agreed with Mr. Szasz that there was sense in starting the constitutional negotiations with the human rights provisions, as the parties appeared to be in general agreement as to those and because satisfactory provisions might ease the negotiations on other points.
>
> "Mr. Buha stated that his delegation needed some clarification on the issue of collective rights. In particular, he wished to know who would determine whether the three nations that make up Bosnia and Herzegovina could each have their own sovereign States, which appeared necessary to him, or whether the Serbs would remain in colonial domination by the other nations. He added that one should keep in mind the rights of peoples to self determination and not to be dominated. What would be the point of departure in dealing with such issues. Mr. Szasz replied that answers to the nature of the future State would have to come out of the negotiations among the parties at the Conference."[80]

A guidance meeting was also held with the Bosnian Croat delegation. It was facilitated by a declaration by its leader, Mr. Mate Boban, in a meeting with Vance, Owen, Ahtissari, with the participation of Szasz and this author, on 21 September, 1992. Mr. Mate Boban had expressed his position on the human rights foundations of the future constitution of Bosnia and Herzegovina as follows:

> "With regard to human rights issues, Mr. Boban stated that all three sides had signed the document of 31 March, 1992 which embraced all relevant international documents on human rights. It was on the basis of those principles that Bosnia and Herzegovina was recognized as a State. His side would sign and abide by any list of human rights instruments that Mr. Ahtisaari came up with."[81]

5. Principles and realities

One can see from the above, how earnest the ICFY negotiators were in striving to build their negotiating package on Bosnia and Herzegovina

[80] ICFY/BH/MTG.13.
[81] ICFY/BH/MTG.8.

on the foundations of human rights. Unfortunately, even as the ICFY negotiators were attempting to take the delegations on the ground of principle, the violence and ethnic cleansing on the ground made these efforts seem unreal.

In a meeting with Mr. Ahtisaari, in the presence of Paul Szasz and this author, on 6 October, 1992, when Ahtisaari asked him for his position on human rights in the new constitution, the Bosnian Serb leader Dr. Radovan Karadzic replied:

> "..All of the Constituent States would have to incorporate human rights guarantees in their constitutions. There could be coordination at the confederal level, with possible participation of the European Community, and human rights would also be written into the agreement between the three Constituent States. He agreed with Mr. Ahtisaari that all the Republics of the FormerYugoslavia should have the same human rights standards."[82]

Two days later, on 8 October, Vance and Owen would have to dress him down as follows in a meeting when they confronted him about the continuing practice of ethnic cleansing:

"Mr. Vance: First of all, ethnic cleansing is getting worse.

"Dr. Karadzic: Need details.

"Mr. Vance: We know that yesterday there had been a meeting of the BH Serb Parliament in Banja Luka at which the local administration had come under heavy attack because ethnic cleansing was not going fast enough; that was a totally unacceptable reaction to the Co-Chairmen's visit the previous week. Furthermore, the Muslim leaders who had talked to the Co-Chairmen during that visit had been called to the Serbian party headquarters for questioning; that too was entirely unacceptable. Finally, reports had reached us that in Kator Varos the entire Muslim population had been arrested.

"Dr. Karadzic: The radicals, i.e. the extreme rightists, in Parliament were not representative of the whole; it was they who had conducted the attack. My party was more moderate.

"Mr. Vance: Did the moderates speak up?

"Dr. Karadzic: The majority in Parliament is opposed to the extreme rightists; however, the radicals are getting more and more influential.

---

[82] ICFY/BH/MTG.19.

I guarantee that the Muslim leaders would be protected. In any event, what is happening to the Serbs in Sarajevo is much worse than anything in Banja Luka. The Muslims had just announced that they had just killed some 250 Serbs.

"Mr. Vance: This cannot justify what is happening in Banja Luka. It was not acceptable to harass those who had spoken to the Co-Chairmen.

"Dr. Karadzic: Mr. Vance is right. If something like that should happen again, Dr. Karadzic would replace the local party leader. But his moderates were losing influence to the radicals.

"Mr. Vance: It wasn't apparent that Mr. Karadzic was losing influence.

"Dr. Karadzic: Showed pictures from a local magazine of foreign Muslims holding heads of slain Serbs.

...

"Lord Owen: Majority of EEC Foreign Ministers are for a War Crimes Tribunal. What about the reported arrest of Muslims in Kator Varos.

"Dr. Karadzic: There is fighting going on around there.

"Mr. Vance/Lord Owen: The horror there is unacceptable to the world community.

"Dr. Karadzic: The world doesn't quite understand what is going on... The European Union shares responsibility for what has happened, for everyone knew the consequences of recognizing Bosnia and Herzegovina prematurely. It must not be forgotten that 50 years ago, 750,000 Serbs were killed. Now his party was preparing a White Book on Muslim war crimes; there are already hundreds of names.

"Lord Owen: History is not the point—the issue is what is happening at present. Right now there is an opportunity to negotiate.

"Dr. Karadzic: I have never committed a war crime. I have publicly condemned those (Serbs) who have committed any; we will try them ourselves.

...

"Mr. Vance: Who are the snipers in Sarajevo?

"Dr. Karadzic: The Serbs have no snipers. Those are the 'green berets', who are commanded by criminals.

...

"Mr. Ahtisaari: Important that the time be used before people start dying in the winter. The political leaders will be blamed. ...."[83]

---

[83] Excerpted from a Note on the Meeting by Paul C. Szasz, PCS, 09/10/92. Text in the possession of the author.

The following day, in a meeting of Ahtisaari with Foreign Minister Silajdzic in the presence of Szasz and this author, Mr. Pejenovic of the Bosnian delegation pleaded:

> "Our position is an extremely difficult one regarding our responsibilities to the citizens of Bosnia and Herzegovina. It has been burdened by the fall of another town while we are here. The basis for being here is being eroded."[84]

At an earlier meeting on 29 September, 1992, between Vance, Owen, and Ahtisaari on the one hand, and President Alija Izetbegovic and Foreign Minister Silazdjic on the other, Silazdjic had pleaded:

> "Foreign Minister Silajdzic stated that his Government was being forced to talk while being attacked. Bosnian Serbs were worse than the Khmer Rouges; very soon there would be no Muslims left in Bosnia and Herzegovina. He did not understand the Western Powers. The situation in his country was being used for domestic political purposes in some countries, for example in the United States. He did not find it normal to treat an aggressor as a regular party to negotiations. Some circles were already speaking about a fait accompli in Bosnia and Herzegovina. Both Mr. Vance and Lord Owen said that such a position was unacceptable to them. They had both recommended the resumption of humanitarian flights.
>
> "Foreign Minister Silajdzic stated: 'I know that around this table we have the best in the world. You went to Banja Luka; the previous team would never have done this. The essential question is: who is going to enforce what we agree upon here?' "[85]

In a meeting with Ahtisaari on 12 October, 1992, Foreign Minister Silajdzic gave a clearer hint where he was headed:

> "In the course of a lengthy, and rather forceful presentation, he stressed that, in view of the critical situation prevailing in Bosnia and the recrudescence of attacks perpetrated by Serb forces, his government wondered whether the Co-Chairmen of the Conference had the authority to stop the aggression. If this was not the case, the Bosnian government had the intention to request, on the basis of article 51 of the Charter as well as or moral grounds, the lifting of the arms embargo imposed on Yugoslavia in 1991.
>
> "The Bosnian government felt that the International Conference was being used as a cover by the 'aggressor' and had not received the political

---

[84] ICFY/BH/MTG.21.
[85] ICFY/BH/MTG.14.

> support it deserved by the international community.... If this situation did not change, his delegation would be obliged, unwillingly, to leave the talks."[86]

Conclusion

Effectively, the Bosnian Serbs, at this stage, had achieved their war aims. They had taken most of the territory of Bosnia and Herzegovina and were still continuing their campaign of ethnic cleansing. The Croats had largely achieved their aims as well, even if they wished to take additional territory from the Muslims. They also were engaged in ethnic cleansing. The Muslim side had been the aggrieved party and wished to have the arms embargo lifted so that they could fight for their cause. Karadzic was smug in his affirmation of human rights. So was Boban. Izetbegovic and Silajdzic felt that they were fighting for their lives and wanted the means to fight.

The ICFY negotiators were taking principled positions on human rights through their contacts with the parties, their public statements, and the incorporation of human rights in the peace package. But Mr. Silajdzic's question was a fair one: Did the Co-Chairmen have the authority to stop the aggression? The plain and simple answer was that they did not. Only the major powers had such authority and the conflict would not end until, three years later, the USA and other major countries marshalled their power on the ground.

What was Vance and Owen to do in this situation? They could have thrown in their hats and given up. But there was danger of continuing conflict and of its spreading to other republics, especially Macedonia. While seeking, with limited effectiveness, to exercise moral authority, they continued to favour the approach of negotiated solutions, the continuation of the arms embargo on all parties, and the prevention of conflict elsewhere in the former Yugoslavia. As Marrack Goulding would appropriately write in his memoirs later, the negotiatiors were required "to establish good working relations with the faction leaders, however wicked they were. As we were being reminded in Yugoslavia at the time, peacemakers must eat with long spoons, for they are obliged to sup with many devils."[87]

---

[86] ICFY/BH/MTG.23.
[87] M. Goulding, Peacemonger. London, John Murray, 2002, p. 278.

Co-Chairman Thorvald Stoltenberg was very much mindful of these issues when he addressed the Security Council in the following terms:

> "... Mr. President, it is important to note that—along with the constant activity of the Geneva Conference—Lord Owen and I have sought to keep certain basic principles clearly in view.
>
> "The Council and the General Assemby have spelled out the guidelines for devising solutions to problems in the former Yugoslavia. You have called for a political settlement consistent with the principles of the Charter and of international norms on human rights. You have rightly condemned forcible expulsions, illegal detentions, and all attempts to change the demographic composition of territories. You have invoked the principles of the OSCE, in particular the inviolability of borders—both internal and external—and the non-recognition of attempts to alter such borders unilaterally.
>
> "The General Assembly has also called for peaceful solutions in line with the Charter and the principles of international law. It has expressly mentioned respect for the sovereignty and the territorial integrity of States, non-recognition of the spoils of aggression and of the acquisition of territory by force.
>
> "I mention these statements of principle in order to emphasize a simple, but crucial point: the international community cannot accept non-compliance with these guidelines.
>
> "As Co-Chairmen of the Steering Committee, our mandate requires that we maintain lines of communication with all sides, while preserving our neutrality and independence. Other United Nations bodies are looking into violations of human rights and humanitarian law. We are cooperating with them—and will continue to do so. I do, however, want to underscore my firm conviction that there can be no compromise when it comes to respect for the principles of the Charter, and of the international norms of human rights and humanitarian law."[88]

Yes, the Co-Chairmen sought to negotiate on the basis of principles. Yes, the parties were all unprincipled and opportunistic. And yet, the search for peace had to go on. How could the peace negotiators take forward their quest for peace? One approach was to try preventive strategies, to the extent that the parties would allow them. In the next chapter we see how the peace negotiators went about in trying to head off conflicts and atrocities.

---

[88] Text in the possession of the author.

CHAPTER 5

PREVENTIVE STRATEGIES

Introduction

In this chapter we shall look at preventive strategies considered, pursued, or possibly missed during the peace operations. We shall look first at an internal ICFY think-piece for the establishment of a regional conference on human rights and the rights of peoples in the region of the former Yugoslavia. We shall look at preventive dimensions of the work of ICFY's Working Group on Ethnic and National Communities and Minorities. We shall then look at the successful initiative for a preventive deployment on the borders between Serbia and Albania. We shall finally look at what might have been a missed opportunity for a preventive deployment in Kosovo.

1. Preventive human rights strategies: discussion paper on establishment of a Regional Conference on Human Rights and the Rights of Peoples in the Former Yugoslavia

In light of experience in the early stages of the ICFY, a senior adviser to the Co-Chairmen of ICFY, submitted a Discussion Paper suggesting the establishment of a Regional Conference on Human Rights and the Rights of Peoples and Minorities to perform the following functions in the area of the Former Yugoslavia:

(a) To promote respect for human rights and the rights of peoples and minorities in the region.
(b) To investigate situations where human rights and the rights of peoples and minorities appeared to be in difficulties.
(c) To promote regional cooperation on the protection of human rights and the rights of peoples and minorities in the area of the former Yugoslavia.
(d) To maintain contacts with the United Nations, the Council of Europe, the European Community, and the CSCE for the purpose of advancing the promotion and protection of human rights and the rights of peoples and minorities in the region.

(e) To promote ratification by the participating Republics of international and regional conventions on human rights and the rights of minorities and to monitor their compliance in the participating states.
(f) To cooperate with the CSCE High Commissioner on National Minorities.

The paper suggested that the Standing Conference would consist of an independent expert of the highest renown and impartiality designated in his or her personal capacity by each participating Republic. Each Republic would establish a national secretariat for the Regional Conference in order to carry out its decisions within that Republic. The Regional Conference would meet once a month, in each Republic in turn, following the English alphabetical order and starting with B-H.

The costs of the Regional Conference would be borne by the participating Republics in equal proportions. The Regional Conference would issue an annual report on its activities, which would be submitted to the government of each participating Republic, to the Secretary-General of the UN, the Secretary-General of the Council of Europe, the President of the European Community, and the CSCE High Commissioner on National Minorities.

The rules of procedure of the Regional Conference would be prepared by the Co-Chairmen of ICFY and would be applied by the Regional Conference for an initial period of five years. Alterations thereafter would be decided by consensus of the Regional Conference.[89]

These ideas were received with understanding by the senior ICFY leaders but a more classical peacemaking approach would be pursued and one never came back to these ideas. Here was a situation in which classical peacemaking efforts might have been complemented by more innovative approaches mindful of the human rights issues at the heart of the conflict. This issue of peacemaking strategies was never really discussed or debated within ICFY. That might have been a missed opportunity. However, ICFY's Working Group on Ethnic and National Communities and Minorities would do much to foster discussions, confidence building and practical solutions to situation-specific issues of human and minority rights as we shall see next.

[89] Paper in the possession of the author.

2. ICFY's Working Group on Ethnic and National Communities and Minorities

The Working Group on Ethnic and National Communities and Minorities was one of the unheralded preventive mechanisms of ICFY during its efforts for peace with justice in the former Yugoslavia. In line with the arrangements established at the London Conference in August, 1992, the Working Group started its extensive work with a plenary meeting in Geneva on 15 September, 1992 with the participation of delegations from Slovenia, Croatia, Bosnia and Herzegovina, and Macedonia. The framework for the discussions was Chapter 2 of the Treaty Provisions for a Convention that the Carrington Conference had been working on. All those present reconfirmed their commitment to the principles of the Convention. The delegations from Serbia, Montenegro and the Croatian Serbs were not able to travel to the meeting.

During the same week there were talks in Geneva with Albanians from Kosovo, Albania, and Macedonia, Muslims from Serbia, Muslims and Albanians from Montenegro, Hungarians from Vojvodina, Croats from Vojvodina, and Serbs from Croatia. A note on these meetings reported:

> "These talks showed, probably with the exception of Macedonia, pictures of continuous and at places dangerous ethnic conflicts that were to be taken up urgently with the Governments concerned. There will be another Working Group Plenum on 2 November in Geneva."[90]

For the next three and a half years, this Working Group, under its able chairman, German Ambassador Geert Ahrens, would patiently and persistently foster discussions on all of these situations, keeping parties talking, and endeavouring to work out negotiated solutions to perceived problems.

In order to discuss complaints and to hear the opinion of the Belgrade Government on matters falling within the province of the Working Group, a delegation travelled to Belgrade in the following week, 22–24 September. It reported that talks with Federal Ministers showed a general readiness to address critical issues, but also hesitation to accept ICFY mediation on some issues. "Moreover, there has so

---

[90] Note dated 27 October, 1992 by Geert Ahrens, Chairman of the Working Group. Text in the possession of the author.

far not been a clear commitment of the Belgrade Governments, the Federal or the Serbian, to all of Chapter Two of the Treaty Provisions for the Convention"[91]

The Sub-Group on Macedonia held two meetings between Government representatives and Albanians in Geneva on 17 September, and in Skopje on 15 October. Ambassador Ahrens reported that although progress had been achieved, the overall situation of the Republic (economic blockade in the eyes of the Government), nonrecognition, an upsurge of nationalism, made it increasingly difficult for the moderate Government to compromise on ethnic questions. He advised: "In my opinion, everything has to be done to uphold the so far positive internal development in Macedonia which is in real danger."[92]

The Sub-Group on Vojvodina and on the Sandzak was due to meeting soon to start trilateral talks but there had been some hesitation in Belgrade. However, meetings had been held in Geneva, Belgrade and Subotica with Hungarians and Croats. Ambassador Ahrens reported that the situation in the Sandzak, "which is related to the Bosnian war, is alarming. Large numbers of Muslims have already left. Hopefully, the presence of CSCE observers there will help to defuse the tense situation on the ground which is a serious obstacle to meaningful dialogue."[93]

On the Serbs in Croatia, the Working Group had held talks with Mr. Goran Hadzic "President of the Republic of Krajina" and several meetings with Croatian representative. Mr. Hadzic had said that he was quite prepared for talks on human rights, economic and communication issues, but not on any form of Serb autonomy inside Croatia. "The Krajina would rather resort to renewed warfare than become a part of Croatia again. It was not possible so far to convince Mr. Hadzic or any other Knin representative that a solution has to be found on the basis of the London Principles."[94] Ambassador Ahrens would—and did—continue his efforts.

Ambassador Ahrens reported that the most intensive work had been done in the Special Group on Kosovo. The basic approach agreed to by both sides was to try a pragmatic breakthrough in one important

[91] Ibid.

[92] Ibid. It bears mentioning that thanks in part to the efforts of ICFY, Macedonia never descended into conflict.

[93] Ibid.

[94] Ibid.

sector in order to improve the political atmosphere for talks on more fundamental issues where positions were still irreconcilable. The Albanians had chosen education. Ambassador Ahrens reported that after difficult and tedious preparations, in which the release from prison of the Chairman of the Albanian Teachers Federation was achieved, the first ICFY-sponsored talks between the Federal and the Serbian Governments from Belgrade, on one side, and Albanian representatives from Kosovo on the other, had taken place. On 14 October, all the parties had agreed on a statement which read as follows:

> "1. Representatives of the Government of the FRY and Serbia led by the Federal Minister of Education, Mr. Ivic, and representatives of the Albanians met in Pristina on 13/14 October with the participation of the Geneva Conference Special Group on Kosovo, under the Chairmanship of Ambassador Ahrens. A representative of the CSCE mission was also present.
>
> "2. After detailed discussion of the problems of education in the Albanian language, the participants agreed that the present situation must be changed. They further agreed on the urgent desirability of the return to normal working conditions for schools and other educational institutions.
>
> "3. It was agreed that, to achieve this, it would be necessary to adopt a pragmatic approach requiring urgent resolution, without prejudice to the positions of the parties on broader political issues.
>
> "4. The Albanian representatives agreed to provide a list of schools and other educational institutions to be covered by the measures mentioned in (2); as well as a list of teaching plans and programmes.
>
> "5. The Group agreed to meet again in Belgrade on 22 October. At that meeting discussions will be held on all the issues mentioned above and on the equal working status of teaching and educations personnel with the aim of reaching the necessary decisions for immediate action."[95]

Further talks were indeed continued on 22 October in Belgrade with meetings held with President D. Cosic, President of the FRY and with Mr. I. Rugova, the Kosovar Albanian leader. They had both reaffirmed their commitment to the necessity of changing the then prevailing situation in the field of education, and to the urgent need for a return to normal conditions in schools and other educational institutions in Kosovo as set out in the statement of 14 October.

---

[95] Ibid.

Ambassador Ahrens and his Working Group would patiently and persistently continue working on the foregoing and similar issues for the next four years and would help nurture agreements on practical issues of human and minority rights on the ground.

3. Preventive peacekeeping in Macedonia

The initiative for a preventive deployment of UN peacekeepers in the Former Yugoslav Republic of Macedonia first came from the Co-Chairmen of the International Conference on the Former Yugoslavia. They had discussed this idea with President Kiro Gligorov who, in turn, wrote to the Secretary-General of the United Nations on 11 November 1992 asking for such a preventive deployment. In a letter of 18 November 1992, to the United Nations Secretary-General, Co-Chairmen, former US Secretary of State Cyrus Vance and former British Foreign Minister Lord David Owen, told him there was growing need to take preventive measures to avoid the outbreak of violence in Macedonia and Kosovo. They recalled that they had warned the Security Council a few days earlier, on 13 November 1992, that a tragedy of dreadful proportions could occur if conflict were to break out in Macedonia and Kosovo, engulfing the neighbouring countries.

Elaborating upon their idea, the Co-Chairmen stated that in terms of preventive diplomacy it would be desirable to put United Nations personnel, under the aegis of UNPROFOR, into Macedonia so as to provide a calming influence for all sides and give a sense of stability. They suggested to the Secretary-General:

> The deployment of a contingent of UNPROFOR personnel within Macedonia, who could have their headquarters in Skopje and be distributed in the main population centres, as well as on the Macedonian borders with Serbia (including Kosovo) and Albania. Their efforts would be complemented by those of the CSCE, which already had a small 'spill-over mission' in Skopje.

The Co-Chairmen suggested that, as a start, about a dozen United Nations military and police officers, with supporting political staff, be sent. They could be stationed in Skopje and could travel to the border areas. In the light of their experience and recommendations, the United Nations presence could be built up as needed. The Co-Chairmen were conscious of the scarcity of United Nations resources and they were seeking to indicate a way to implement their recommendation even in the face of that scarcity.

Upon receipt of the Co-Chairmen's recommendation, Secretary-General Boutros Boutros-Ghali advised the Security Council that he would be sending an exploratory mission to the FYR of Macedonia to look into the possibility of establishing a preventive deployment of United Nations peace-keepers in the country. Following its visit, the exploratory mission made the following recommendations:

> that a small UNPROFOR presence be established on the Macedonian side of the Republic's borders with Albania and the Federal Republic of Yugoslavia (Serbia and Montenegro) with an essentially preventive mandate of monitoring and reporting any developments in the border areas which could undermine confidence and stability in Macedonia or threaten its territory.
>
> that a small group of United Nations civilian police be deployed in the border areas to monitor the Macedonian border police.

The rationale for the latter deployment was that incidents arising from illegal attempts to cross the border had led to increased tension on the Macedonian side. The Mission believed that the presence of a small United Nations civilian police detachment would have a calming effect.

In December 1992, the Secretary-General reported to the Security Council on the findings of the exploratory mission, together with his recommendations.[96] On 11 December 1992, the Security Council authorized the Secretary-General to establish a presence of the United Nations Protection force (UNPROFOR) in the FYR of Macedonia. The Council requested that the Secretary-General deploy immediately the military, civil affairs, and administrative personnel he had recommended in his report, as well as police monitors.

In mid-December 1992 a United Nations team discussed practical arrangements with the Government in Skopje. The first UNCIVPOL monitors arrived on 27 December 1992. They were eventually deployed along the northern and western borders. On 28 December, a reconnaissance team went to the country to make arrangements for the interim deployment of a Canadian company. On 7 January 1993, a Canadian company arrived in the country pending the arrival of a joint battalion from Finland, Norway and Sweden. On 25 January, Brigadier-General Finn Saermark-Thomsen of Denmark, who had been designated Commander of the Macedonia Command of

[96] S/24923.

UNPROFOR, arrived in Skopje. On 18 February, the Nordic battalion took over the operation from the Canadian company.

The Nordic battalion was 434 strong, composed of three rifle companies. It was deployed on the western border from Debar northward and on the northern border up to the border with Bulgaria. At the beginning there were 19 United Nations Military Observers (UNMOs) in the area of operations. The western border south of Debar was covered solely by UNMOs.

From early January 1993, the northern border and the western border north of Debar were constantly monitored from observation posts and by regular patrols, with a view to reporting any activities that might increase tension or threaten peace and stability. The UNMOs conducted regular patrols in their area of operations to monitor the situation. They also carried out a programme of visits to border villages aimed at gaining the confidence of their inhabitants and assisting in defusing possible inter-ethnic tensions.

While carrying out their border visiting programme, the UNMOs were approached by representatives of different ethnic groups who lodged various complaints about alleged discriminatory practices by the authorities. In those cases where the complaints were relevant to the mandate of the mission, they were brought to the attention of the appropriate authorities. Some were also brought to the attention of the competent international bodies, such as the International Conference of the Former Yugoslavia.

UNCIVPOL also conducted regular patrols to specific crossings and the border areas in general on a daily basis. In the course of doing so, it received through local mayors a number of complaints concerning the local border police. In those cases where there appeared *prima facie* to be a basis for the complaint, UNCIVPOL took up the matter with the relevant police authorities.

The Civil Affairs component of the mission established, from the outset, an information programme to explain the role of UNPROFOR in the country. UNPROFOR maintained close coordination with the CSCE mission in the country.

By the middle of 1993, UNPROFOR's assessment was that it had been successful in its preventive mandate in the country. It was concerned, however, about the internal situation and the possibility of instability should there be an increase in the inter-ethnic tensions, a possibility which, it reported, was repeatedly mentioned by local and international sources. A related concern of UNPROFOR was about the deterioration of the economic situation stemming from the implementation of sanctions which, it was felt, could contribute to heightened inter-ethnic tensions.

By September 1993, the Secretary-General reported to the Security Council that the FYROM Command of UNPROFOR consisted of 1,190 military and civilian, including UNCIVPOL, personnel. A Nordic battalion was based at Kjojila, east of Skopje, and a United States contingent of 315 troops had arrived in Skopje in early July, deploying to the FYROM side of the border with the Federal Republic of Yugoslavia on 20 August 1993. United Nations Military Observers, UNCIVPOL and Civil Affairs officers were also continuing their activities. UNPROFOR reported: 'This first venture in the field of preventive peace-keeping on the part of UNPROFOR continues to be successful, and to enjoy an excellent cooperative relationship with the FYROM Government, and to be fully supported by the people of the country."

The leadership of the preventive deployment would come to conclude that "the increasing internal instability in the FYROM cold prove to be more detrimental to the stability of the country than outside threats". UNPROFOR would therefore need "to consider what its role should be, if any, in the event that internal stability results in some form of civil conflict."[97]

Thus it was that the deployment developed the second of its three pillars, as presented by Sokalski: good offices and political action, alongside troop deployment and the human dimension. As Sokalski has written, the mission developed and maintained active contacts with political forces and ethnic groups in the country as a means of promoting domestic stability. Efforts were made to reduce the level of mistrust among the country's political and ethnic actors and UNPREDEP set in place a dialogue on questions regarding the rights of ethnic communities and national minorities. Sokalski has written:

> UNPREDEP was recognized as a significant instrument for facilitating dialogue, restraint and practical compromise between the different segments of Macedonian society. UN troop patrols along the northern and western borders of the country effectively complemented such activities; this outreach had a calming and stabilizing effect throughout the area.

[97] Background paper submitted by the FYROM Command to Brainstorming Exercise on the future of UNPROFOR, Zagreb-Mokrice, 15-17 February 1994. Paper in the possession of the author, who participated in the exercise.

> The contingent of UN military observers and the team of civilian police monitors rendered equally invaluable services.[98]

The preventive deployment in the FYR of Macedonia worked effectively—externally as well as internally. The model of United Nations observers patrolling sensitive areas where ethnic tensions were high, receiving complaints, transmitting them to the authorities, and serving as an intermediary and confidence builder is one that clearly has great relevance to situations of ethnic and religious tension, in situations where there are minority populations or in other situations where internal strife or conflict could result in gross violations of human rights. The establishment of a UN rapid reaction force would certainly help facilitate the dispatch of preventive deployments of UN peacekeepers in situations of urgent need.

4. Missed opportunities for preventive action on Kosovo?

As we saw in the preceding section, it was an initiative from Vance and Owen on 18 November, 1992 that led to the eventual establishment of UNPREDEP. There is among the ICFY papers a letter from the President of Albania, Sali Berisha, dated 25 December, 1992, addressed to Cyrus Vance as ICFY Co-Chairman, expressing growing concern over the situation then prevailing in Kosovo. President Berisha referred to the idea of a preventive deployment outlined in Secretary-General Boutros-Ghali's report, An Agenda for Peace, and continued:

> "The Republic of Albania has hailed the UN Security Council Resolution 795 to send UN forces to Macedonia, as a guarantee of preserving the delicate peace there. Urged by the same ends, I take the opportunity to request from you…the support of ICFY to send these forces to Kosovo. Time is running very fast. Peace is hinging on rapidity and cooperation."[99]

On 29 December, 1992, Vance and Owen replied to President Berisha in the following terms:

> "Regarding the specific proposal contained in your letter, namely a preventive deployment in the province, this will require, as you will

[98] H. Sokalski, *An Ounce of Prevention: Macedonia and the UN Experience in Preventive Diplomacy* (Washington, D.C.: United States Institute for Peace, 2003), 108. See also, A. Williams, *Preventing War: The UN and Macedonia* (Lanham, MD: Rowman & Littlefield, 2000).

[99] Text in the possession of the author.

> appreciate, the consent of the Federal Republic of Yugoslavia, followed by an affirmative decision by the United Nations Security Council.
>
> "It seems to us that it might be advisable for you to initiate an exchange with the authorities of the Federal Republic of Yugoslavia on measures that all sides could take to maintain calm, to promote confidence and stability and to defuse the situation in Kosovo. Your proposal for a preventive deployment in Kosovo could be raised in that context.
>
> "You and your government can play a very crucial role in calming the situation by promoting restraint on all sides, particularly the Kosovo Albanian leadership. The positions and actions of your Government are, of course, very important in this regard."[100]

Earlier in the letter, Vance and Owen recalled their meeting with President Berisha in Tirana on 29 October, 1992, in which they had explained to him their view that stability in Kosovo should be secured through genuine autonomy for the province rather than secession or unilateral declaration of independence.

At the end of December, 1992, Vance and Owen, in addition to having proposed a preventive deployment in Macedonia, had invited the leaders of the Federal Republic of Yugoslavia and Croatia, and of the three Bosnian parties, to commence peace talks in Geneva on 2 January, 1993. They thus had their hands full. In addition, President Slobodan Milosevic of Serbia, whose state had jurisdiction over Kosovo at the time, was clearly indicating that he would not agree to the internationalisation of the Kosovo issue.

Whatever the factors that influenced Vance and Owen at the time, given the subsequent history of the province, the grievous human rights violations that took place, the prolonged massive NATO air assault on Serbia, one would be forgiven for asking whether Vance and Owen might have used President Berisha's letter as an opportunity to explore the idea of a preventive deployment in Kosovo and engaged in some diplomacy to this end. Might this, with hindsight, have been a missed opportunity?

One will never know whether the initiative might have made any headway. There had been a CSCE long-term monitoring mission in Kosovo but Belgrade had asked them to leave in July, 1993, following the CSCE's exclusion of Belgrade from the Organization. On 7 April, 1994, the US Permanent Mission in New York gave to the UN

---

100 Text in the possession of the author.

Secretariat a paper proposing the deployment of international monitors in Kosovo. They apparently had also raised the idea in Moscow and in the capitals of EU countries. The US initiative proposed a joint EU/Russian/US demarche urging Belgrade to reconsider its refusal to accept international monitors in Kosovo.

According to the US note, "Monitors in Kosovo", the Americans said that they would be willing to show flexibility on the nature of the proposed observer mission. While they would prefer a return of the CSCE, if a CSCE mission remained unacceptable to Belgrade, the US would propose sending monitors from the United Nations. The US made it clear, however, that it was not willing to admit Serbia into the CSCE or improve Serbia's status at the UN as the "price" for readmitting CSCE monitors or allowing UN monitors. The US ideas paper given to the UN Secretariat stated, however:

> "Belgrade can be assured that none of the nations participating in the demarche favors independence—as LDK has proposed—for Kosovo."[101]

At a later stage, in 1994, the Kosovar Albanian leader Ibrahim Rugova asked Thorvald Stoltenberg, when they met in Oslo, to facilitate a meeting between himself and President Slobodan Milosevic. Stoltenberg and Owen raised the matter with Milosevic and he agreed on condition that Rugova would approach him directly. Stoltenberg and Owen drafted the following letter and gave it to Rugova for him to send to Milosevic:

> "Mr. President,
>
> "Some time ago I had a conversation in Oslo with Mr. Thorvald Stoltenberg, Co-Chairmen of ICFY. We both recognized the importance of dialogue to deal with issues. I have since been informed by the Co-Chairmen, Lord Owen and Thorvald Stoltenberg, that you yourself support such dialogue and would be ready for us to meet. May I therefore suggest that we meet at a mutually convenient time, possibly in the week beginning 28 November, 1994?
>
> "Yours sincerely,
>
> "Ibrahim Rugova."[102]

As far as we are aware, Rugova never sent the letter, and an idea that he himself had suggested did not go forward. We believed at the time

---

[101] Text of the US paper in the possession of the author.
[102] Text in the possession of the author.

that Rugova could not persuade the hard-liners in his entourage who preferred a more robust approach to achieving their objective of the independence of Kosovo.

Conclusion

The preventive deployment in Macedonia was, without doubt, a major initiative on the part of Vance and Owen that had a direct bearing on the protection of human and minority rights. The peace-building activities that we shall recount in a later chapter also had preventive dimensions, as indeed, did the overall thrust of the Co-Chairmen and other ICFY actors in highlighting the centrality of human rights. The efforts of the Working Group on Ethnic Communities, Nationalities and Minorities also contributed to prevention of atrocities. The reports of Special Rapporteur Tadeus Mazowiecki, which we recounted in a previous chapter, probably contributed to limited prevention as well.

The question deserves to be posed, however, whether ICFY might have given a higher profile to the prevention of gross violations of human rights in the former Yugoslavia. Whether such an effort would have succeeded is far from clear. But, looking back nearly two decades from the London Conference of 1992, it is a fair question to pose. We would tend to the view that in a similar situation in the future it would be important to have a deliberate strategy to help prevent gross violations of human rights.[103]

[103] See, generally, B.G. Ramcharan, Preventive Human Rights Strategies. Routledge, 2010.

CHAPTER 6

PEACEMAKING

Introduction

In earlier chapters we saw that the protection of human rights was at the heart of the concept of UN Protected Areas (UNPAs). Cyrus Vance, Personal Envoy of the UN Secretary-General, together with Marrack Goulding, UN Under-Secretary-General, drafted what is known as the Vance Plan that introduced this concept. Vance would become the lead UN negotiator alongside Lord David Owen in the International Conference on the Former Yugoslavia. We saw UNHCR struggling with human rights violations while being called upon to provide assistance and protection to the innocent victims of conflicts in the former Yugoslavia. We saw the UN Special Rapporteur, Tadeusz Mazowiecki performing the function of a UN flag-bearer against ethnic cleansing and other human rights violations and we saw the Principles of the London Conference and the efforts of ICFY negotiators to build their negotiating efforts on the foundations of these principles.

Turning to the role of human rights in peacemaking, the evidence will show the ICFY negotiators pursuing the following approaches: giving a central role to human rights in the formulation of peace plans; taking on a leading role in guarding against ethnic cleansing; making strong representations to the leaders on the ground about human rights issues; calling on the aid of UN peacekeepers to protect people against ethnic cleansing; speaking out against violations of human rights; working for human rights monitoring during and after the conflict; seeking to provide for strong institutions for the protection of human rights in Bosnia and Herzegovina and elsewhere in the former Yugoslavia; working for peace-building in the long term through respect for and protection of human rights; striving for the protection of group and minority rights. We devote a separate chapter later to the role of human rights in peace-building. The other approaches are discussed below.

1. Human rights in the peace plans

Early in the existence of ICFY, on 25 September, 1992, a senior advisor to the Co-Chairmen of ICFY, submitted the following Confidential Discussion Paper marked "Eyes Only" to the lead negotiator on Bosnia and Herzegovina:

"Discussion Paper on National Institutions for the Promotion and Protection of Human and Minority Rights in Bosnia and Herzegovina.

> "The aim of the ICFY is to help bring peace to B-H and to promote security and respect for human rights in the long-term. Both the processes of peace-making and the long-term security of the country would be influenced by the kinds of arrangements that are made to deal with issues of human and minority rights in the country.
>
> "Normative provisions on human and minority rights in a future constitution of B-H are being discussed in the Working Group on B-H. Also being discussed in that Working Group is the idea of a special court to deal with problems affecting the enjoyment of human and minority rights.
>
> "Beyond normative guarantees and a special court, it would seem necessary to envisage arrangements and institutions within the country that could serve to head off conflicts among the three main groups and provide for confidence-building, dispute resolution and redress of grievances that can help and ensure that problems arising in the future do not boil over. The question therefore arises: What kind of arrangements or institutions can one envisage in B-H in the future to perform these functions? One would need to think about national, regional and local institutions.
>
> "At the national level, one could think in terms of arrangements or institutions that would fulfil the following functions:
>
> - Regular review of legislative provisions affecting human and minority rights.
> - The promotion of confidence-building measures at the national level.
> - Coordination of the activities of regional and local bodies.
> - Monitoring and supervision of arrangements for assuring respect for the language, religion and culture of the different groups.
> - Early-warning and preventive action.
> - Dispute resolution.
>
> "At the regional and local levels, institutions and arrangements would need to keep all of the preceeding functions in mind and also undertake fact-finding, mediation and conciliation.

> "The arrangements made should be so devised as to attract confidence throughout the country and to win the respect and the trust of all parts of the community.
>
> "If one examines national arrangements and institutions for the promotion and protection of human and minority rights which exist in other States one could ask the question: What models are there that might provide some guidance for devising arrangements and institutions in B-H. United Nations reports and studies on national institutions for the promotion and protection of human rights offer the following relevant models:
>
> - National and provincial human rights commissions.
> - Human Rights Commissions.
> - Commissions on racial equality.
> - Ombudsmen.
> - Minorities Commissioners.
>
> "Taking into account the circumstances prevailing in B-H, it would seem advisable to think in terms of an integrated structure of institutions and arrangements for guaranteeing protection of human and minority rights. One might therefore think about a structure encompassing the following elements:
>
> - A supreme court of human, minorities, and peoples' rights.
> - A council on the equality of peoples in B-H.
> - A national conference on human and minorities rights.
> - A national core of investigators, mediators and conciliators.
> - Local community relations commissions.
> - A commission on national cultures.
> - A Commission on freedom of religion or belief."

Many of these ideas would form key planks of the plans subsequently advanced by ICFY. Human rights were thus at the centre of the peacemaking process in ICFY from its very commencement in September, 1992. This approach ran throughout the peacemaking process.

2. Emphasizing the Centrality of Human Rights in the Peace Process

After about six months of their efforts, Vance and Owen sought to highlight the importance they attached to human rights by including in their report to the UN Security Council an Annex titled, "The Co-Chairmen of the Steering Committee and Human Rights

Issues in the Former Yugoslavia".[104] This section reproduces the essence of the document.

Vance and Owen stated that from the outset of their Co-Chairmanship of the Steering Committee of the ICFY they had placed human rights and humanitarian issues at the core of the peacemaking process in the former Yugoslavia. At a press conference on 23 October, 1992, they had insisted that the international community would not tolerate the taking of territory by force, nor acquiesce in ethnic cleansing. Responding to reports that Bosnia and Herzegovina had in fact been carved up by Serbian and Croatian forces, the Co-Chairmen had said that the status quo on the ground was not acceptable and that international recognition and lifting of sanctions would not take place until a political solution had been found.

"This is not going to be settled by people who have taken up arms, and have abandoned humanitarian principles, and trampled upon international law", Lord Owen had told assembled correspondents. "We do not accept this status quo as permanent", he added, "and we intend to see that it is changed." Mr. Vance had agreed, adding "this is the way that we will act; that is what we expect to happen; and we will not be turned back in our determination to see that happen."

On 13 November, 1992, Mr. Vance had told the Security Council:

> "You have called for a political settlement consistent with the Principles of the Charter and of international norms on human rights. You have rightly condemned forcible expulsions, illegal detentions, and all attempts to change the demographic composition of territories.
>
> …
>
> "I mention these statements of principle in order to emphasize a simple but crucial point: the international community cannot accept non-compliance with these guidelines.
>
> "As Co-Chairmen of the Steering Committee, our mandate requires that we maintain lines of communication with all sides while preserving our neutrality and independence. Other bodies are looking into violations of human rights and humanitarian law. We are cooperating with them and will continue to do so. I do, however, want to underscore my firm conviction that there can be no compromise when it comes to respect for the Principles of the Charter, and of the international norms of human rights and humanitarian law".[105]

---

[104] S/25221, Annex I.
[105] S/PV. 3134.

Lord Owen had stated to the Security Council the same day:

> "How can we as Co-Chairmen and you as members of the Council implement the principles and objectives agreed at the London Conference at the end of August?
>
> "European history is, sadly, no stranger to conflict nor to ethnic disputes. Memories of the Holocaust are still with us. The odious practice of 'ethnic cleansing' that we are witnessing in the former Yugoslavia is not something therefore which any European can ignore, merely passing by on the other side.
>
> "Europe knows that, were this flagrant 'ethnic cleansing' to be tolerated, were all its perpetrators to be allowed to escape without being brought to justice, and were its victims not to be helped to return to their homes and land, then we Europeans would pay a terrible price."[106]

On the issue of prisoners and detainees, the Co- Chairmen said that they had worked closely with the International Committee of the Red Cross to ensure the release of prisoners and detainees in the former Yugoslavia. They had used every occasion to highlight the plight of prisoners and detainees in their contacts with Governments and with the parties in their pubic statements and in the reports submitted to the Security Council and the General Assembly. At the commencement of the peace talks on Bosnia and Herzegovina on 2 January, 1993, the Co-Chairmen had made the following appeal to the parties to the conflict.

> "...Your immediate release of all detainees is essential. It would not only be an indication of your peaceful intentions, but could also help to stop the drums of war, which are beating so loudly around us as we meet here today."[107]

On the issue of grave breaches of international humanitarian law, the Co-Chairmen said they had been in frequent contact with the Chairman of the Committee of Experts established by the Secretary-General to examine information pertaining to those breaches. Working level contcts had also been maintained between the Co-Chairmen's staff and the staff of the Commission of Experts. The Co-Chairmen had held meetings with the Commission of Experts, the Secretary-General and the Special Rapporteur for Yugoslavia of the Commission

106 S/PV.3134.
107 (S/25050, annex II).

on Human Rights to help bring about a forensic examination of the mass grave site at Ocvara in Croatia. The Co-Chairmen's efforts had helped bring about a decision by the Commission of Experts to arrange for a prompt forensic examination of the mass grave site. In a public statement on 17 December, 1992, the Commission of Experts had stated:

> "A major step taken by the Commission has been to request an NGO, Physician for Human Rights, to investigate a mass grave near Vukovar, taking into account calls made by…the Co-Chairmen of the Conference on the Former Yugoslavia."

On the idea to establish an international criminal court, Vance and Owen said that they had repeatedly advocated the establishment of an international criminal court to deal with grave breaches of humanitarian law. On 16 December, 1992, Vance had stated to the Ministerial Meeting of the Steering Committee of ICFY:

> "Lord Owen and I believe that atrocities committed in the former Yugoslavia are unacceptable, and persons guilty of war crimes should be brought to justice. We therefore recommend the establishment of an international criminal court."

On future constitutional arrangements for Bosnia and Herzegovina, the Co-Chairmen recalled that they had placed human rights issues at the core of their proposals. They had proposed that the Constitution set out a number of human rights grouped into three categories:

(a) General human, especially civil and political, rights as expressed in instruments such as the 1966 International Covenant on Civil and Political Rights and the Protocol thereto, and in the 1950 European Convention for the Protection of Human Rights and Fundamental Freedoms and in the Protocols thereto.
(b) Group and especially 'minority' rights, as expressed in instruments such as the 1992 UN Declaration on the Rights of Persons belonging to National, or Ethnic, Religious and Linguistic Minorities and in the 1990 Recommendation 1134 (1990) on the rights of minorities of the Parliamentary Assembly of the Council of Europe.
(c) Economic, social and cultural rights, as expressed in the 1966 International Covenant on Economic, Social and Cultural Rights and in the 1961 European Social Charter and the Protocol thereto.

With a view to ensuring the protection of human rights, the Co-Chairmen had proposed that:

(a) All persons in Bosnia and Herzegovina, whether citizens or not, would at all times have unimpeded access to the courts.
(b) Both the provincial and the national courts would be required to apply the constitutionally guaranteed human rights, as set out in the Constitution or in the international instruments incorporated therein by reference as directly applicable law.
(c) There would be four ombudsmen, one representing each of the recognized groups. The ombudsmen would have wide powers to investigate, either on the basis of complaints or on their own initiative, all questions relating to the implementation of human rights, including those arising out of ethnic cleansing, and to report to the legislature and to other appropriate governmental bodies. Initially, the ombudsmen would be appointed by ICFY and later by the Lower House of the national legislature.
(d) There would be a Constitutional Court and a Human Rights Court.
(e) There would also be an International Commission on Human Rights for Bosnia and Herzegovina. The Commission would be authorized to investigate and to hear complaints and to report thereon to the appropriate international bodies.
(f) Bosnia and Herzegovina would be required to become a party to a number of international human rights treaties that established supervisory monitoring and dispute-settlement mechanisms.

Addressing the Organization of the Islamic Conference on 1 December 1992, Lord Owen had stated:

> "You have already seen in our proposals for a new constitution for Bosnia and Herzegovina that we are not prepared to accept that land can be taken by force by the Bosnian Serbs—land which far exceeds anything they could justifiably claim in the past to have contained a majority of Serbs.
>
> "You will have seen in these same constitutional proposals the toughest provision for enforcing human rights and interlocking mechanisms for the reversal of the odious practice of ethnic cleansing.
>
> "I can assure you that the citizens of the European Community did not live through the trauma of the 1930s and 1940s without vowing to themselves that they would never again tolerate within Europe the vile things which we have seen practised in Bosnia and Herzegovina. We are determined, with your help, to end the practices and reverse the consequences."

On human rights and humanitarian problems being encountered in the former Yugoslavia, Vance and Owen noted in their abovementioned report to the Security Council that they had cooperated closely with the Special Rapporteur of the UN Commission on Human Rights. The day after their arrival in Geneva, on 4 September 1992, they had had an extensive meeting with the Special Rapporteur. They had met with the Special Rapporteur again on 8 October. Working-level contacts had been maintained throughout by the Co-Chairmen's staff and the staff of the Special Rapporteur.

In a message that the Co-Chairmen had sent to a special session of the Commission on Human Rights on 30 November, 1992, they had stated:

> "Regrettably, the disgraceful practice of ethnic cleansing has not ceased and violations of international norms on human rights and humanitarian law are rampant. We condemn these violations in the most categorical terms.
>
> "We hope that your session will help in bringing an end to the violations of human rights and humanitarian law taking place. We also hope that you will give attention to the importance of protecting the rights of minorities. This issue is of great importance to the future stability and security in the area of the former Yugoslavia."

The Co-Chairmen recalled that they had used their influence to highlight the importance of human rights issues. They had initiated contact with the Council of Europe immediately after they started operations, so as to draw upon the expertise and assistance of the human rights machinery of the Council of Europe. Addressing the Council on 3 October, 1992, Lord Owen had made the following proposal:

> "Let me put one practical suggestion to this body.
>
> …
>
> "A non-member State could subscribe to the Council of Europe *ad hoc* mechanism by means of a unilateral declaration which would then be in its Constitution, but which would have to be accepted by the Committee of Ministers of the Council of Europe. The mechanism could consist of a body which would be set up for a transitional period pending the accession of the subscribing State to the Council of Europe fully and to the European Convention on Human Rights. The body might be composed of judges of the European Court of Human Rights, members of the European Commission on Human Rights and persons from the subscribing States. The body could receive communications from any subscribing State, individual, group of individuals or non-governmental organizations alleging violations of human rights in a subscribing State. The body

would be able to examine the admissibility and merits of the allegations received. It could make findings of fact and state its opinion, in the first place by reference to the European Convention on Human Rights and the case-law developing under it, but also by reference to other international human rights treaties and agreements to which the subscribing State was already a contracting party—for example, United Nations covenants—and other legal instruments relating to human rights. The opinion of the body could be made binding on the subscribing State. I hope that they would not choose it to be only an advisory opinion but that they would entrench this body in their Constitution until such time as they were able to become members of the Council of Europe."

The Co-Chairmen noted that as a result of an initiative of theirs the Human Rights Committee (established under the International Covenant on Civil and Political Rights) had requested reports from the Federal Republic of Yugoslavia (Serbia and Montenegro), Bosnia and Herzegovina and Croatia on human rights matters of international concern. The Human Rights Committee had undertaken searching examinations of the human rights situations in those countries from 3 to 6 November, 1992 and had made important recommendations to the three States.

The Co-Chairmen recalled that they had, on a number of occasions, reacted to urgent humanitarian situations. On 24 September, 1992, they had issued a public statement expressing their deep concern about reports they had received from the Banja Luka region indicating a build- up of tension, bomb incidents and intimidation with the potential threat of violence and the development of an ethnic-cleansing campaign. In view of the urgency of the situation, the Co-chairmen had travelled to Banja Luka the following day to assess the situation on the ground and to speak to representatives of the local communities and humanitarian agencies.

The Co-Chairmen had continually emphasized the importance and urgency of humanitarian relief and protection. Addressing the Security Council on 13 November, 1992, Vance had stated:

> "…on humanitarian aid, countless thousands of lives depend on our help and, despite the increasing pressure upon the UNHCR and the International Committee of the Red Cross (ICRC), we cannot afford to slacken our efforts. To this end, the international community must insist on unhindered access to persons who need humanitarian aid, especially food, medical supplies and shelter—particularly in view of the approaching winter. The release of prisoners and detainees, particularly from Bosnia and Herzegovina, now depends primarily on providing immediately refuge for them abroad." (S/PV.3134)

Addressing a special meeting of the ICFY Humanitarian Issues Working Group on 4 December, 1992, Vance had also stated:

> "What we are faced with in the former Yugoslavia is a situation that challenges interntional standards of conduct for the protection of human rights internally as well as externally. Internally, the vile practice of ethnic cleansing has led to terrible human loss and suffering. The rule of law and the reign of principle have been replaced by disgraceful forms of behaviour. Externally, notwithstanding the generosity of many countries and organizations, basic principles have come under stress, including the principles of non-refoulement of refugees, and of solidarity with human beings in distress."

Any objective reader of the foregoing record of the Co-Chairmen would agree that they were providing courageous human rights leadership while forging ahead with the search for negotiated solutions. Vance and Owen were particularly vehement on the importance of safeguarding against ethnic cleansing, as we shall see in the next section.

3. Taking on a Leading Role in Guarding against Ethnic Cleansing

On 2nd October, 1992, Vance and Owen had a meeting in Geneva with the Director of Operations of the ICRC and its Delegate General for Europe. This writer attended the meeting and this account is based on the note he prepared on it. The purpose of the meeting was for the ICRC officials to brief Vance and Owen on a document that had recently been signed by the leadership of the three warring parties in Bosnia and Herzegovina on the movement of people. According to the ICRC officials, there were different groups of civilians living in a totally unsecured situation. Humanitarian organizations could not provide them with the necessary protection. The ICRC was very concerned that with the approach of winter these people would be without protection or subsistence. Based on this assessment, which was shared by all of the ICRC delegates in the field, the ICRC as a humanitarian organization had had to consider how it could help the people involved. That was why it had taken the position that it would have to take immediate steps to move the people involved to areas where they would have natural protection and to start soon a huge plan of action to help them face a very difficult situation during the winter. The ICRC was aware—and had taken into account—that it could be accused when it came to the issue of ethnic cleansing but it had nevertheless felt that it had to take this risk. The ICRC was ready to undertake the supervisory role involved in checking upon the wishes of the people involved. Even the plenipotentiaries of the three sides had come to the same conclusion and President Izetbegovic himself personally had supported the recommendation.

Vance and Owen immediately raised concerns about the issue of ethnic cleansing. Vance warned that the plan encouraged ethnic cleansing. What worried him was to suddenly find a document which some well-meaning people had concluded but without thinking the issues through. Everyone shared the anguish about the situation. However, to bring the people out and not to provide protection on the ground—as well as not knowing where the people involved would be going to—raised serious difficulties of principle.

According to the author's note of the meeting, "Lord Owen stated that the Co-Chairmen recognized that the moral and ethical problems were formidable. However, one had to resist ethnic cleansing. There were dangers in taking people out in an uncontrolled situation. Mr. Vance said that if the question entered the public domain, he would have to say that the document concerned was premature; that the alternatives were not considered; that there ought to be an opportunity for Mrs Ogata to sit down and talk about these issues; and that the Co-Charimen also had to be given an opportunity to participate in the discussion."

The ICRC Delegate-General for Europe responded that what the ICRC had done was in response to a serious problem. It had sought to put the problem on the table. It was an embarrassing issue for the international community but the humanitarian dimensions nevertheless remained.

Ambassador Herbert Okun, Senior adviser to Vance, commented that "the line between ethnic cleansing and safe havens was a thin one. One would need to think about where the people would go." The ICRC Delegate-General for Europe replied that the ICRC had a number of ideas about this. Mr. Vance commented that somebody ought to be giving thought about which international body would be responsible to check the will of the people."[108]

---

[108] BGR Notes of a Meeting with Representatives of the International Committee of the Red Cross, Friday 2 October, 1992, 4-15—5.20 pm.". Document in the possession of the author.

One could see from the above how vigilant and attentive Vance and Owen were on the dangers of ethnic cleansing. In a cable that Vance had sent to Secretary-General Boutros-Ghali on 3 October, following a visit to Banka Luka and Zagreb, he had warned:

> "2. I am sorry to report that we did find in Banja Luka disturbing evidence of pressure upon the Muslim population of that city as well as solid indications of ethnic cleansing actually going on in the neighbouring regions. Matters were worse than we had expected. We received confirmation of reports that ethnic cleansing of thousands of Muslims was underway at Bosanski Petrovac and Kljuc. We also saw sign of hope, however: while Banja Luka itself was tense, violence had not erupted and there was still the possibility that its reputation for tolerance could be preserved.
>
> …
>
> "5. In view of what we had found in Banja Luka, David and I decided to travel to Belgrade on Monday, 28 September, to discuss some of our concerns….In Belgrade we met Federal President Cosic, Vice-President Kontic, General Panic, Serbian President Milosevic and his Foreign Minister Jovanovic….
>
> **"Ethnic cleansing: David and I insisted that ethnic cleansing had to stop. All parties were involved, and all had to stop. We noted that the international community saw the Serbs as the major perpetrators, and unless their record improved markedly there would be no question of lifting sanctions or taking other positive steps."**
>
> "7. …On the morning of Monday 28 September, David and I met for over two hours with President Izetbegovic…
>
> "9. During our discussions with President Izetbegovic we also sought his thoughts on ways and means of guaranteeing respect for human rights in Bosnia and Herzegovina."

The Co Chairmen could, here again, be seen taking a strident position against ethnic cleansing. Vance, as the UN Co-Chairman, pressed the issue with the UN Secretary-General and sought a protective role for UN peacekeepers, as we shall see next.

4. Calling on the aid of UN peacekeepers to protect people against ethnic cleansing

On 13 October, 1992, USG for Peacekeeping, Marrack Goulding, sent the following cable to General Satish Nambiar, the Commander of UNPROFOR, based in Zagreb:

> "1. At a meeting with SecGen this morning Mr. Vance expressed his grave concern about continued abuses by the Bosnian Serb authorities in

and around Banja Luka. Large numbers of Muslims were being rounded up and bussed to the Travnik area and made to walk through no-man's land into Muslim-controlled territory, many being shot as they went. Mr. Vance felt that early deployment of UNPROFOR troops could help to deter such activities. This would be achieved when the new Canadian contingent was deployed for humanitarian protection duties. Meanwhile, was there any possibility of temporarily detaching some elements from Canadian battalion in Sector West to Banja Luka, ostensibly as advance party for new Canadian battalion?

"2. SecGen agreed that your views should be sought on this idea."[109]

We shall discuss the role of UN peacekeepers in the chapter following this one.

5. Making strong representations to the leaders on the ground about human rights issues

We saw in the opening pages of this book, setting out some of the humanitarian pleas, examples of Vance and Owen making strong representations to the Bosnian Serb leader, Radovan Karadzic about ethnic cleansing taking place in Bosnia. The Co-Chairmen also made similar representations on human rights issues on different occasions to President Alija Izetbegovic and the Bosnian Croat leader, Mate Boban.

6. Speaking out against violations of human rights

We also saw, earlier in this book, instances of Vance and Owen speaking out publicly against violations of human rights. We repeat here the following statement cited earlier:

"Vance and Owen Warn That Carve-up of Bosnia and Herzegovina Will not be Tolerated"

"The international community will not tolerate the taking of territory by force, nor acquiesce in ethnic cleansing, Lord Owen and Cyrus Vance said at a press conference today. Responding to reports that B-H in fact had been carved up by Serbian and Croatian forces, the two Co-Chairmen of the International Conference on the Former Yugoslavia said that the status quo on the ground was not acceptable, and that international

[109] Cable in the possession of the author.

recognition and the lifting of sanctions would not take place until a political solution had been found.

"This is not going to be settled by people who have taken up arms, and have abandoned humanitarian principles, and trampled on international law," Lord Owen told the assembled correspondents. "We do not accept this status quo as permanent", he added, "and we intend to see that it is changed." While some advocated the use of force, he went on, the Geneva Conference would use other methods that in the end would triumph. Mr. Vance agreed, saying, "That is the way we will act; that is what we expect to happen; and we will not be turned back in our determination to see that happen."[110]

7. Working for human rights monitoring during and after the conflict

Vance, Owen, and Stoltenberg worked assiduously to put human rights monitors on the ground during the conflict in Bosnia and Herzegovina. We discuss this in a separate chapter on human rights monitoring later in this book.

8. Seeking to provide for strong institutions for the protection of human rights in Bosnia and Herzegovina and elsewhere in the former Yugoslavia

We cited earlier in this chapter, the emphasis of Vance and Owen, and later Owen and Stoltenberg, to provide for strong human rights institutions in Bosnia and Herzegovina.

9. The Z-4 Plan: Draft Agreement on the Krajina, Slavonia, Southern Baranja and Western Sirmium

ICFY negotiators worked hard for an agreement on autonomy for the Krajina and other Serb areas in Croatia grounded in extensive human rights provisions. In order to give impetus to the negotiations, it was agreed that a specialized group would assist the ICFY negotiators, consisting of the Ambassadors in Zagreb of France,Germany, Russia and

[110] Press Release of the International Conference on the Former Yugoslavia, 23 October, 1992.[7]

the USA who would constitute the "Z-4 Group" focusing on the Serb areas in Croatia. The late Paul Szasz prepared for the Group a Draft Agreement on Krajina, Slavonia, Southern Baranja and Western Sirmium that was presented to the Governments in Belgrade and Zagreb.[111] President Franjo Tudjman of Croatia wanted full integration of the Serb areas within the Croatian State and was less than lukewarm about the proposals. When it was presented to President Milosevic, he asked for a week to study it, and when Owen and Stoltenberg saw him the following week, he advised: "Gentlemen, please do not press today ideas that might work in five years time". The plan never took roots, but its human rights provisions were striking.

The plan called for the application throughout Croatia of the highest level of internationally recognized human rights and fundamental freedoms provided in the constitution of the Republic of Croatia, in the Constitutional Law on Human Rights and Freedoms and the Rights of National and Ethnic Communities or Minorities in the Republic of Croatia, and in a detailed set of instruments listed in an Annex to the Plan. All persons within the Republic of Croatia would enjoy the rights to life, liberty, equality before the law and various other enumerated rights.

The Republic of Croatia would, as soon as possible, become a party to each of the international treaties listed in an Annex to the Plan. The Republic of Croatia would make arrangements with the Council of Europe for the establishment of a Human Rights Court of Croatia in accordance with Resolution 93(6) of the Committee of Ministers of the Council of Europe and as specified in an Annex to the Plan. The Government of the Republic of Croatia would provide for the appointment of Ombudsmen to assist in implementing the rights and freedoms specified. There would be a Special Constitutional Court for the Krajina to which would be submitted for final disposition all disputes arising under the proposed agreement. Detailed provisions for the protection of minority rights were included. Provisions were also made for domestic and international prosecutions related to the conflict.

---

[111] The version presented is dated 18 January, 1995. Text in the possession of the author. In a collection of documents of the International Conference on the Former Yugoslavia that this author edited in 1997 the Z-4 document was not included because the compendium included only documents that had been made public. The Z-4 Plan has, as far as the author is aware, never been made public.

As mentioned above, the Z-4 Plan did not go forward because neither President Slobodan Milosevic nor President Franjo Tudjman encouraged it, but its provisions did influence the Eastern Slavonia agreement that was negotiated by Thorvald Stoltenberg, Co-Chairman of ICFY and US Ambassador in Zagreb Peter Galbraith.

10. Should the negotiators have drawn 'consequences' from the fact that systematic violations of human rights were being committed during the peace negotiations?

In an article written in the Polish Yearbook of International Law in 1992, the principal aide to Special Rapporteur Mazowiecki, my good friend Prof. Roman Wieruszewski, thought that the Special Rapporteur should play an important role within the framework of ICFY. He noted that the Co-Chairmen of the Steering Committee of the Conference had on various occasions stressed that human rights standards should be observed and that within the proposed peace agreement the human rights provisions had been 'very carefully elaborated and specified.' Within the framework of ICFY there had been discussions on a broad human rights monitoring operation. He added, however:

> "Nevertheless, one cannot escape the impression that human rights were treated instrumentally within that context. They have always been used as an additional element of diplomatic pressure. Negotiators were unable to draw any consequences from the fact that systematic violations of human rights have been committed during the peace negotiations. In spite of verbal declarations, the Co-Chairmen were very reluctant to envisage any kind of close cooperation with the Special Rapporteur. The instrumental treatment of human rights standards may be very dangerous. As Mazowiecki said in one of his reports, the good faith and credibility of the parties to the conflicts should be measured by their proven commitment to human rights."[112]

Wieruszewski thus recognized that the peace plans had detailed human rights provisions and that the negotiators had spoken out against violations of human rights. Nevertheless, he thought that human rights had been used 'instrumentally', as an element of diplomatic pressure and that the negotiators were unable to draw any consequences from the fact that systematic violations of human rights

[112] R. Wieruszewski, "International Response to the Human Rights Violations in the Territory of the Former Yugoslavia", XIX Polish Yearbook of International Law 1991–1992, pp.203–225, at p.219.

were committed during the peace negotiations. He felt that the good faith and credibility of the parties to the conflicts should have been measured by their proven commitment to human rights.

These were understandable criticisms from someone who was so close to the Special Rapporteur but do they stand up to scrutiny? How can one assess them? On the charge that human rights had been used instrumentally, the author, unfortunately, cited no evidence to back it up and it is simply not true.

On the charge that human rights had been used as an element of diplomatic pressure, here again, no evidence was adduced to back this up and it remained in the realm of the opinion of the author. This criticism does not deserve further consideration.

The charge that the negotiators were unable to draw any consequences from the fact that systematic violations of human rights were committed during the peace negotiations was understandable,coming from the vantage point of the author. It goes to the heart of a discussion of the role of human rights in peace negotiations. But, in our view, it is a charge born of frustration rather than judgment. We propose to discuss it in the light of the relevant facts.

By the time Vance and Owen came to lead the negotiations in the former Yugoslavia in September, 1992, war had already raged in Croatia the previous year and war had ranged in Bosnia and Herzegovina since the spring of 1992. The Security Council, with the participation of the leading governmental powers, had ordered an arms embargo on all parts of the former Yugoslavia and had called for negotiated solutions to the different conflicts. The 'Carrington Conference' had been negotiating a comprehensive peace treaty but Lord Carrington felt that his efforts had been undermined by the premature recognition of the constituent republics. Then had come the London Conference in August, 1992, which had mandated continuous negotiations among the Bosnian parties for a solution to the conflict in that country. The London Conference had put down some basic principles, including the principle of respect for human and minority rights, but all the negotiators had to work with to implement those principles was persuasion and diplomacy.

What could the peace negotiators do in the circumstances apart from what they actually did: stating publicly that they would not accept the results of ethnic cleansing or ratify those results in the peace agreement; point out violations to the parties and the international community; call for discussions of human rights violations in pertinent bodies such as the UN Commission on Human Rights and the

UN human rights treaty bodies; call for and work for the establishment of an international criminal tribunal; call for and actively support forensic investigations of mass-grave sites; and negotiate the establishment of future institutions for the protection of human and minority rights in the future?

Should the negotiators have called off their efforts to negotiate peace and let the killings and atrocities continue? Should the negotiators have called for the use of force against offending parties? Prior to becoming a lead negotiator representing the European Community, Lord Owen had called for the use of air power against the Bosnian Serbs but the London Conference, which gave him his mandate, had chosen the route of negotiated solutions. And even if the negotiators had abandoned their efforts and called for the use of superior force, who would have been willing to use such force against, for example, the Bosnian parties?

No Government at the time was willing to go to war against the Bosnian Serbs or Croats. When the Clinton Administration proposed the lifting of the arms embargo to allow the Bosnian Muslims (now called Bosniacs) to arm themselves, EU Governments chose not to back them on this. For argument's sake, it would have counted for nothing had the negotiators supported the call for lifting of the arms embargo. Had they done so their negotiating role would have been over and it would have necessitated another negotiating team which, again, would have had to choose between facilitating negotiations or abandoning their role.

I have among my papers a Note prepared at the request of Vance and Owen dated 7 December 1992 with the title, "Questions About Lifting the Arms Embargo for the Government of Bosnia and Herzegovina". The Note acknowledged that given the tragic situation in that country, it was natural that many concerned observers wondered not only about the advisability, but even the necessity, of lifting the arms embargo. It was also understandable that this question arose in view of the ethnic cleansing taking place and the world's apparent inability to end the fighting.

One also had to look, however, the Note argued, beyond those concerns and ask what the lifting of the arms embargo would mean on the ground. In this respect, a number of questions arose:

1. 'Would the lifting of the arms embargo really enable the Government (in reality the Muslim side) to defend itself, or would it rather

lead to an escalation of the conflict with greater loss of lives on all sides—even for the Muslims?

2. 'Would the lifting of the arms embargo not be tantamount to licensing the war and thereby give the Bosnian Serbs a pretext to use maximum force as soon as possible to achieve their aims before the Muslims could be armed?
3. 'Even now it is difficult to get the leadership of the three sides to talk about peace while the fighting goes on. Would it be possible to pursue efforts for peace after licensing the escalation of the war? Would not peace-making come to a halt?
4. 'Would it be possible to maintain United Nations peace-keeping forces in Bosnia and Herzegovina to protect humanitarian convoys while the conflict was escalating? It is hard to conceive the continuation of the UN peace-keeping role in such circumstances. Would humanitarian relief agencies such as UNHCR and the ICRC still be able to function in the midst of all-out warfare?
5. 'With the lifting of the arms embargo leading to increased hostilities in Bosnia and Herzegovina, how could we contain the situation in the United Nations Protected Areas in Croatia? Could a spill-over of the conflict be avoided?
6. With arms flowing freely into Bosnia and Herzegovina, would they not reach groups in Kosovo and Macedonia, thereby increasing the risk of conflict in those areas?
7. 'If there were a free-for-all in the provision of arms, would Serbia not be able to acquire sophisticated weapons from Republics of the former USSR? Would Bosnia and Herzegovina not be able to acquire such arms from the Muslim Republics of the former USSR?
8. 'If arms were flowing freely into Bosnia and Herzegovina and in the area of the former Yugoslavia, what would stop radical or fundamentalist religious groups from getting involved in the supply of arms and even in terrorist activities? What would such a situation mean for the Balkan region as a whole?
9. 'As a matter of international public policy the United Nations Charter, while granting the inherent right of self-defence, emphasizes the principle of the non-use of force. What constitutes international morality: putting the emphasis on peace or providing the means for increased bloodshed and death?'[113]

---

[113] Questions About Lifting the Arms Embargo for the Government of Bosnia and Herzegovina, December 7, 1992. Note in the possession of the author. The Note was

Vance and Owen, and then Stoltenberg and Owen, in fact, chose the honourable route: persisting with negotiations in the face of great odds. It is easy to say that the negotiators were unable to draw any consequences from the fact that systematic violations of human rights were being committed while the peace negotiations were under way. But what practical consequences could one have drawn in the circumstances?

Likewise, arising out of frustration and genuine concern, it is understandable that Mazowiecki and Wieruszewski felt that the good faith and credibility of the parties to the conflicts should have been measured by their proven commitment to human rights but what, if anything, could this have meant in practice? In his book on the negotiations, Lord Owen reveals that when he met Lord Carrington to discuss the passing of the dossier from him as the lead EC negotiator, Carrington's views on the leadership of the Bosnian parties were 'unprintable' and that 'there was not much to choose between them on his scale of perfidy'.[114] Carrington had no illusions about the integrity of the Bosnian leaders but his task was to help negotiate a peace agreement and that would become the task of Vance, Owen and Stoltenberg. If the truth be told, few, if any, of the Bosnian leaders had a 'proven commitment to human rights'. What could the negotiators do about this in practical terms, other than trying to put their human rights responsibilities before the Bosnian leaders, while continuing to facilitate negotiations?

Conclusion

This chapter will hopefully have shown that the peacemakers did their utmost to grapple with human rights challenges in the course of their negotiations. But it would be a fair question to ask whether their approaches to peacemaking in such a situation was too traditional, and whether it might have been possible for them to adopt more dynamic approaches to peacemaking taking account of the gross violations of human rights on the ground. Among the papers of the ICFY there is a confidential discussion paper, written around October, 1992, "Strategic Options for Finding Solutions to the Problems

---

also used by the Spokesman of ICFY in briefing journalists and was shared with some of them.

[114] David Owen, Balkan Odyssey, London, Victor Gollancz, 1995, p. 29.

in the Republics of the Former Yugoslavia" where one finds the following written:

> "7. The situation in the former Yugoslavia seems to be indicating that one would need to devise innovative approaches and strategies; in short, one would need to break new ground in handling problems involving the application of the principle of self-determination. If one is to be able to tackle the problems of the former Yugoslavia meaningfully, one would need to start building up confidence on the part of the different groups of the population that *their* wishes will be taken into account in devising new arrangements. This would seem to be the key to a durable solution of the current conflict.
>
> "8. Can the Co-Chairmen of the International Conference on the Former Yugoslavia set in motion a process that would lead people to believe that solutions could be worked out based on their wishes and on negotiations involving them? Two options may be considered. The first would be for the Co-Chairmen to hold a series of hearings in Geneva, and on the ground in selective parts of the former Yugoslavia, so as to give the people involved, their governments, associations, representatives, academics and community leaders opportunities to offer their views and suggestions. The second possibility could be for the Co-Chairmen to designate a high level international committee of experts to conduct such hearings and to draw up a report giving an account of the hearings, together with their recommendations.
>
> "9. Between these two options the first would seem to be preferable. In the first place, time is pressing and it may not be possible to afford the delay that would be involved in setting up a commission of experts. In the second place, it could be extremely useful for the Co-Chairmen to conduct hearings themselves so as to listen to the different perspectives and views at first hand and to take them into account in distilling strategies and future courses of action.
>
> "10. Should the Co-Chairmen decide to hold such hearings, that decision could be widely disseminated and four weeks set aside for the conduct of the hearings. An internal report could be written by the Co-Chairmen's staff for use by the Co-Chairmen and for the information of the Secretary-General. In light of insights gained during the hearings, the Co-Chairmen could then proceed to map out a long-term course of action.
>
> "11. It may be mentioned, finally, that the holding of such hearings could have value as a confidence-building process as well as a process calculated to gain time in the search for peace."[115]

[115] Text in the possession of the author.

This was an internal think-piece and it was never pressed with the Co-Chairmen, who had their hands full from the outset. But, when we came across this paper in the files of ICFY, we could not help thinking that it might have been a way of blending classical negotiating approaches with innovative approaches to negotiations in the midst of crimes against humanity on the ground. We leave it to the reader to ponder this matter.[116]

[116] We owe it to the reader to admit that we are the author of this think-piece.

CHAPTER 7

PEACEKEEPING

Introduction

United Nations peacekeeping changed for ever in the former Yugoslavia. At the outset of UNPROFOR the peacekeeping doctrine was the classical one: that UN forces were interposed between warring parties who wished them to help keep a peace that they had agreed to. With a stretch, one could say that there was such an agreement in respect of the deployment in the UNPAs in Croatia.[117] One could not, however, say this of the subsequent deployments in Bosnia and Herzegovina and the Former Yugoslav Republic of Macedonia. The leadership of the peacekeeping force was reluctant to have to deal with human rights issues. From the very outset of the deployment of UNPROFOR, however, it would be called upon to contribute to the human rights effort. As the duration of the Force's deployment increased it would come to accept a role in reporting on human rights violations, in speaking out on human rights violations, and in being ready to use force if needed for the protection of those at risk. Yugoslavia established the principle that UN peace forces had a duty to contribute to the defence of human rights.

In chapter 1 above, we saw how UNPROFOR discharged its mandate as a protection force in the UNPAs in Croatia. In this chapter we shall see how the human rights-related role of the force would develop dramatically over time. For background, we provide an overview of the contributions of UN peacekeeping forces in the former Yugoslavia.

1. The contributions of UN peace operations in the former Yugoslavia

In a briefing to the UN Security Council, meeting in Informal Consultations on 23 February, 1995, Thorvald Stoltenberg, Co-Chairman of the ICFY and during 1993 the SRSG in charge of all UN

117 See on this, M. Goulding, Peacemonger, London, John Murray, 2002.

operations in the former Yugoslavia, addressed head on criticism of UNPROFOR in the media and proceeded to provide a dramatic account of the force's contribution in the area. Noting that there had been charges that the UN and UNPROFOR had not fully implemented their mandate, he admitted that, to a certain extent, this had been true. But, he pointed out, a UN withdrawal from areas of the former Yugoslavia would make the world realize that what it had accomplished there had been of 'capital importance'. Since the Council's adoption of resolution 713 in September 1991, 62 resolutions had been adopted and more than 50 Presidential statements had been issued. UNPROFOR, whose authorized strength was 50, 433 personnel, barely mustered 43, 547. Its casualties then stood at 1,340, 139 of them fatal.[118]

The UN High Commissioner for Refugees, he continued, had spent more than 1 billion in direct assistance to some 4 million refugees and displaced persons. The Sarajevo airlift was the longest in history. UNPROFOR units were stationed along the 712 kilometre cease-fire line in Croatia, along a 1,205 kilometre line inside Bosnia, and along the 290 kilometre FYROM border. ICFY monitors were operating in a 500-kilometre arc between the Federal Republic of Yugoslavia (FRY) (Serbia and Montenegro) and Bosnia and Herzegovina and along a 245 kilometre line between Croatia and the FRY. There were no UN personnel along the 850 kilometre border between Croatia and Bosnia and Herzegovina.

There had been close to 100 ceasefire agreements in Bosnia and a dozen in Croatia. Those figures, Mr. Stoltenberg said, illustrated the seriousness of the threat that would arise if UNPROFOR were compelled to withdraw from Croatia. There had been successes through the five successive blueprints for an overall regional settlement and the two plans for Croatia, the latest of which was the "Z-4" Plan emanating from a Zagreb group in which ICFY participated. An economic agreement between Croatia and the Croatian Serbs had led to the reopening of the highway between the Croatian and Serbian areas of Croatia, permitting renewed contacts among people and among families. Four thousand five hundred vehicles were then using the highway daily. The oil pipeline had been opened on 26 January, 1995,

[118] See UN Secretariat Note: Proceedings of the Security Council. Thursday 23 February 1995. Informal Consultations. Briefing by Mr. Stoltenberg. Members of the Council welcomed this briefing as 'comprehensive' and ' comprehensible'.

and agreement reached on its joint operation by Croatia and the Knin authorities. The Croatian authorities had recently delivered the spare parts needed for the Obrowsz power plant, which would resume operation in a few weeks. Mine-clearance operations had begun along two railway tracks.

On the political front, Mr. Stoltenberg continued, the "Z-4" document was a basis for political negotiations. The parties were all familiar with the document's contents and with time he was confident that talks would take place on them. What might result from them was a new mandate for UNPROFOR and possibly a new deployment and reinforcement.

Turning to Bosnia and Herzevovina, the bulk of the negotiations at that stage were being carried out by the Contact Group, with ICFY's support and assistance. The most significant event inside Bosnia had been the creation of an ICFY Mission on the Bosnia-FRY border after the FRY had indicated its willingness to isolate the Bosnian Serbs by sealing that border. Within four hours of Mr. Milosevic's decision, ICFY had received financial and manpower support from donor countries. Within a week, the first 60 ICFY personnel were in place. With 190 personnel from 17 countries manning 21 border posts, the mission acted promptly on all information received.

Mr. Stoltenberg next drew the Council's attention to the Former Yugoslav Republic of Macedonia (FYROM), where the situation was of serious concern. Domestic tensions were high because of differences between Macedonians and Albanians and also because the country was under severe external pressure due to the effects of sanctions against the FRY;. A critical economic situation had developed following a Greek embargo.

Nevertheless, one of the most positive and stimulating aspects of UN action in the FYROM had been the preventive deployment of UN troops, which could serve as a model for future operations. Stoltenberg added that he had reached agreement with the FYROM Government on holding tripartite talks between the Government, the Albanian opposition, and the Albanian party taking part in the Government. At a meeting in Geneva that week, donor countries and governments had indicated their readiness to support multi-media Albanian broadcasts. A few weeks before that, at an educational conference in the Hague, education in the FYROM had specifically been discussed, in concert with ICFY and UNESCO. Participants were hopeful that their discussions might lead to the establishment of an

Albanian Pedagogical Institute in Skopje, which would be of great importance to the Albanians.

Stoltenberg continued that he had checked with President Milosevic regarding Mr. Rugova's interest in meeting him in order to discuss the situation in Kosovo. President Milosevic had replied in the affirmative. That had been conveyed to Mr. Rugova who had said that he would have to discuss it with his people.[119]

We have set out the content of this briefing in some detail because it provides a dramatic snapshot of UN peace operations in the former Yugoslavia, taken from the Notes on the proceedings of the UN Security Council done by its Secretariat staff.

2. Development of a human rights role

Thorvald Stoltenberg, who, at one stage, served simultaneously as ICFY Co-Chairman and SRSG in charge of all UN operations in the former Yugoslavia, played a decisive part in bringing about a human rights role for United Nations peacekeepers in the midst of a conflict—the first time this had ever been done. How this came about is a story not well known.

Professor Torkel Opsahl, a member of the Commission of Experts gathering information into possible crimes in the Former Yugoslavia, was a fellow Norwegian and a good friend of Stoltenberg. He had served brilliantly as a member of the European Commission on Human Rights, on the UN Human Rights Committee, and on other international human rights bodies. This writer had been fortunate to have him as Director of Studies when the author participated in the Research Centre of the Hague Academy of International Law and he and the author had done a United Nations mission together to visit prisoner of war camps in Iran and Iraq in 1988 during the war between those two countries.

Opsahl, a man of principle, was outraged by the atrocities being committed in the former Yugoslavia and he conveyed his views with some passion to Stoltenberg. When Stoltenberg became the SRSG in charge of all UN operations, including the peacekeeping forces,

[119] Note by the author: Rugova made this request and after Stoltenberg informed him of Milosevic's positive response he said he would have to discuss it with 'his people' and never came back to the subject.

he asked this author, as Director of his office as SRSG, to look into what might be done by the peacekeepers on the human rights front.

It will be remembered that the force had been established initially as a stabilization and protection force and carried the name the United Nations Protection Force (UNPROFOR). The concept was that it would be placed around the Serb enclaves in Croatia with the idea that there would be protection through presence. The main role in human rights related issues was played by the Civilian Police (CIVPOL) but this was, again, largely a role of protection through presence.

The United Nations peacekeeping doctrine at the time did not envisage an active human rights protection role for United Nations peacekeepers and the UN Department of Peacekeeping Operations was far from having made the intellectual or policy leap into the notion that peacekeeping troops could play a role on human rights matters. The cable traffic in the early days of the force bears this out.

This prevailing culture came out very much in this author's meetings with the Force Commander, Deputy Force Commander and other senior peacekeeping personnel when the author met with them to discuss the issue of a human rights role for the peacekeepers. The first meeting was in May, 1993, with the Deputy Force Commander, Major-General Gaudreau of Canada and other senior leaders at the force headquarters in Zagreb. It was a cooperative and constructive meeting. The Deputy Force Commander, a seasoned UN peacekeeper, explained that peacekeeping forces had never been called upon to gather information and report on atrocities committed by the parties among whom they were stationed. If it became known that they were doing this it would make their relations with the parties on the ground difficult. Moreover, across the former Yugoslavia, the force, though cumulatively large, was thinly distributed on the ground.

This author, in turn, explained that we were dealing with a situation that had not arisen before. The forces were on the ground and serious violations of human rights were taking place in their midst. Members of the international community were harsh in their criticism and the situation we were in was untenable. We had to be seen as attentive to the human rights issues involved.

The Deputy Force Commander was a gentleman and he clearly absorbed these arguments even though he maintained his position during the meeting. This author sought to make the case for the forces to at least report on what they were aware of, confidentially. One could see the discomfort of the peacekeeping leaders over the idea that they should report on violations to non-peacekeeping entities and that this would become known to the parties on the ground. They were thinking about the fact that they had to operate among the very parties on the ground and they were, at the end of the day, vulnerable, being so thinly spread out. This author nevertheless pressed the point for at least reporting.

It must be said that one was dealing with leaders of goodwill and they reflected on our discussions. In the end one could see a softening of their position on reporting, even if there was not an immediate change. Eventually, Yasushi Akashi took over as SRSG following Stoltenberg's request to Boutros-Ghali that he be relieved of the SRSG position so that he could concentrate on the negotiations, and a unit was established in the Office of the SRSG to gather information on violations of human rights and to report thereon to the SRSG. Thus it was that the first human rights component was established in a United Nations peacekeeping force operating prior to the conclusion of a peace agreement. It was a small step, but an important one. It began with the insistence of a peacemaker/peacekeeper, Thorvald Stoltenberg.

Stoltenberg was in a strong position because he doubled as SRSG and chief UN negotiator and therefore had considerably more leverage. But there are ways for the peacemaker to exert influence on people of goodwill in charge of peacekeeping forces. A peace negotiator who comes to the conclusion that there is need for human rights monitoring on the ground, even while peace negotiations are carried on, can and should exert such influence.

3. Peacekeepers report on atrocities

On 13 May, 1993, the Force Commander, General Lars-Eric Wahlgren, sent a communication to Kofi Annan, USG for Peacekeeping Operations, on alleged Bosnian Croat (HVO) forces atrocities in the Lasva Valley. He provided advance notice of the outcome of investigations conducted in central Bosnia by the human rights staff of the related bodies based with UNPROFOR. In brief, they were reporting a major, well-coordinated and planned exercise in ethnic cleansing conducted by the HVO at various locations in the valley of the river Lasva, including Vitez and Ahimici, involving hundreds of Muslim civilian deaths "in circumstances which will certainly be described as atrocities, and may involve breaches of the Genocide Convention. The evidence is detailed, extensive and convincing."

According to Wahlgren's report, a major sequence of events took place from 16 – 20 April. They had been witnessed by about 60 identified persons, of whom many had given statements, including members of the British battalion, who seemed fully informed. The purpose was to drive all Muslims out of a number of towns and villages physically and by terror. HVO burned villages, telling the Muslim inhabitants that the area under the Vance-Owen plan was to become a part of Croatia.

The communication continued that the pattern of alleged behaviour was "tragically familiar, but entails especial levels of barbarity". 18 HVO members were specifically accused. The number of persons killed was unknown as, in some villages such as Ahimici, several hundreds of persons were said to be missing still. Grenade and petrol-bomb attacks on houses were said to have been followed in some instances by house-to-house massacres. "It is concluded by the investigators, who had Britbatt protection and logistical assistance throughout their work, that the practice was to spread terror by engaging in public massacres, followed by vigorous pressure in the area to leave it". The communication continued that some later retaliation by Bosnian forces had taken place, but not on a large scale.

The foregoing was the gist of the report given to the Centre for Human Rights in Geneva for the attention of the Special Rapporteur.[120]

On 21 December, 1993, Stoltenberg as SRSG in charge of UNPROFOR sent a communication to Kofi Annan, USG in charge of the Department of Peacekeeping Operations on alleged massacres committed by Bosnian Presidency forces. On the night of 14 September, 1993, the Major of Prozor had requested UNPROFOR to witness the results of an alleged massacre by Bosnian Presidency forces in the village of Kriz. A company of UNPROFOR had attended the scene on 15 September and reported that it appeared that, the previous day, an attack had been made by 70–100 Bosnian Muslim forces whose aim was to pin down HIV troops on their frontline positions and to draw the remainder of the men out of the village of Kriz. During the offensive, an HVO command post had been located and attacked in the village and, as the Bosnian troops withdrew back through Kriz, they had systematically killed a number of civilians. A total of 35 civilian bodies had been identified including elderly men and women, and a

[120] Communication in the possession of the author.

fourteen year old female. Some of the elderly had been killed in their beds or while cowering for cover elsewhere. The majority of those killed had been shot but a small number had been stabbed, one had possibly been axed to death, and a number of bodies burned. There were reports of 'Mujahideen' involvement.

The communication noted that Special Rapporteur Mazowiecki had written to President Izetbegovic on15 October to condemn this and other unacceptable massacres of civilians by Bosnian forces and had urged an investigation of the matter and punishment of the perpetrators. UNPROFOR had no information of any action on this front by the Bosnian Presidency.[121]

4. Peacekeepers speak out about atrocities

On 6 October, 1993, Stoltenberg, in his capacity as SRSG in charge of UNPROFOR, sent a communication to the Secretary-General transmitting a report drawn up by Civil Affairs Sector South on behalf of various components of UNPROFOR in respect of the incursion into the "Medak pocket" by the Croatian Army on and after 9 September, 1993. The report had been endorsed by Force Commander Jean Cot and the Head of Civil Affairs Cedric Thornberry. The report described a series of grave breaches of international law.

Stoltenberg informed the Secretary-General that he endorsed the report's recommendation that it be transmitted to the Human Rights Commission's Special Rapporteur Mr. Tadeusz Mazowiecki, and to the Commission of Experts on War Crimes for their consideration. The report had been hand-carried to those two recipients in Geneva that very day. Stoltenberg approved a press statement on the grave breaches.

Stoltenberg further informed the Secretary-General that a copy of the report was being transmitted to the Croatian Minister of Defence, Mr. Susak, in Zagreb, requesting appropriate action on his part. Furthermore, UNPROFOR had details of the senior command structure of the units responsible for the actions described in the report which, as could be seen from the report, "appear in large measure to have been premeditated and planned."[122] The press statement issued by UNPROFOR was blunt in its content and tone.

---

[121] Communication in the possession of the author.
[122] Communication in the possession of the author.

Another occasion when UNPROFOR spoke out forthrightly occurred later that month. On 27 October, 1993, UNPROFOR issued the following remarkable press release on a massacre that had taken place in the Muslim village of Stupni Do:

> "UNPROFOR troops succeeded in entering the Muslim village of Stupni Do on the afternoon of 26 October 1993 and have confirmed that a massacre has occurred there.
>
> "Stupni Do…was attacked by Croatian Defence Council (HVO) troops on Saturday, 23 October, allegedly as a reprisal for a Muslim attack on the nearby Croat village of Kopjari on Thursday, 21 October, during which all the inhabitants were driven out of the village.
>
> "The Nordic Battalion (Nordicbat) of the Bosnia-Herzegovina Command of UNPROFOR found that all 52 houses of the village had been burned to the ground. At last report, the UNPROFOR soldiers had searched half the houses and had found the bodies of 15 persons who had either been shot or burned to death. This included a group of women holding each other's arms, who had been shot. In addition, two young women from a group of 25 refugees who escaped from the village have made accusations of rape.
>
> "The whereabouts of many of the village's inhabitants is still unknown, but it is believed that some succeeded in escaping into the surrounding hills.
>
> "The UNPROFOR troops initiated attempts to reach Stupni Do almost immediately after the HVO attack began on 23 October. Throughout the three-day stand-off with the HVO, they were constantly blocked by the Bobovac Brigade. The UNPROFOR troops were threatened with rocket-propelled grenade anti-tank weapons, small arms and anti-tank mine barriers. Several of the UNPROFOR armoured personnel carriers (APCs) were damaged by small arms fire and grenades.
>
> "UNPROFPOR's Force Commander General Jean Cot, said: 'Despite the valiant efforts of Nordicbat, the HVO troops systematically prevented the UN soldiers from entering the village of Stupni Do for three days. It is unacceptable that we were forced to delay our entry into the village for such a period. It is clear that the HVO troops were attempting to hide from us the atrocities they had committed.
>
> "At the same time, UNPROFOR is deeply concerned about the safety of more than 200 Muslims being held in two school buildings in the town of Vares. There has been some evidence of mistreatment of some of the prisoners by HVO soldiers. UNPROFOR troops with APCs are stationed near these locations.
>
> "The Force Commander said these tragedies impeded moves towards reconciliation among the parties involved. He said it was another example

of the need for all the parties to the conflict to make a solid commitment towards the protection of minorities within the areas they controlled.

"The investigation into the massacre and the collection of further evidence regarding war crimes will continue. UNPROFOR troops, UN Civilian Police, members of the European Community Monitoring Mission, representatives of UNHCR and other humanitarian agencies will visit the village."[123]

On 5 September, 1994, UNPROFOR issued the following Press Statement by the SRSG for the former Yugoslavia, Yasushi Akashi on "Recent Mass Expulsions and Other Severe Violations of Human Rights in Bosnia and Herzegovina":

"I am deeply concerned by reports over the past several days of the continued mass expulsion of people from the Bosnian Serb controlled areas of Bijeljina and Banja Luka. I strongly condemn these extremely serious violations of international humanitarian law and universally recognized principles of human rights.

"Since the middle of July, over 2,400 people are believed to have been expelled from the Bijeljina area to Tuzla as part of a deliberate policy of rendering the area ethnically homogeneous. These expulsions have continued throughout the past six weeks but have increased dramatically in size in recent days. On Sunday 4 September alone, more than 750 people were reported to have been expelled from the Bijeljina area to Tuzla. Smaller numbers of people are also reported to have been expelled from the Bijeljina area to central Bosnia.

"More than 750 people have also been forcefully expelled from Banja Luka over the past two weeks and of these, 500 are now at the camps of UNPROFOR's Jordanian and Nepali battalions in Sector West of the United Nations Protected Areas of Croatia. 250 others, mainly ethnic Romany, have crossed into Croatia proper.

"Many of those who have been expelled have reported the systematic practice of forced labour in the areas from which they have arrived, as well as other severe human rights violations including torture, rape and sexual assault, arbitrary arrest and detention and arbitrary deprivation of property.

"Recalling the Security Council Presidential Statement on Bosnia of 2 September 1994 as well as other relevant presidential statements and Security Council resolutions, I demand the immediate cessation of these

[123] Statement signed by Shannon Boyd, UNPROFOR Spokesman, Zagreb HQ, 1800053. Text in the possession of the author.

practices and remind those who commit these violations of international humanitarian law that they are personally responsible."[124]

On the same day, 5 September, 1994, Nicholas Morris, the Special Envoy of the UN High Commissioner Refugees for the former Yugoslavia, wrote the following letter to Dr. Radovan Karadzic, the Bosnian Serb leader:

"Dear Dr. Karadzic,

Already this month, over 1,300 members of the minority communities in the Bijeljina area have been forced to leave their homes by your authorities and expelled towards Tuzla. Similar departures continue from the Banja Luka region to Croatia: almost 1,000 in the last two weeks. The expulsions from the Bijeljina area are combined with the exaction of significant sums of money (reportedly by a man known as 'Vojkan') and take place in circumstances that create great hardship for, and sometimes threaten the lives of, the old and the vulnerable. Able-bodied males are separated from their families and apparently detained by your authorities.

On many occasions UNHCR has expressed the gravest concern to you at these practices. The ICRC has done likewise. We have been assured by you and your colleagues that resolute correction action would be taken by your authorities, yet the expulsions continue and even intensify. Once more, I write to urge you to take immediate action to provide proper protection to the minorities in the areas that you control, and for whose safety you are directly responsible.

Yours sincerely,
Nicholas Morris."

On 6 September, 1994, SRSG Akashi wrote to USG Annan and USG Gharekan that he had raised with Dr. Karadzic at their last meeting in Pale the ongoing abuses of human rights around Bijeljina. At that time, Dr. Karadzic had attributed the problem to criminals and had undertaken to replace the Chief of Police due to what he had acknowledged was a very unsatisfactory situation in the area with respect to security and crime.

Akashi continued that he had subsequently learned that the Chief of Police had indeed been replaced. The UNHCR office in Tuzla nevertheless continued to report the arrival of large numbers of refugees who had been forced to leave the Bijeljina area. As a result he had issued the statement reproduced above.

---

[124] Statement in the possession of the author.

He continued that he had telephoned Dr. Karadzic to ensure that he was aware of the events around Bijeljina, and to express strong concern. He reported:

> "Dr. Karadzic has advised me that he has taken measures to identify, arrest, and prosecute those responsible. I urged immediate action as the frequency of expulsions indicates that more are likely to follow. I also advised him of my statement of yesterday and that a statement might also be issued from Geneva by the ICRC."[125]

5. The Rapid Reaction Force (RRF)

On 28 February, 1994, NATO planes fired the first ever shots in the history of the military alliance when it shot down four Serb jets flying in a no-fly zone. The Serb jets had ignored orders to land or be shot down. Two other planes escaped. The Serb planes had apparently gone on a bombing run against a Bosnian Muslim ammunitions factory in Novi Travnik.[126] According to NATO sources, the no-fly zone had been violated hundreds of times by all three warring factions using helicopters to ferry men and materiel and to evacuate the wounded. But NATO's Admiral Boorda reportedly said that the incident involved the first confirmed violations by fixed-wing aircraft since NATO, acting under Security Council authorization, began operating Opertion Deny Flight. Russia supported NATO's action in shooting down the planes.[127] This could be classified as part of a conflict containment strategy, rather than a protection strategy as such.

The following year would see UNPROFOR's establishment of a Rapid Reaction Force (RRF) after Bosnian Serb forces had attacked UN safe areas and chained UNPROFOR personnel to military installations to deter NATO response to their aggression. Like the policing of the No-Fly Zone, the RRF was more of a conflict containment measure but it did have a protection dimension inasmuch as it was meant to deter future Bosnian Serb attacks against Muslim positions.

The setting up and deployment of the RRF was authorized by Security Council resolution 998, voted after the hostage problem following earlier NATO air strikes against Bosnian Serb targets. The purpose of the RRF was to permit UN peace forces to support theatre forces in conducting their peacekeeping mandate. It consisted of

---

125 Communication in the possession of the author.
126 Four Serb Jets Shot Down by Nato, The Times, London, 1 March, 1994.
127 Ibid.

three main units: a multinational brigade, a 24-hour airmobile brigade reinforced by Royal Air Force helicopters, and a French brigade on alert in France.

Its general mission was to be prepared to conduct operations in order to enhance the security of UN forces, to facilitate freedom of movement in Bosnia and Herzegovina and thereby maintain the credibility of the UN peace forces. The concept of operation took account of the political environment (the need for impartiality, the risk of escalation in the war, and the element of reversibility of operations.). The RRF was considered a second echelon element while the in-theatre forces made up the first echelon. The second-echelon was meant to support the first-echelon in the achievement of its mandate. The RRF was under the overall command of Force Commander General Janvier based in Zagreb and the operational command of General Rupert Smith in charge of UN forces in Sarejevo.

To begin with, the multinational brigade was deployed mainly in Bosnia, particularly Mount Igman. The airmobile brigade was deployed to Ploce. The French brigade remained on alert in France. The multinational brigade had 1000 troops deployed on Mount Igman and, during the night of 27th to 28 July, 1995, conducted successful deterrent action in order to dislodge Serb encirclement of the locality of Krupac. The RRF conducted a silent infiltration of the area which obliged Serb forces to withdraw. The RRF thus carried a distinct preventive protection function in this instance.[128]

6. Protection from ethnic cleansing

As we saw in the previous chapter, on 13 October, 1992, USG for peacekeeping, Marrack Goulding, sent the following cable to General Satish Nambiar, the Commander of UNPROFOR, based in Zagreb:

> "1. At a meeting with SecGen this morning Mr. Vance expressed his grave concern about continued abuses by the Bosnian Serb authorities in and around Banja Luka. Large numbers of Muslims were being rounded up and bussed to the Travnik area and made to walk through no-man's land into Muslim-controlled territory, many being shot as they went. Mr. Vance felt that early deployment of UNPROF OR troops could help to deter such activities. This would be achieved when the new Canadian

[128] This account is based on a "Rapid Reaction Force Brief", circa August, 1995 in the possession of the author. See, generally, R. Smith The Utility of Force: The Art of War in the Modern World. 2008.

> contingent was deployed for humanitarian protection duties. Meanwhile, was there any possibility of temporarily detaching some elements from Canadian battalion in Sector West to Banja Luka, ostensibly as advance party for new Canadian battalion?
> "2. SecGen agreed that your views should be sought on this idea."[129]

UNPROFOR would come to accept, over time, that it should take account of considerations such as these in its deployment, operations, and strategies.

7. Cooperation with the Commission of Experts

On 23 November, 1992, USG for peacekeeping, Marrack Goulding sent a cable to UNPROFOR Force Commander Nambiar on the subject "Human Rights". It read as follows: "Following the establishment of the Commission of Experts under Security Council resolution 780, I should be grateful if you would ensure that any information relating to human rights matters is passed to Geneva for the attention of both the Special Rapporteur and the Commission. Please relay such material directly through your Geneva LO, keeping us informed. X and Y (names withheld by BGR) are hereby authorized to serve as UNPROFOR liaison to the Commission, whose Secretary, Ms. J. Dauchy, will contact (them) later this week."[130]

UNPROFOR gave its fullest support to the Commission of Experts.

8. The human rights of the peacekeepers

While pushing for a human rights role for the UN peacekeeping forces, UN leaders were not unmindful of the human rights of peacekeepers themselves as could be seen in a cable from Vance to the Secretary-General on 14 September, 1992. Reporting on a Mission to the former Yugoslavia, from September 9 to 13, 1992, Vance informed the Secretary-General:

> "We left Izetbegovic in no doubt of our concern over attacks on UNPROFOR personnel and called on him to bring the perpetrators of such attacks to justice. This he agreed to do."[131]

---

[129] Communication in the possession of the author.
[130] Communication in the possession of the author.
[131] Report in the possession of the author.

Conclusion

From the foregoing, it could be seen that the challenges facing UN peacekeepers were formidable. UN peacekeeping evolved to incorporate a role in the defence of human rights. The methods used were reporting, investigations, statements of concern, condemnations. In the end, UN forces were forced to go into fighting posture in order to help uphold the principles of the Universal Declaration of Human Rights. That was perhaps the most important lesson for UN peacekeeping and the defence of human rights that came out of the Yugoslav experience.

CHAPTER 8

PEACEBUILDING

Introduction

Peacebuilding in the former Yugoslavia was not a straightforward issue. As the Socialist Federal Republic of Yugoslavia was on the verge of breaking up, the most powerful country in the world, the USA, walked away from it. The then US Secretary of State paid a one-day visit to the area and then left the problem to the European Community. His famous words were 'We have no dog in this fight'.[132]

Then, as Lord Carrington and his colleagues were working on the framework for a loose confederation anchored in respect for human and minority rights, Germany pressed for recognition of the successor republics and, in the assessment of Carrington, wrecked his efforts.[133] The London Conference on the Former Yugoslavia, held at the end of August, 1992, sought to anchor the peace effort in a set of principles that looked good on paper but were difficult to uphold in practice.

The International Conference on the Former Yugoslavia, which the London Conference had established, had a Confidence Building Working Group[134] and an Economic Issues Working Group.[135] The former, led by Vicente Berasategui, a senior official from the UN disarmament secretariat, concentrated, while it lasted, on the regulation and control of weapons and never had occasion to address broader confidence-building measures that would come under the heading of today's concept of peacebuilding measures. The Economic Issues Working Group, led by a senior economist from the secretariat of the European Community, Jean Durieux, sought to plan for the economic future of the area but, in the end, was overtaken by fighting on the ground.

---

[132] J. Baker III, The Politics of Diplomacy, Revolution, War and Peace 1989–1992.

[133] See M. Goulding, Peacemonger, London, John Murray, 2002.

[134] See B.G.Ramcharan, The International Conference on the Former Yugoslavia. Collected Papers. 2 Vols. Martinus Nijhoff, 1997.

[135] Ibid.

A Succession Issues Working Group[136] of the ICFY did groundwork for the eventual negotiations among the successor republics on the division of assets and liabilities. It thus contributed to peacebuilding in the long term but there was little in the way of human rights within its activities.

Earlier chapters in this book have recounted the role of human rights considerations in efforts for conflict prevention, peacemaking and peacekeeping. It is our submission that the foundation work of the ICFY was the basis for the human rights provisions of the Dayton Conference, that the Dayton blueprint on human rights based on ICFY's design was the real contribution to peacebuilding in Bosnia and Herzegovina. It is also our submission that ICFY's groundwork on an autonomy regime for Eastern Slavonia was another major pillar of peacebuilding in Croatia. Third, we submit that, ICFY's Working Group on Ethnic Communities, Nationalities and Minorities[137] did invaluable peacebuilding work in the Former Yugoslav Republic of Macedonia and elsewhere in the former Yugoslavia on issues of group and minority rights.

In this chapter we shall outline these different contributions.

1. ICFY WORKS FOR THE HUMAN RIGHTS TREATY BODIES TO REQUEST URGENT REPORTS FROM THE SUCCESSOR REPUBLICS

A major contribution of the peacemakers to peace-building in the successor republics in the former Yugoslavia was the work of Lord Owen, in particular, using his relationship with a member of the Human Rights Committee, to get the Committee to ask for urgent reports from the successor republics. Thanks to the initiative of Lord Owen, the Human Rights Committee, which functions under the International Covenant on Civil and Political Rights, asked successor republics in the former Yugoslavia to submit urgent reports on their efforts to protect the rights guaranteed under the Covenant. Reports were submitted by Bosnia and Herzegovina, Croatia, and the Federal Republic of Yugoslavia (Serbia and Montenegro). This author worked personally on this initiative and submitted reports to the Co-Chairmen on the Human Rights Committees discussion of the reports of the successor republics.

---

[136] Ibid

[137] Ibid.

1.1. *Human Rights Committee examination of the report of Bosnia and Herzegovina*

The report of Bosnia and Herzegovina was considered on Tuesday 3 November, 1992 from 15.00 to 17.45. The report of Bosnia and Herzegovina was introduced by Professor Filipovic. He was accompanied by Mr. Trnka, their legal expert. In his introductory remarks, Professor Filipovic drew attention to genocide, mass executions, and ethnic cleansing which, he said, was being perpetrated by "the aggressor" on the territory of the Bosnia and Herzegovina.

Members of the Human Rights Committee asked the following questions or made the following observations:

- Would the Government confirm that its submission of the report, and the presence of the delegation, amounted to its formal acceptance of obligations under the Covenant?
- What was the Government doing to fulfil its duties to curb excesses, even in a situation of civil war?
- Why had the Government made no declaration of an emergency under Article 4 of the Covenant?
- What preventive measures was the Government taking to assure that violations of human rights were not committed by its agents?
- What investigations had the Government carried out into violations of human rights?
- Had the Government notified places of detention to the ICRC? Was the ICRC being allowed access to visit detainees?
- What had the Government done to protect the rights of arrested persons in the face of allegations, including by the CSCE, that such persons had been ill-treated?
- What had the Government done about allegations that some villages with Serb populations had been rendered into virtual concentration camps?

In reply to these questions, the delegation stated that it accepted internationally recognized norms on human rights, including those in the Covenant and that the Government was committed to observing those rights. It did not deny that some excesses had taken place on its side. It said that some investigations had been carried out and some perpetrators of excesses had been sanctioned.

With regard to places of detention, it stated that, although belatedly, they had by the time of the Committee's discussion of the report of

Bosnia and Herzegovina, been notified to the ICRC and that the Government was cooperating with the ICRC.

The delegation's introduction of the report and its response to questions won it wide praise in the Committee. Members of the Committee expressed their appreciation of the Government's acceptance of responsibility for the implementation of the Covenant; its acceptance of responsibility for violations in areas under its control; and its willingness to pursue a dialogue with the Committee even in the difficult circumstances prevailing in the country.

The members of the Committee reiterated their recommendations that the Govenrment should:

- Dismantle all "concentration camps".
- Grant ICRC access to places of detention.
- Reinstate the rule of law.
- Be constantly vigilant about violations of human rights and monitor the human rights situation constantly.[138]

This author reported to the ICFY Co-Chairmen:

> "All in all, from the Government's point of view, this was a very successful occasion. It clearly won the respect, and the appreciation of the Members of the Human Rights Committee who were struck by the fact that although the Government could have come with a tale of atrocities committed by the other side, it had accepted responsibility to ensure respect for human rights in areas under its control—and had even accepted some lapses."[139]

1.2. *Human Rights Committee examination of the report of Croatia*

The report of Croatia was considered on 4 November, 1992. This author reported to the Co-Chairmen that the questions asked by members of the Committee touched upon the following points: The duties

---

[138] This account is based on the author's Note on the Human Rights Committee's Examination of a Report from the Government of Bosnia and Herzegovina submitted to the ICFY Co-Chairmen and other senior officials on 3 November, 1992, the very day of the Committee's examination of the report. Text in the possession of the author.

[139] Ibid. Unfortunately, there is little evidence that the Government actually followed up on its commitments. This is probably explained by the fact that Professor Filipovic was a very decent delegate who believed in Bosnia and Herzegovina and made his commitments in good faith whereas some of those in actual political and military control of the Government were, to say the least, less principled and had different agendas.

of Croatia to respect human rights even during a situation of conflict; preventive measures that the Government had taken, if any, to avert violations of human rights; whether there were detention camps in Croatia; whether ethnic cleansing had taken place in Croatia; the behaviour of Croatian forces in Bosnia and Heryegovina; the existence and numbers of minorities in Croatia; the role of the office for ethnic relations. This author concluded his report with the following comment:

> "...the facts cited by the Members of the Committee seemed to leave little doubt that ethnic cleansing had taken place in Croatia and that there were detention centres in the country about which the Government had not been forthcoming."[140]

1.3. *Human Rights Committee examination of the report of the FRY*

The report of the FRY was considered on 4 November, 1992. This author reported to the Co-Chairmen that the members of the Human Rights Committee had been severe in their questions and comments. The Members of the Committee had insisted that the international responsibility of the FRY was engaged in Bosnia and Herzegovina because of the role of the Yugoslav army, the role of Serbian leaders, and the role of other agents whose actions were attributable to the Government. The author reported:

> "If there is one thing that the Human Rights Committee did in its examination of the report of the FRY, it was to establish in an authoritative form, and with impeccable reasoning, that the Federal Republic of Yugoslavia could not evade international responsibility for events taking place in Bosnia and Herzegovina.
>
> "The Members of the Committee were quite caustic in the terms they used to characterize what was taking place in Bosnia and Herzegovina: Genocide, holocaust, unbelievable horrors, atrocious crimes against humanity. The Members told the representative of the FRY bluntly that they found it hard to believe that the Government could come before the Committee and pretend that these events were not taking place."[141]

---

[140] Note on the Human Rights Committee's Examination of a Report from the Government of Croatia, 4 November, 1992, 10.00 to 13.00. Document in the ICFY archives and in the possession of the author.

[141] Note on the Human Rights Committee's Examination of a Report from the Federal Republic of Yugoslavia (Serbia and Montenegro), 4 November, 15.00 to 20.00. Document in the ICFY archives and in the possession of the author.

1.4. *Assessment of the consideration of the reports in the Human Rights Committee*

This author advised the Co-Chairmen that from the Human Rights Committee's examination of the reports of the three countries "one could offer the following assessments":

(a) In all three instances the process was valuable. It recorded the international community's concerns over specific human rights problems.
(b) It registered the point clearly that each government was responsible for taking measures to assure protection for human rights in areas under its control. Each Government was left in little doubt that it was expected to establish arrangements to prevent violations of human rights and to deal effectively with excesses that took place.
(c) The need for governments, especially Croatia and Bosnia and Herzegovina, to cooperate with the ICRC came across strongly.
(d) The reports on human rights issued by the CSCE, Mr. Mazowiecki, and Amnesty International, were used repeatedly as sources of information in putting questions to the Governments. They served a very useful purpose. **The Co-Chairmen may well wish to consider how they could enhance cooperation with Mr. Mazowiecki.** (Emphasis in original).
(e) The Human Rights Committee's examination of the report of the Federal Republic of Yugoslavia has laid down normative benchmarks on issues such as ethnic cleansing, criminal responsibility for gross violations of human rights, and international responsibility for events taking place in Bosnia and Herzegovina. **It confirms that the Co-Chairmen of the International Conference were absolutely correct in taking positions of principle about events taking place in Bosnia and Herzegovina.** (Emphasis in original). After the Human Rights Committee's examination of the report of the Federal Republic of Yugoslavia, **it may well be that the Co-Chairmen would have to take an even more strident position regarding issues of principle related to gross violations of human rights and international crimes taking place in Bosnia and Herzegovina. There is no room for ambiguity on these issues.** (Emphasis in original).[142]

---

[142] Ibid. The author's note was copied to Vance, Owen, Amb. Okun, Amb. Hall, the Chairmen of Working Groups, and all members of the Office of the Co-Chairmen.

2. A framework for autonomy in the successor republics

In their search for peace in the former Yugoslavia, the Co-Chairmen of ICFY, Stoltenberg and Owen, explored possibilities for arranging schemes of autonomy for certain national groups in the former Yugoslavia. In October, 1993, they floated a set of draft principles for Special Autonomous Areas within UN Member States in the former Yugoslavia, to be agreed at a future international conference. The draft principles dealt with the following issues:

Functions: The following functions would be carried out exclusively by Special Autonomous Areas (SAA): police and law and order; health care and social services; housing; education at all levels with the exception of the curriculum; cultural and religious institutions and activities.

The following functions would be carried by the SAA in cooperation, as provided for in national legislation, with competent authorities of the central government: transportation (road, sea, rail and air); environmental protection and resource management; financial institutions; taxation; customs and excise.

The following functions would be carried out by the SAA subject to any applicable legislation by of the central government: educational curriculum; licensing of professions; television, radio and communications;

Citizenship: Dual citizenship would be allowed.

Forces: An SAA would not have any military or paramilitary forces.

Police: Police forces of the SAA would have a proportionally balanced ethnic composition. The number and equipment of the police would be in keeping with normal European standards.

Border control: Control of the international frontier would be the responsibility of the armed forces of the central government, who would also be able to deploy within the SAA.

Constitutions: The SAA shall adopt constitutions following negotiations with the central government. The constitution shall provide for democratically elected executive and legislative authorities and for an independent judiciary.

Foreign affairs: Foreign policy and international commercial policy would be the sole prerogative of the central government but the competent authorities of the SAA may establish and maintain informal relations with the authorities of other States and with entities in such States that represent the same ethnic group as form the majority in the SAA. The SAA may constitute agreements with other States or with international organizations with the approval of the central government.

Settlement of disputes: Any disagreement about the implementation of these principles would be referred to the International Conference on the Former Yugoslavia whose decision by a two-thirds would be binding on the SAA and the central government.[143]

Claims for autonomy in the successor republics were being advanced by many groups. The Co-Chairmen thus sought to suggest a framework for negotiating agreements in specific instances. This approach would be concretely tested in the negotiations for an autonomy regime in Eastern Slavonia that we discuss below.

3. ICFY's contribution to group and minority rights

ICFY's Working Group on Ethnic and National Communities and Minorities, chaired by Ambassador Geert Ahrens of Germany, pursued a double-track approach to the situations it dealt with. While noting that claims for autonomy or self-determination would need to be addressed as part of the process of negotiating political solutions in the light of the Principles agreed upon at the London Conference, the Working Group sought to forge ahead in the search for pragmatic solutions to problems on the ground.

The pragmatic approach of the Working Group could be seen in relation to situations in Kosovo and Macedonia. A report that the Co-Chairmen submitted to the Security Council through the Secretary-General on 11 November, 1992 recorded the approach of the Working Group as follows:

> "Intensive work was done in the Special Group on Kosovo. The basic approach agreed to by both sides is to try a pragmatic breakthrough in one important sector—the ethnic Albanian chose education—in order to improve the political atmosphere for talks on more fundamental issues where positions are, at present, irreconcilable. After difficult and

[143] Text, drafted by Paul Szasz, in the possession of the author.

tedious preparations, in which the release of the Chairman of the Albanian Teachers Association from prison could be achieved, the first Conference-sponsored talks between the Federal and Serbian Governments from Belgrade, on one side, and ethnic Albanian representatives from Kosovo, on the other, took place. On 14 October, all parties agreed to the following statement.

1. Representatives of the Government of the FRY and Serbia led by the Federal Minister of Education, Mr. Ivic, and representatives of the Albanians met in Pristina on 13 and 14 October with the participation of the Geneva Conference Special Group on Kosovo, under the Chairmanship of Ambassador Ahrens. A representative of the CSCE mission was also present.
2. After detailed discussion of the problems of education in the Albanian language, the participants agreed that the present situation must be changed. They further agreed on the urgent desirability of the return to normal working conditions for schools and other educational institutions.
3. It was also agreed that, to achieve this, it would be necessary to adopt a pragmatic approach requiring urgent resolution, without prejudice to the positions of the parties on broader political issues.
4. The Albanian representatives agreed to provide a list of schools and other educational institutions to be covered by the measures mentioned in (2), as well as a list of teaching plans and programmes.
5. The Group agreed to meet again in Belgrade on 22 October. At that meeting discussions will be held on all the issues mentioned above and on the equal working status of teaching and educational personnel with the aim of reaching the necessary decisions for immediate action."[144]

Unfortunately, in a report that the Co-Chairmen submitted to the Security Council on 30 March, 1993, they reported that in the talks on Kosovo, fundamental issues were continuing to hinder the pragmatic approach for solutions in the field of education. The Group would persist in its efforts but, at the same time, it was necessary to address fundamental issues in the light of the principles agreed at the London Conference.[145]

In the end, though the pragmatic approach did yield some practical results such as on the re-opening of Albanian-language schools, the refusal of the principal parties to negotiate a political solution for Kosovo would lead to a major conflict in 1999. The pragmatic approach did, however, yield more positive results in Macedonia, where the

[144] UN doc. S/24795, para. 90.
[145] S/24590, paras. 19–20.

confidence-building work of ICFY would help avoid a feared conflict in that country. On 26 January, 1994, the Co-Chairmen reported to the Security Council that the Working Group had negotiated "Agreed Minutes" between the Government of the Former Yugoslav Republic of Macedonia and a representative of the Serbs in the country. In these Agreed Minutes:

> 1. The Government representative declared that the Serbian nationality will be treated completely equally with other nationalities living in Macedonia. The Government and the representative of the Serbs from Macedonia agreed to support consistent implementation in Macedonia of all rights formulated and made effective by the Charter of the United Nations and by the Conventions formulated under its auspices, as well as CSCE's, the Hague Declaration, the Charter of Paris and other instruments, especially the document of the Copenhagen Meeting on the Human Dimension.
>
> 2. The Serb representative declared that the Serbs in Macedonia would fulfil their aspirations only within the framework of the existing Republic of Macedonia."

The fact that Macedonia was largely spared from conflict and could pursue its search for negotiated solutions among its different ethnic groups owes a great deal to the efforts of the ICFY Working Group as well as to the efforts of the CSCE High Commissioner on National Minorities. The efforts of the ICFY Co-Chairmen for a preventive deployment of UN peacekeepers in Macedonia, which we discussed in an earlier chapter, also played a capital role in the avoidance of conflict. A report submitted by the Co-Chairmen to the Security Council on 24 December 1992 recorded the Chairman of the Working Group recommending that "in the interest of the endangered stability of the Republic (the FYROM), the early arrival of United Nations Peacekeeping troops as well as the presence of long-term CSCE Observers, which include members of the European Community Monitoring Mission (ECMM) would be most helpful."[146]

4. ICFY's contribution to the Erdut Agreement for Eastern Slavonia (1995)

The peace agreement that settled the conflict in Eastern Slavonia, the Erdut Agreement, originated in efforts by ICFY Co-Chairman Thorvald Stoltenberg who, in the summer of 1995, engaged in secret

---

[146] S/25015.

shuttle diplomacy between the leadership of Belgrade and Zagreb. At one stage, he used a UN plane to take a senior Croatian leader, Mr. H. Sarinic, from Zagreb to Belgrade for secret discussions with then Yugoslav President Slobodan Milosevic. This laid the political groundwork for an eventual agreement.

The US Ambassador in Zagreb, Peter Galbraith, also did useful ground work in Zagreb in facilitating negotiations. Eventually, Stoltenberg and Galbraith teamed up, together with their staff, and succeeded in steering the Government of Croatia and the Croatian Serbs in Eastern Slavonia to an agreement that had notable human rights provisions. At first, Galbraith and Stoltenberg persuaded the parties to adopt a statement of principles that they later fleshed out in a more detailed agreement. This author worked on the drafting of the statement of principles.[147] The first draft was written during a five-hour stop-over at the passenger lounge at Frankfurt airport!

The Basic Agreement on The Region of Eastern Slavonia, Baranja, And Western Sirmium (The Erdut Agreement) of 12 November, 1995, provided for a transitional period of 12 months, extendable for another period of the same duration if so requested by one of the parties. It requested the UN Security Council to establish a Transitional Administration to govern the Region during the transitional period in the interest of all persons resident in or returning to the Region.

It further requested the Security Council to authorize an international force to deploy during the transitional period to maintain peace and security in the Region and otherwise to assist in implementation of the Agreement. Article 4 stated:

> "The Transitional Administration shall ensure the possibility for the return of refugees and displaced persons to their homes of origin. All persons who have left the Region or who have come to the Region with previous permanent residence in Croatia shall enjoy the same rights as all other residents of the region. The Transitional Administration shall also take the steps necessary to re-establish the normal functioning of all public services in the Region without delay."

Article 5 added:

> "The Transitional Administration shall help to establish and train temporary police forces to build professionalism among the police and confidence among all ethnic communities."

---

[147] He is grateful to the cooperation and friendship of US diplomat Jeff Hovenier of the US Embassy in Zagreb, with whom he pursued work on the draft statement of principles.

The human rights provisions of the Basic Agreement[148] built on earlier human rights drafts of ICFY and on the Z-4 plan for autonomy of the Croatian Serbs. The Basic Agreement provided that the highest levels of internationally-recognized human rights and fundamental freedoms shall be respected in the Region. All persons would have the right to return freely to their places of residence in the Region and to live there in conditions of security. All persons who had left the Region or who had come to the Region with previous permanent residence in Croatia would have the right to live in the Region. All persons would have the right to restoration of any property taken from them by unlawful acts, or that they were forced to abandon, and to just compensation for property that could not be restored to them. The right to recover property, to receive compensation for property that could not be returned, and to receive assistance in reconstruction of damaged property would be equally available to all persons without regard to ethnicity.

Article 10 of the Basic Agreement requested interested countries and organizations to take appropriate steps to promote the accomplishments of the commitments in the Agreement. After the expiration of the transition period, and consistent with established practice, the international community should monitor and report on respect for human rights in the Region on a long term basis. In addition, under Article 11, interested countries and organizations were requested to establish a commission that would be authorized to monitor the implementation of the Agreement, particularly its human rights and civil rights provisions, to investigate all allegations of violations of the Agreement, and to make appropriate recommendations.

The Security Council acted positively on this Agreement and established a Transitional Administration (UNTAES),[149] which did invaluable work on its implementation, and contributed to the promotion and protection of human rights in very challenging circumstances. UNTAES deployed to the area in April, 1996 and continued until 15 January, 1998. It consisted of military, police, civilian observer, and civilian components. The different components all contributed to implementation of the human rights mandate. In early August, 1997,

[148] Basic Agreement on The Region of Eastern Slavonia, Baranja, And Western Sirmium (The Erdut Agreement), Signed in Erdut, Croatia and in Zagreb, Croatia, November 12, 1995.

[149] Security Council resolution 1037 of 15 January, 1996.

somewhat late, a Human Rights Monitoring Unit of UNTAES became fully functional on the basis of arrangements agreed with the Office of the United Nations High Commissioner for Human Rights.[150]

A report of the Secretary-General submitted to the Security Council on 2 October, 1997 noted that numerous cases of human rights violations had been identified. While there was no pattern of gross human rights violations, the cumulative effect of the violations and discriminatory practices were such that Serbs in the Region had little confidence in the will of the Croatian authorities to protect them after the departure of UNTAES. Confirmed human rights violations included unfair trial procedures in war crimes cases; attacks on Serb displaced persons from the region in other parts of Croatia either by Croat police officers or with their apparent collusion; abuses by Croatian Transitional Police Force officers, usually involving harassment of Serb displaced persons, and discrimination against Serbs in areas such as education, employment, pensions, and health care.[151]

A later report of the Secretary-General submitted to the Security Council on 4 December, 1997, noted that in relation to human rights there was evidence that Serbs, in particular displaced persons, continued to be subject to administrative discrimination. Obstacles were often overcome with the help of UNTAES personnel, but they suggested a pattern, initially of arbitrary decisions and deliberate misinformation by local officials. The report urged that the Government must ensure that its decisions and policies were communicated and implemented at all administrative levels. In several reported cases, officers of the Transitional Police Force had participated in harassment. The Government's response to complaints of police misconduct had, at times, been disappointing.[152]

This was a situation that, on the facts, required stronger human rights protection. ICFY had by then been disbanded and senior international statespersons such as Vance, Owen or Stoltenberg[153] were no longer around to make the case to the international community for stronger human rights machinery such as an International Human Rights Commission. The idea in the Erdut Agreement that friendly

[150] S/1997/767, Chapter 4, Human Rights.
[151] Ibid, para. 37.
[152] S/1997/953.
[153] Carl Bildt was then preoccupied with the responsibilities of High Representative for Bosnia and Herzegovina.

Governments should cooperate in the establishment of a human rights commission was not pursued by UN Secretary-General Kofi Annan. Rather, he recommended to the Security Council that UNTAES should complete its work, as originally envisaged, and that its mandate should be terminated on 15 January, 1998. However, he did recommend that the Security Council establish a support group of 180 civilian police monitors whose task would be to continue to monitor the performance of the Croatian police in the Region. The civilian police monitors would be stationed in the main Croatian police headquarters and the 20 Croatian police stations throughout the Region and would maintain a 24-hours-a-day coverage of police activities.

5. The Dayton Human Rights Blueprint Builds on the ICFY Design

The human rights provisions of the peace accords concluded in Dayton, Ohio, on 21 November, 1995, and later signed again at a ceremony in Paris in December, 1995, built on work first done within ICFY. In November, 1992, following the election of President William J. Clinton, this author drafted a letter that Cyrus Vance, ICFY Co-Chairman sent to Warren Christopher, Head of the Transition Team of the incoming President, and later appointed Secretary of State by President Clinton. The letter explained the thinking behind the Vance-Owen peace plan, and sent a full set of the documentation, including the detailed provisions on human rights.

Later, on the eve of the Dayton peace conference, this author, as Director of the International Conference on the Former Yugoslavia, wrote to the US State Department transmitting a full set of the human rights provisions that the ICFY negotiators had developed. This author was present at the Dayton peace conference and has in his possession the texts on human rights presented to the Bosnian parties. They built largely on the ICFY drafts but were even more expansive initially. However, the Bosnian parties eventually whittled them down and in the end, though important, they were not as extensive as the human rights proposals of ICFY.

In particular, ICFY's idea for the establishment of an international human rights monitoring mission was replaced by more vague provisions in Article XIII of Annex VI to the Dayton accords titled

'Organizations Concerned with Human Rights'. Under Article XIII the Parties joined in inviting the United Nations Commission on Human Rights, the OSCE, the United Nations High Commissioner for Human Rights, and other intergovernmental or regional human rights missions or organizations to monitor closely the human rights situation in Bosnia and Herzegovina, including through the establishment of local offices and the assignment of observers, rapporteurs or other relevant persons on a permanent or mission-by-mission basis and to provide them with full and effective facilitation, assistance and access.

Article XIII acknowledged ICFY's idea of establishing an international human rights monitoring mission with a vague provision whereby all competent authorities in Bosnia and Herzegovina were expected to cooperate with and provide unrestricted access to 'any international human rights monitoring mechanism established for Bosnia and Herzegovina'. In the end result, such a mission, as proposed by ICFY, was never established.

The Agreement on Human Rights concluded at Dayton did, as had been proposed by ICFY, contain a statement of fundamental rights and freedoms. It also provided for the establishment of what was strangely termed a Commission on Human Rights consisting of two parts, the Office of Ombudsman and the Human Rights Chamber. The Agreement provided that allegations of violations of human rights received by the Commission would generally be directed to the Office of the Ombudsman, except where an applicant specified the chamber. The Ombudsman was given the competence to investigate, either on his or her own initiative, or in response to an allegation by any Party or person, NGO, or group of individuals claiming to be the victim of a violation by any Party or acting on behalf of alleged victims who were deceased or mission, alleged or apparent violations of human rights.

The Human Rights Chamber was composed of fourteen members. The Chamber was given the competence to receive by referral from the Ombudsman on behalf of an applicant, or directly from any Party or person, NGO, or group of individuals claiming to be the victim of a violation by any Party or acting on behalf of alleged victims who were deceased or missing, for resolution or decision, applications concerning alleged or apparent violations of human rights. At the outset of a case or at any stage during the proceedings, the Chamber might attempt to facilitate an amicable resolution of the matter on the basis of respect for the rights and freedoms referred to in the Agreement.

Article XI provided that following the conclusion of proceedings before the Chamber it would promptly issue a decision addressing whether the facts found indicated a breach by the Party concerned of its obligations under the Agreement; and what steps must be taken by the Party to remedy such breach, including orders to cease and desist, monetary relief (including pecuniary and non-pecuniary injuries), and provisional measures.

The Human Rights Chamber functioned until 2004 and handed down an impressive body of jurisprudence on human rights issues.[154] Unfortunately, the Governments concerned concluded that the Chamber would end its existence in 2004. This writer, as the person then performing the functions of UN High Commissioner for Human Rights, wrote to the High Representative for Bosnia and Herzegovina, Lord Ashdown, urging that the decision be reconsidered and that the Chamber be continued. This was to no avail and a very useful human rights body first envisaged by ICFY and agreed upon at Dayton, passed from the scene.

Conclusion

The concept of peacebuilding is a dynamic one. When this author wrote the first draft of what became Agenda for Peace (1992), he defined the term peacebuilding as all those activities that were conductive to the maintenance and strengthening of peace. In the final version of Agenda for Peace, and subsequently, the term became identified more with post-conflict peacebuilding activities. Whichever way one views the term, there can be no doubt that the activities of ICFY, as recounted in this chapter, contributed in the end result to helping build up the edifice of peace in different parts of the former Yugoslavia, notably in Bosnia and Herzegovina. It needs to be repeated here, that throughout the life of the ICFY, from September 1992 to the autumn of 1995 when the Dayton Peace accords were signed, war raged in Bosnia and Herzegovina and in Croatia and threatened elsewhere. The ICFY negotiators could not, as explained earlier, succeed in their peacemaking efforts because the USA, in particular, chose to arm the Bosnian

[154] See, Human Rights Chamber of Bosnia and Herzegovina. Digest. Decisions on Admissibility and Merits, 1996–2002. With an Introduction by Manfred Nowak. Kehl/Strasbourg, Engel Publisher, 2003.

Government forces so that they could continue fighting. The efforts of ICFY's Working Groups on Confidence Building and on Economic Issues had, as a result, to be put on hold. Nevertheless, ICFY personnel pursued imaginative approaches to laying and consolidating the foundations for future peace in the region grounded in human rights norms and arrangements.

CHAPTER 9

HUMAN RIGHTS MONITORING AND FACT-FINDING

Introduction

The UN peace operations in the former Yugoslavia saw courageous efforts for human rights monitoring on the part of the peacemakers, the peacekeepers, the UN Special Rapporteur, the Office of UN High Commissioner for Refugees, and the Office of the UN High Commissioner for Human Rights. In this chapter we shall present some highlights of these efforts.

1. The peacemakers

In an earlier chapter on peacemaking we saw how Vance, Owen and Stoltenberg sought earnestly to build their peace plans on the foundations of human rights. They also pushed hard for human rights monitoring even as the conflict in Bosnia and Herzegovina raged and in the midst of their peacemaking efforts.

The Co-Chairmen of ICFY, Cyrus Vance and Lord Owen, convened on Thursday 11 March 1993 an informal meeting on future human rights monitoring in Bosnia and Herzegovina. The purpose of the meeting was to bring together representatives of NGOs working on human rights issues with UN human rights officials and ICFY representatives in order to explore and develop new ideas to make human rights monitoring as effective as possible in Bosnia and Herzegovina. The participants included representatives of Amnesty International, Helsinki Watch, Human Rights Watch, the International Human Rights Law Group, Lawyers Committee for Human Rights, UNA/USA, the World Council of Churches, the UN Centre for Human Rights, the UN Department of Humanitarian Affairs, the UN Department of Political Affairs, the UN Department of Peacekeeping Operations, the UN Office of Legal

Affairs, UNHCR, and officials from ICFY. Martti Ahtisaari, Ambassador Okun and this author took turns in chairing the meeting.[155]

On the need for human rights monitoring in Bosnia and Herzegovina, participants identified the following issues to be borne in mind in the establishment of a future human rights monitoring mission: to observe and report on the human rights situation in all parts of the country immediately; to provide access for existing monitors, including NGOs; to provide protection for current and future human rights monitors; to obtain the agreement of the parties to the conflict for human rights monitoring; to support local human rights groups; to support and reinforce the functioning of the local judicial establishment; to be more victim-oriented; to monitor the treatment of refugees, including those who wished to return; to deal with human rights violations, war crimes and crimes against humanity; and to address the issues of accountability for human rights violations, war crimes and crimes against humanity.

On the possible functions to be performed by an International Human Rights Monitoring Mission, participants thought that it could: collect the information and get it out to the international community; contribute to effective prosecution of those guilty of international crimes; monitor the entire country; address medical and public health aspects (Physician for Human Rights provided a detailed paper on this); draw upon the United Nations experience in El Salvador, Cambodia, Haiti, and South Africa; to address the question of impunity.

On the organization of a future International Human Rights Monitoring Mission, participants advised to: keep it as an independent entity and safeguard its independence; include women in its leadership and its monitors; plan for a large number of human rights monitors (300 to 1,000); coordinate efforts with the Special Rapporteur of the UN Commission on Human Rights; coordinate with NGOs; pay particular attention to publicity and the broadcasting of news; to have a publicity arm; deploy field officers throughout the country; and to designate as the head someone with great prestige world-wide.[156]

---

[155] See ICFY document, Highlights of an Informal Meeting on Human Rights Monitoring in Bosnia and Herzegovina, 11 March, 1993. Text in the possession of the author.

[156] The person ICFY approached to perform this role was Professor Thomas Buergenthal, then Judge on the Inter-American Court of Human Rights and later

On the timing of the establishment of an International Human Rights Monitoring Mission, there were two schools of thought: One, led by Aryeh Neier, argued forcefully that the Security Council should act immediately, before a peaceful settlement had been achieved, and that an international human rights monitoring mission should be deployed immediately. The second school of thought, led by Michael Posner, held that without the cooperation of the parties, a monitoring mission could not function. Hence, one should look to the deployment of a human rights monitoring mission *after* a peace agreement had been signed.

In the light of these two schools of thought it was suggested that the most fruitful way to proceed would be to send a small (3-5 persons) team of independent human rights experts to Bosnia and Herzegovina to assess the feasibility of a human rights monitoring mission (a) before a peace settlement was concluded and (b) as part of an overall peace settlement. The team could also provide concrete proposals on the mandate, structure and operations of any mission to be established.

As it happened, the ICFY negotiators decided to proceed with the establishment of an International Human Rights Monitoring Mission. In a report submitted to the Security Council, through the UN Secretary-General, the negotiators reported that it had been agreed with the Bosnian parties that there should be an International Human Rights Monitoring Mission, to be established by the Secretary-General and to be headed by an Interim Human Rights Commissioner for Bosnia and Herzegovina, who would be based in Sarajevo. Deputy Commissioners would be based in various parts of the country.

The Commissioner would be supported by international human rights monitors, deployed throughout the country and particularly in areas affected by 'ethnic cleansing'. They would observe the situation of human rights throughout Bosnia and Herzegovina, would intercede with the interim Presidency, with provincial authorities and with UNPROFOR to provide protection in urgent cases, would refer issues to the ombudsmen and to other human rights agencies as needed, and would work closely with the Office of the United Nations High Commissioner for Refugees (UNHCR), the International Committee of the Red Cross and other humanitarian agencies. The Commissioner would submit regular reports to the Secretary-General who would, in

Judge on the International Court of Justice. He was supportive but had to decline on personal grounds.

turn, report periodically to the Security Council and to other international bodies, including the United Nations Commission on Human Rights and its Special Rapporteur.[157]

The central and other authorities would be required to give the fullest access, in respect of all relevant persons and places, to the Interim Human Rights Commissioner, the Deputy Commissioners and the human rights monitors, as well as to UNHCR, ICRC and other international humanitarian organizations.[158]

The peace plan also envisaged that as part of the UNPROFOR deployment in Bosnia and Herzegovina there should be a sufficiently large United Nations Civilian Police (UNCIVPOL) element whose task would be to see that the police in all parts of the country had an appropriately balanced ethnic composition; did not oppress members of minority ethnic groups; contribute positively to the reversal of ethnic cleansing by protecting persons returning after having been forced to flee; carry out judgments of courts, in particular the Human Right Court; and assist the Interim Human Rights Commissioner, the deputy Commissioners and the human rights monitors.[159]

The Co-Chairmen actually identified some of the people to fill positions of Ombudsperson and one of them even spent time being briefed by ICFY staff. Unfortunately, as the US and others armed the Bosnian government forces and the fighting intensified it became impracticable to proceed with these plans.

2. The European Community Monitoring Mission (ECMM)

The European Community Monitoring Mission (ECMM) operated in the former Yugoslavia from 1991 onwards on the basis of the Brioni Agreement signed on the 7th July, 1991 in follow up to a decision taken in Prague within the framework of the CSCE as it was then. The republics of the former Yugoslavia agreed that a monitoring mission should become operational as soon as possible. For almost a year, ECMM was the only international peace-making/keeping/monitoring" agency in the region.[160] After the Vance Plan was signed in January, 1992,

[157] S/25403, para. 11.
[158] Ibid, para. 12.
[159] Ibid, para. 18.
[160] ECMM, Brief for Mr. Stoltenberg and Mr. Bildt. Zagreb, Croatia, 20 June, 1995. Senior Brief as at 19 June, 1995, p.1. Briefing Dossier in the possession of the author.

between Croatia and Yugoslavia, ECMM conducted a classic military monitoring role along the Cease Fire line and handed over to UNPROFOR after it was deployed.

Memoranda of Understanding (MOUs) were signed with different constitutent entities of the former Yugoslavia between July and October 1991. Similar agreements were signed later with Hungary, Bulgaria, and Albania. ECMM deployment was made at the request of those countries in order to prevent a spill-over of the fighting and the troubles across borders. ECMM was also present in the Former Yugoslav Republic of Macedonia, working under the auspices of OSCE but had no agreement with the so-called "Republic of Serbian Krajina", nor with the Bosnian Serbs and Bosnian Croat authorities. In late 1991, ECMM undertook a commitment in Bosnia and Herzegovina to help monitor peace and stability. But ECMM had to withdraw in May 1992 due to security reasons, after the murder of a Belgian Monitor and the violent behaviour of the Bosnian Serbs towards the European Community.

During the conflicts in the former Yugoslavia the European Community Monitoring Mission thus operated in different parts of the former Yugoslavia and in the neighbouring states of Hungary, Bulgaria and Albania. ECMM observed and reported in detail on the observance of human rights and actively promoted human rights through their work with the warring parties. The essential role of ECMM was to promote a long-term, peaceful solution to the conflicts in the former Yugoslavia. It had three main areas of interest: political/military and humanitarian matters; the state of infrastructure; and the protection of human rights.

ECMM's main modes of actions were monitoring, reporting and establishing Confidence Building Measures (CBMs) as a neutral party between the warring factions and in close cooperation with UNPROFOR and other international organizations. In a briefing to the ICFY Co-Chairmen in Zagreb on 20 June, 1995, ECMM listed its operations under the following eleven main tasks:

(a) Monitor and report on the political situation.
(b) Monitor and report on the military situation.
(c) Monitor and report on the humanitarian and the human rights situation.
(d) Monitor and report violations of the No-Fly Zone at assigned airfields and assist in air CASEVAC/MEDEVAC in coordination with UNPROFOR.

(e) Participate in Confidence Building Measures such as Tripartite meetings and the activities that evolved from them.
(f) Monitor and report on the particular borders and the political situation in Hungary, Bulgaria and Albania with emphasis on the appropriate borders.
(g) Arrange/assist with humanitarian operations in coordination with humanitarian organizations.
(h) Assist in accomplishing ceasefires and separation of forces by mediation.
(i) Monitor and report on the state of the economy and infrastructure.
(j) Ensure liaison with the UN and other international organizations.
(k) Develop priorities for reconstruction of the economic infrastructure.[161]

The results of ECMM actions were reported to the ICFY in Geneva, to the EU Presidency, and to the different capitals.

ECMM personnel were completely unarmed. But the teams wore white flak jackets and helmets when necessary. Since it began operation to 20 June, 1995, six members of the ECMM were killed on duty.

In a Memorandum dated 1 June 1993 to SRSG Stoltenberg, ECMM provided detailed recommendations on future human rights monitoring. It recommended that the HRMM should be established as soon as possible, with a clear mandate to investigate violations of human rights with a view to prosecution. The legal mechanisms must be established to allow them to do this. The HRMM must have the ability to task UNCIVPOL. The HRMM should be present in all areas of the former Yugoslavia where abuses of human rights had taken place.

The HRMM should provide the focus of expertise for investigating and prosecuting violations of human rights, using its own investigators, UNCIVPOL, and by calling in teams of experts. It should use the extensive networks of monitors already present in the former Yugoslavia (UNHCR, ICRC, UNCIVPOL, ECMM) to monitor and report on observance of human rights.

HRMM teams should liaise with the monitoring agencies to collect and collate their information on observance of human rights. HRMM teams should be led by investigating magistrates and include criminal lawyers, human rights lawyers, police criminal investigators and collators. In order to be effective, the HRMM must be backed up by a judicial system that was seen to be actually prosecuting individuals for

[161] Ibid, pp.2–3.

human rights violations, although this did not have to be directly linked to the HRMM.

HRMM teams should liaise with the monitoring agencies to collect and collate their information on observance of human rights. As well as being passed on to the UN Secretary-General, this information should be used to direct the efforts of the various monitoring agencies onto problem areas as they were identified and to direct investigators.[162]

These ideas also could not go forward due to the increase of fighting fuelled by the supply of arms to the Bosnian government forces from the USA and others.

3. The peacekeepers

In an earlier chapter we saw how UN peacekeepers eventually came to play a role in human rights monitoring. They also did courageous fact-finding exercises. A case in point was UNPROFOR's report on the Medak Operation and Assessment of Human Casualties and Material Damages. This report and annexes extended over 160 pages and provided detailed evidence of a Croatian Army incursion into the Medak pocket in Croatia from 9 September, 1993. Early in the morning of 9 September shelling began along both sides of the the confrontation line in Sectors North and South. UNPROFOR Force Commander Cot mediated a cease-fire agreement that was to have gone into effect at 11.00 am. However, at that time, Croatian Army units launched a surprise offensive with heavy artillery and mortar fire into the region south of Gospic, attacking the area of Licki Citluk, Strunici (Divo Selo) and Donji Selo near the confrontation line in the 'pink zone'. On 10 September there were further Croatian Army attacks against Medak and south of Licki Citluk. The Croatian Army seized the village of Njegovani. Serbian artillery fired at the Sisak oil refinery, which prompted Croatian artillery retailiation retaliation and rocket fire over Turanj. UNPROFOR intensified efforts to mediate a ceasefire. The Croatian President, Franjo Tudjman, told the Special Representative of the Secretary-General, Thorvald Stoltenberg, that he had ordered a cessation of shelling but could not order a withdrawal from the occupied villages until a generalized cease-fire agreement was signed.

---

[162] HQ ECMM, Zagreb, Memorandum to Mr. Stoltenberg, 1 June, 1993: Human Rights Monitoring in Former Yugoslavia. Text in the possession of the author.

Fighting continued until 15 September when both sides signed a cease-fire agreement providing for UNPROFOR control of the Medak pocket. Notwithstanding this, on 16 September Croatian forces in the pocket systematically burnt houses. On 18 September the Croatian side handed over to the Serb authorities 51 bodies found in the Medak pocket. On 25 September four French soldiers were injured by mine explosions in two incidents in the Poljari area.

An UNPROFOR team was formed to search the main roads and inhabited areas for survivors and bodies, and to give an authoritative assessment of the destruction. UNPROFOR conducted a systematic investigation of conditions in the Medak area and concluded that the Croatian Army attack in the area on 9 September "was fully coordinated and planned". It had met little or no Serb resistance. Croatian troops had killed most of those who were unable to make good their escape, regardless of age, sex or status. A number were still missing.

Massive destruction to property had been conducted by the Croatian forces during their advance, and particularly during their withdrawal. Virtually all houses and outbuildings in the villages and surrounding hamlets had been destroyed, many by explosion. Wells had been destroyed or damaged. Household chattels had been deliberately destroyed, and almost all remaining domestic animals killed. During a period in which UNPROFOR personnel had been prevented from moving into the areas, in accordance with a prior agreement with the Croatian Army, the destruction had been completed. UNPROFOR members had heard explosions and shooting, and, shortly after, had observed houses in flames.

The report ended:

> "While the commanding officers in charge of the Croatian Army in this undertaking are not identified in this report, these details are available. It is recommended that the report be transmitted to the Special Rapporteur of the Human Rights Commission, and to the Acting Chairman of the Commission of Experts on War Crimes."[163]

This was duly done.

---

[163] The text of the report is in the possession of the author. The report was duly transmitted to the Special Rapporteur and the Commission of Experts.

4. The UN Special Rapporteur

On 23 October, 1992, Amnesty International wrote an Open Letter to Foreign Ministers of States participating in or members of the European Community, the UN Commission on Human Rightas, the CSCE, the International Conference on the Former Yugoslavia (ICFY), the Organization of the Islamic Conference Contact Group on the Situation in Bosnia-Herzegovina,and the UN Security Council. The letter was titled "Intergovernmental Initiatives to Protect Human Rights in the Former Yugoslavia".[164] Amnesty International, *inter alia* welcomed the appointment by the UN Commission on Human Rights of a Special Rapporteur on the former Yugoslavia, Mr. Tadeusz Mazowiecki.

Amnesty International considered that Mr. Mazowiecki should play a central role in documenting the human rights situation and making recommendations about preventive measures. He must therefore be an integral part of any coordination process. Amnesty International also urged the UN to examine closely the results of his fact-finding missions and take urgent steps to implement relevant recommendations. Amnesty International supported the recommendation of the Special Rapporteur in his first report that, as a matter of urgency, some members of his staff should be able to remain in the region for as long as the Special Rapporteur considered necessary.[165]

Roman Wieruszewski, the principal aide to Special Rapporteur Mazowiecki, has written that when Mazowiecki accepted the mandate of Special Rapporteur he had to determine his priorities. He decided to concentrate on victims of human rights violations and to contribute to solving the existing crisis. He was "less concerned about with detailed documentation concerning committed crimes, including the identification of perpetrators, but rather concentrated on organizing help for the victims. His personal background and life experience contributed to that approach. He was criticized by various, mainly American NGOs for neglecting the investigatory aspect of his mandate."[166]

---

[164] AI Index: EUR 48/27/92, 23 October, 1992.

[165] Ibid, pp. 3-4.

[166] R. Wieruszewski, "International Response to the Human Rights Violations in the Territory of the Former Yugoslavia", XIX Polish Yearbook of International Law 1991-1992, pp.203–225, at p.214.

Wieruszewski complained about the paucity of resources allocated to the Special Rapporteur by the then UN Centre for Human Rights for the deployment of field personnel, which did eventually take place with considerable delay.[167] Nevertheless, he maintained that:

> "The Special Rapporteur embarked upon very intensive activity. He managed to persuade world public opinion of the dimensions of the human rights drama in the former Yugoslavia. His reports contributed to a number of resolutions adopted by various UN bodies. Nevertheless, he has not been able to achieve his main objectives: to put an end to the massive violations of human rights. This failure should be partly attributed to the inherent weakness of the mechanism which he represented. The mandate of the Special Rapporteurs were very limited. Consequently his position vis-à-vis other actors proved to be rather weak."[168]

5. The Office of UN High Commissioner for Refugees

As we saw in an earlier chapter, Mrs Sadako Ogata, UN High Commissioner for Refugees considered that in the absence of adequate legal principles or effective enforcement mechanisms that covered internally displaced persons, international presence was, for her agency the only available tool for their protection. UNHCR's presence sought to respond to the concerns of those who had not yet moved from their homes but feared they might be removed. UNHCR placed colleagues in conflict zones instead of evacuating them out from insecure situations. UNHCR posted large contingents of field protection officers throughout Bosnia and Herzegovina and opened as many as twenty seven sub-offices. Their functions ranged from responding to the safety and assistance needs of the fleeing people to negotiating with the local authorities to counteract displacement and to publicly denouncing abuses as a last resort.[169]

During the year that Thorvald Stoltenberg was SRSG in charge of all peace operations in the former Yugoslavia, this writer doubled as Director of ICFY and Director of the Office of the SRSG. He thus saw numerous reports written by UNHCR officers in the field and

---

[167] See on this, M. O'Flaherty and G. Gisvold, Post War Protection of Human rights in Bosnia and Herzegovina. The Hague, Martinus Nijhoff, 1998. See especially Chapter 4 by M. O'Flaherty, International Human Rights Operations in Bosnia and Herzegovina.

[168] R. Wieruszewski, "International Response to the Human Rights Violations in the Territory of the Former Yugoslavia", XIX Polish Yearbook of International Law 1991–1992, pp. 203–225, at p. 214.

[169] The Turbulent Decade…, p. 55.

submitted to the Special Representative. The Office of the SRSG had a dedicated officer from UNHCR who liaised with UNHCR and other humanitarian agencies. The Special Envoy of the UN High Commissioner for Refugees reported both to Mrs Ogata and the SRSG. He was in regular contact with this author. The author has in his possession courageous reports written by UNHCR officers in the field drawing attention to widespread gross violations of human rights and ethnic cleansing in the areas that they covered.

On 30 June, Knut Vollebaek, Stoltenberg's Deputy, sent a confidential cable to Stoltenberg and Owen on the subject, "UNHCR in Bosnia. Meetings with Nicholas Morris, HCR's Special Envoy to Former Yugoslavia, and Karin Landgren, Chief of Mission for Bosnia". The UNHCR officials had reported on the 'Actual Situation' on the ground as follows:

> "(a) In Central Bosnia, outside Sarajevo, more than one million people are cut off from all commercial activities...1.5 million wholly or largely dependent on relief supplies. The situation for the Moslems is desperate. With no fuel the economic life will come to a stand-still. Harvests are not gathered, processed or distributed...
>
> UNHCR sees an increasingly close cooperation between Croats and Serbs, said to be a reprisal for previous Moslem offensives.
>
> "(b) 'Safe areas' are a major problem. They are not viable as of now. In some (i.a. Srebrenica) it will be necessary to move out a large portion of the actual population in order to enable those remaining to survive the winter. However, the parties have not been willing to facilitate such a move, not even the Moslems who appear to want the situation to reach a crisis for the purpose of their own propaganda. **The reason for this being that they still believe in a possibility of intervention or lifting of arms embargo/air strikes**.
>
> "(c) UNHCR knows that their supplies of food and fuel for humanitarian purposes are being pooled together at the receiving end and distributed to the combatants. It is difficult to distinguish a civilian from a combatant as most men do a rotation of six days of fighting and three days of rest.
>
> "(d) Humanitarian assistance has ceased to be humanitarian as it is being used for military purposes. There is an urgent need for negotiated political and military decisions to create a basis and an environment for truly humanitarian assistance to the civilian population. Until then the parties will continue to treat relief supplies as part of the war effort; denying access to and obstructing convoys as a tactic of war."[170]

---

[170] Text in the possession of the author.

We saw in an earlier chapter the heart-wrenching letter written on 5 September, 1994, by the Special Envoy of the High Commissioner, Nicholas Morris, to Dr. Radovan Karadzic about ethnic cleansing by the Bosnian Serbs. Morris pleaded:

> "On many occasions UNHCR has expressed the gravest concern to you at these practices. The ICRC has done likewise. We have been assured by you and your colleagues that resolute correction action would be taken by your authorities, yet the expulsions continue and even intensify. Once more, I write to urge you to take immediate action to provide proper protection to the minorities in the areas that you control, and for whose safety you are directly responsible."

6. The ICRC

The ICRC, for the most part, kept publicly to a 'humanitarian' posture. However, it also performed a monitoring and fact-finding role. In March 1994 the ICRC issued a compilation of its Press releases and communications to the press covering the period 2 July 1991 to 4 March 1994.[171] It is a wrenching compilation of the humanitarian and human rights problems encountered in the former Yugoslavia.

On 27 May, 1992, the ICRC issued a statement under the title "ICRC: Humanitarian Situation in Bosnia-Herzegovina Intolerable". In it, the ICRC stated that it was forced to recognize that, despite the commitments made under its auspices in Geneva on 22 May by the parties involved in the conflict in Bosnia-Herzegovina to respect and ensure respect for the fundamental principles of international humanitarian law, the terrible escalation of violence in that strife-torn republic showed no sign of abating. In those circumstances, when the most basic rights of the victims and of especially vulnerable groups were being constantly and deliberately violated, the ICRC was no longer in a position to carry out its humanitarian tasks and was therefore obliged temporarily to withdraw its delegates from Bosnia-Herzegovina. The ICRC announced that it was calling a meeting in Geneva on 30 May to work out the details of a plan of humanitarian action which would allow it to return to the republic as soon as possible.

---

[171] Former Yugoslavia. Press releases and communications to the press by the International Committee of the Red Cross (ICRC), 2 July 1991 – 4 March 1994. Compilation in the possession of the author.

The ICRC did return to Bosnia and Herzegovina on 7 July, 1992 but, barely a month later, it issued a statement on 2 August, 1992, titled "Bosnia-Herzegovina: ICRC's Growing Concern." It pleaded that despite public appeals and many confidential representations the ICRC had made at all levels during more than a year of fighting, "it has been forced to acknowledge that violations of humanitarian law and of basic human rights perpetrated by all parties to the conflict have reached such a point that they have become common practice." ICRC President Cornelio Sommaruga had issued a public warning the previous week about "the terrible ravages of 'ethnic cleansing'", saying that "whole populations are being terrorized, minorities intimidated and harassed, civilians interned on a massive scale, hostages taken, and torture, deportation and summary executions are rife."[172]

On 2 April 1993 the ICRC issued a statement about the death of seventeen detainees from Batkovic Camp killed near the front line.[173] This lead to a public statement by the UN Security Council on 8 April, 1993:

> "The members of the Security Council express their concern at the report of the International Committee of the Red Cross, according to which 17 detainees lost their lives on 26 March, 1993 in the Republic of Bosnia and Herzegovina, when the vehicle transporting them from the Batkovic Camp under the control of the Serb forces) for work at the front was ambushed.
>
> "The members of the Council, recalling all relevant resolutions and statements of the Council, remind all the parties that they are responsible at all times for the detainees' safety and that they must not compel detainees to do work of a military nature or destined to serve a military purpose. The ICRC had already repeatedly called on all parties to the conflict in the Republic of Bosnia and Herzegovina strictly to observe the provisions of international humanitarian law.
>
> "The members of the Council condemn all violations of the Third and Fourth Geneva Conventions, which the parties have undertaken to respect, and reaffirm once again that those who commit or order the commission of such acts will be held personally responsible.
>
> "The members of the Council request the Commission of Experts established pursuant to Security Council resolution 780 (1992) to carry out an investigation of these abominable practices and to make a report."[174]

---

[172] Ibid.
[173] Ibid.
[174] S/25557, 8 April, 1993.

7. The UN High Commissioner for Human Rights

The first UN High Commissioner for Human Rights, Jose Ayala Lasso, entered into office in the spring of 1993 and immediately had his hands full with the situation in Rwanda, where he established the first UN human rights field office. He would also play a leading role in the development of the second human rights field office, for Bosnia and Herzegovina, which was based in Sarajevo.

On 3 February, 1995, the High Commissioner organized a meeting with representatives of the Departments of Peace-keeping Operations and Political Affairs, as well as of Mr. Richard Goldstone, the Chief Prosecutor of the International Tribunal on war crimes in the Former Yugoslavia, UNHCR, representatives of the Special Rapporteur on the Situation of Human Rights in the former Yugoslavia and Special Representative of the Secretary-General for the Former Yugoslavia. The meeting, in which this author participated, recommended in the short term the placement of a representative of the High Commissioner for Human Rights in the office of the SRSG with a view to facilitating the coordination and enhancement of human rights activities in Bosnia and Herzegovina. The meeting also discussed the possibilities of an expanded human rights operation through the deployment of human rights field officers in the medium and long term.

The meeting strongly supported the development by the High Commissioner of training programmes in human rights for field officers of the various agencies in close cooperation with those agencies. The meeting endorsed the concept that an expanded human rights operation would service the Special Rapporteur and that guidelines would be developed for the cooperation of this operation with the work of the international tribunal on war crimes. The meeting also considered the desirability of developing comprehensive technical cooperation and human rights education programmes.[175]

The High Commissioner, on occasions, drew the attention of the international community to situations of concern. Thus, on 8 August, 1995, the High Commissioner issued a statement expressing his grave concern over the human rights situation in the Krajina region in Croatia resulting from the recent military operations in that area. He said that he was appalled at the loss of life, injury and hardship suffered

---

[175] See UN Press Release, 3 February, 1995, Note for Correspondents, Note/95/07.

by the civilian population. He was particularly concerned at the loss of life, injury and hardship suffered by the civilian population. He was also very concerned by the exodus of a great number of people from their homes under extremely hazardous and difficult circumstances.

The High Commissioner said that he was cooperating with the UN Peace Forces (UNPF) in the former Yugoslavia in monitoring the human rights situation. In order to help ensure respect for human rights in the difficult situation then prevailing, human rights monitoring teams had been set up by the SRSG. Those teams would be reporting on the situation both to the SRSG and to the High Commissioner and they would be taking appropriate action to prevent violations. Elements of the teams were already present in Knin and it was expected that team members would go the following day to the former Sector North if security conditions permitted.

The High Commissioner said that he was following closely the rapidly changing situation and was ready to take further action within the framework of the operations of the United Nations in the region.[176]

In an address to the Social and Humanitarian Committee of the UN General Assembly on 21 November, 1995, the High Commissioner, Jose Ayala Lasso, assessed that in the process of restoring peace and reconciliation in the former Yugoslavia, human rights had played a role of great importance. However, the proper infrastructure needed to be established in the region in order for the process of reconstruction and reconciliation to be to be fruitful. His Office was prepared to make great efforts in the region, and he hoped for a spirit of cooperation, and not of competition, with other UN bodies. Personal and direct contacts with governments, he continued, were essential in order to gain trust and ensure their support.[177]

8. The Commission of Experts[178]

By its resolution 780 (1992), the Security Council decided to set up a Commission of Experts to examine and analyze evidence of grave

---

[176] UN Press Release HR/95/37, Statement by the UN High Commissioner for Human Rights on the Situation in Krajina.

[177] UN Press Release GA/95/31, 21 November, 1995, pp. 1–2.

[178] See, generally, A. de Zayas, "The Kalshoven Commission", Leiden Journal of International Law, vol. 6, April 1993, pp. 131–134.

breaches of the Geneva Conventions and other violations of international humanitarian law. Amnesty International, which had campaigned for an international criminal tribunal, issued a briefing paper advising its sections on the importance of this development.[179] Amnesty International believed that anyone in the former Yugoslavia responsible for human rights violations or abuses within its mandate should be brought to justice. The most important question for Amnesty was whether an act fell within its mandate, such as torture, cruel, inhuman or degrading treatment of punishment and extrajudicial executions/deliberate and arbitrary killings. If so, Amnesty took the position that the perpetrator should be brought to justice and it did not matter whether the act was technically characterised as a violation of human rights law or humanitarian law. Amnesty International would support a prosecution under humanitarian law principles because it was another way of bringing to justice those responsible for acts within its mandate and could also act as a deterrent to possible future violations of that nature.[180]

Conclusion

War raged in Bosnia and Herzegovina from 1992 to 1995 and in Croatia during 1994 and 1995 because the USA, in particular, willed it so. ICFY peacemakers and peacekeepers kept doing their utmost to highlight the human rights concerns and to devise ways of monitoring criminal violations of human rights. This was not easy. Putting down monitors in the midst of war is not an easy matter. But this chapter will have shown, we hope, the persistence and inventiveness of UN and partner actors.

In the next chapter we look at the quest for justice.

[179] Bosnia-Herzegovina: 'War Crimes' in the Former Yugoslavia. Weekly Update NWS 11/42/92, 22 October, 1992. This internal paper of ten pages was given to the author by Amnesty International's Legal Adviser, the late Nicholas Howen, on 6 November, 1992.

[180] Ibid, p. 8.

CHAPTER 10

JUSTICE

Introduction

When Vance and Owen began their negotiating efforts in Geneva at the beginning of September 1992, crimes against humanity and war crimes were pervasive in Bosnia and Croatia. When they met the UNPROFOR Force Commander, General Satish Nambiar, in Zagreb in the middle of September, he told them that all three sides in the Bosnian conflict were committing war crimes and attacking UN forces. He asked them, when they saw President Alija Izetbegovic in the coming days to protest to him about recent Bosnian Government forces attacks on UN troops that had killed two soldiers.[181]

The London Conference held at the end of August, which had established the International Conference on the Former Yugoslavia, had given Vance and Owen a mandate to engage in continuous negotiations for the settlement of the Bosnian conflict. The London Conference had adopted principles calling for respect of the highest standards of human rights, declared that claims to territories acquired through use of force would not be upheld, and asked Vance and Owen to "carry forward a study of the creation of an international criminal court."[182] But the London Conference had said nothing concrete about bringing the perpetrators of war crimes and crimes against humanity to justice. The peace negotiators would have to tread their way carefully on this issue of bringing the perpetrators to justice.

In the end, Vance and Owen would take a stance of principle in favour of bringing the perpetrators to justice. This was consistent with the position they took from the outset, as we saw in an earlier chapter, of helping to place the spotlight on human rights issues in bodies such as the Human Rights Committee and the Council of Europe.

In this chapter we look at how the justice issue was handled in the peace process.

---

[181] When Vance and Owen saw President Izetbegovic in Sarajevo they pressed him on this and asked him to bring the perpetrators to justice. He promised to do so, but nothing ever came of this promise.

[182] Specific Decisions of the London Conference (LC/C7 (FINAL)), para. 8.

1. The question of the establishment of an international criminal tribunal arises early on the table of Vance and Owen

On 17 September, 1992, barely two weeks after Vance and Owen had arrived in Geneva, the Government of the Netherlands circulated a telegram to its European partners recalling that during the past months the importance of accurate and systematic data gathering on war crimes and gross violations of human rights in the former Yugoslavia had been emphasized in several international fora on different occasions. It expressed the view that the call for international fact-finding and possible persecution of the severe crimes that had taken place could not go unheeded.

The Government of the Netherlands therefore submitted to its partners a proposal for the establishment of *ad hoc* machinery for the investigation and possible prosecution of war crimes and serious human rights violations in the former Yugoslavia. It recalled the example of the War Crimes Commission established in London in 1943 and proposed the establishment of such a commission (WCC) for the former Yugoslavia. In its view, the Commission could catalogue and analyse information received on war crimes as well as serious human rights violations. The collection of information in the field of human rights and international humanitarian law would be coordinated by the Special Rapporteur of the UN Commission on Human Rights, Mr. Tadeusz Mazowiecki, assisted by a data-gathering bureau (DGB). All Missions and agencies in the former Yuguslavia would be invited to make relevant information available to the WCC. The population in the region, as well as those who had been forced to leave the region as refugees should also be made aware of the possibility to submit information to the WCC.

Lord Owen, as the EU-designated Co-Chairman, circulated the Dutch telegram within ICFY and sought the views of different officials, including this author. Lord Owen expressed very tentative views that he could see advantage in public pressure being brought to bear, given that atrocities were still being committed and others very likely would be committed. He favoured an International Court of universal application instead of a Yugoslav-specific body. He added:

> "I see merit in an international fact-finding body which may or may not have to prosecute, as proposed by the Dutch, namely an *ad hoc* UN War Crimes Commission.

> "I believe such a Commission would buttress any investigation undertaken by the Human Rights Committee..."[183]

One of the addressees of the memorandum replied that the Dutch proposal sought to respond, as a matter of urgency, to what was considered an issue of principle, namely, that persons guilty of war crimes or serious violations of human rights should not go unpunished. He considered that while this was a commendable objective, neither the procedure suggested, nor the timing, seemed appropriate. In the midst of a war, laden with propaganda on all sides, charges flew in all directions. The Commission on Human Rights had appointed a Special Rapporteur who had already prepared an interim report. He was expected to prepare a follow-up report to the General Assembly that was just beginning, and to the Commission on Human Rights later that year.

It would, the official continued, seem to be the proper course of action to allow the Special Rapporteur to examine the situation and the available evidence and to come up with recommendations on the possible prosecution of persons accused of international crimes. In short, the appropriate course of action seemed to be to let the Rapporteur get on with his job but to invite him to pay particular attention and to include a chapter in his report, if he considered this necessary, on this issue.

The official continued:

> "From the point of view of timing, to launch the initiatives proposed by the Dutch when the Co-Chairmen are exploring avenues for making peace in the area would not seem the wisest course of action. The activities of the Co-Chairmen could even be complicated by setting up an elaborate mechanism which could take on a life and momentum of its own. This would seem to be all the more reason to follow the course of action of letting the Special Rapporteur of the Commission examine the issues calmly and dispassionately."[184]

The late Paul Szasz, legal adviser, submitted his views in a Memorandum dated 29 September, 1992. He noted that the Dutch proposal would have the Statute of the proposed tribunal prepared, as part of its

---

[183] Memo from Lord Owen to C. Vance, P. Hall, H. Okun, P. Szasz, and B. Ramcharan, 18 September, 1992. Text in the possession of the author.

[184] Note to Lord Owen dated 21 September, 1992. Text in the possession of the author. Name of the author withheld for the sake of discretion.

terms of reference to be established by the Security Council, by an *ad hoc* UN War Crimes Commission for the Former Yugoslavia (WCC). That would, in effect, remove this task from the ICFY Co-Chairmen. If the Co-Chairmen were content to have the WCC undertake this task they might request to be consulted in due course. If, however, the Co-Chairmen considered that the work should be done under their auspices, as apparently foreseen by the London Conference, it could be done within ICFY. In that case it might be useful to engage the assistance of Professor Cherif Bassiouni, the leading expert in this field, as a consultant.[185]

2. Vance and Owen take a principled stance

In the end, the Co-Chairmen took a principled position from the outset on dealing with war crimes in the former Yugoslavia, while maintaining a distinction between the role of peacemakers and those of investigators/prosecutors. Immediately after commencing their activities in Geneva, the Co-Chairmen, Vance and Owen, began internal discussions on the possible establishment of an international criminal court. They maintained contacts on this subject with the European Community, the Council of Europe, and Governments particularly interested, such as those of the Netherlands and the USA. They commissioned papers on the subject from their Legal Adviser, the late Paul Szasz, who provided options to the Co-Chairmen on this topic.

Throughout, the Co-Chairmen maintained an active discussion on this subject with the President of ICFY's Arbitration Commission, Mr. Robert Badinter. Several meetings were held to discuss this subject. On 14 October, 1992, Mr. Badinter advised the Co-Chairmen that it was important that the perpetrators of crimes against humanity should not go unpunished. Even if amnesties were declared at the national level eventually, the perpetrators of international crimes should know that they were vulnerable to arrest and prosecution abroad. He encouraged efforts to establish an international criminal court to try the perpetrators of crimes against humanity. With the concurrence and support of the Co-Chairmen, Mr. Badinter discreetly

[185] Text in the possession of the author.

contacted concerned Governments seeking to promote the establishment of an international criminal court.

The Co-Chairmen also maintained contacts on this subject with the Secretary-General of the United Nations who went on record as being in favour of the establishment of a tribunal to deal with the perpetrators of war crimes and crimes against humanity in the former Yugoslavia. On 30 December, Secretary-General Boutros-Boutros Ghali told a news conference in Geneva that he was in favour of the establishment of a three-man tribunal on war crimes to examine violations of human rights committed by all three sides in the Yugoslav conflict. Noting that a five-member Commission previously established by the Security council was examining reports on human rights violations and grave breaches of the international human rights conventions, the Secretary-General said that the work of the tribunal and the Commission would be coordinated.

The Co-Chairmen continued to use their influence discreetly and publicly in order to promote the establishment of an international criminal court. In a statement to the Steering Committee of the ICFY on 16 December, 1992, they stated:

> "We have…taken action on allegations of war crimes and other breaches of international humanitarian law. We have sought to help the Commission of Experts bring about a forensic examination of the mass grave site at Ovcara near Vukovar… (We) believe that atrocities committed in the former Yugoslavia are unacceptable, and persons guilty of war crimes should be brought to justice. We therefore recommend the establishment of an international criminal court."[186]

Also in December, 1992, Lord Owen wrote the following to partners:

> "1. Vance and I have concluded that given the continued existence of ethnic cleansing an *ad hoc* tribunal should now be introduced urgently. We understand the Security Council could establish a War Crimes Tribunal for Yugoslavia by vetoable decision under Chapter 7 of the Charter. Pursuant to Charter Articles 25 and 48(1), such a War Crimes Tribunal could be given the power to demand cooperation from all states, e.g. on extradition of accused persons, the production of witnesses and the punishment of those convicted as well as of uncooperative and perjured witnesses.

---

[186] See ICFY Aide Memoire: Policy of the Co-Chairmen on War Crimes in the Former Yugoslavia Text in the ICFY archives and in the possession of the author.

> 2. The alternative we preferred some months ago of the General Assembly establishing an International Criminal Court, with general jurisdiction, i.e. not only in respect of a particular state and not necessarily restricted to war crimes, is now going to take years and it is obviously not going to be done in a timescale which is remotely defensible."[187]

3. Support for forensic investigation of mass graves

The ICFY negotiators not only supported the establishment of an international criminal tribunal, they actively supported forensic investigations of mass grave sites. Cy Vance took a special interest in the mass grave site at Ovcara, near Vukovar. On 25 November, 1992, Vance wrote to the Special Rapporteur of the Commission on Human Rights Tadeusz Mazowiecki on the issue of the mass grave site near Vukovar, informing him that the Co-Chairmen had been striving for weeks to get work started on the required forensic examination of this site. UNPROFOR had placed guards around the site and had been waiting for weeks for the arrival of experts to conduct the examination. He stated: "David Owen, I, and General Nambiar feel strongly that the examination of the graves should take place straightaway."

Vance informed Mazowiecki that forensic experts from governmental and non-governmental sources were available right away. They could commence work immediately and could be placed at the disposal of the United Nations. What was needed was a United Nations framework whereby those experts, accompanied by United Nations staff, and with the assistance of UNPROFOR, could proceed immediately to do an examination of the graves. He continued:

> "Therefore, I would strongly request that you authorize a team of forensic experts to do an examination of the site at Vukovar before the onset of the winter freeze which, we are told, could lead to the destruction of the evidence."[188]

---

187 Full cable in the possession of the author. Dated December 1992, but day date unclear.

188 Memorandum in the possession of the author. The author worked on this issue and helped facilitate contacts with Physicians for Human Rights, who were ready to undertake the forensic examination. However, before they could be given access to the site, they needed the imprimatur of the UN. Hence, Vance was seeking Mazowiecki's sponsorship of the forensic examination. Mazowiecki readily cooperated.

On 26 November, 1992, Vance wrote to UN Secretary-General Boutros-Boutros Ghali on the subject, "Forensic Examination of the alleged mass grave site at Ovcara, near Vukovar". He wrote:

> "1. We consider it of great importance that a forensic examination be made of the alleged mass grave site at Ovcara, near Vukovar, as soon as possible. As a matter of principle it is important that we discover what has taken place. As you know, UNPROFOR set guards at the site several weeks ago and the sooner the forensic examination can be made, the faster it will be possible for UNPROFOR to be relieved of this responsibility. The best expert opinion available indicates that after the winter freeze the evidence might be damaged and therefore lost. Moreover, the risk cannot be excluded that internal forces might attempt to destroy the evidence.
>
> "2. We have, therefore, been seeking to find the fastest way of initiating a forensic examination of the alleged mass grave site. We discussed this matter with USG Blanca on Monday, November 23. On Wednesday, November 25, I sent (a) cable to the Special Rapporteur of the Commission on Human Rights, Mr. Mazowiecki, urging him to authorize a team of forensic experts to do an examination of the site before the onset of the winter freeze.
>
> "3. We met today, Thursday November 28, with the Chairman of the Commission of Experts, Professor Kalshoven, to make the same point to him, namely that it would be extremely important to have a forensic examination done as soon as possible. Professor Kalshoven was very helpful and took the view tht the examination should be done under the auspices of the Commission of Experts.
>
> ...
>
> ...
>
> "5. I thought I would report to you on my efforts so that you might indicate to all concerned the importance and the urgency of this matter and the need for pragmatic approaches and solutions so as to get the forensic team to the site straight away. I would hope very much that the dispatch of the forensic team would not get caught up in any procedural snags."[189]

The decision to establish a Commission of Experts to gather information on possible international crimes being committed in the conflicts in the Former Yugoslavia was taken by the United Nations Security Council. It had the full support of Vance and Owen from the very

[189] Cable in the possession of the author.

beginning. I have seen some accounts arguing otherwise that I consider unfounded and unfortunate.

Shortly after the members of the Commission assembled in Geneva, Vance asked me to arrange a meeting with the Chairman, Professor Fritz Kalshoven of The Netherlands. I knew Kalshoven well and went over to his office in the Palais des Nations and arranged for him to meet with Vance. It was a cordial meeting during which Vance raised with Kalshoven his determination to do everything he could to support investigations into the massacre that had taken place at Vukovar hospital.

When reports came in of a mass grave site at Ovcara, near Vukovar, Vance had asked this author to contact Physicians for Human Rights for them to do a forensic examination of the site. I did so, using the good offices of a friend in a human rights NGO, who facilitated the contacts. In order for Physicians for Human Rights to proceed with the forensic examination they needed the imprimatur of the Commission of Experts. Again I contacted Professor Kalshoven who readily agreed that Physicians for Human Rights could act under the auspices of the Commission of Experts.

This is how the first forensic examination of a mass grave site in the Former Yugoslavia began. It stemmed from a direct initiative from the UN peace negotiator, Cyrus Vance. By the time the examination actually got under way, Vance had moved on and had been succeeded by Thorvald Stoltenberg. After the Vance-Owen plan was signed by the parties in Athens, in April, 1993, Secretary-General Boutros Boutros Ghali designated Stoltenberg as Special Representative in charge of all UN operations in the Former Yugoslavia. Boutros-Ghali thought that the implementation stage had been reached but, unfortunately, within a week of signing the accords in Athens, the Bosnian Serbs repudiated their signature and Stoltenberg went on, during 1993, to double as special representative and as negotiator.

As Special Representative of the Secretary-General, Stoltenberg was in charge of the peace-keeping troops, the largest force ever assembled in the history of the United Nations. This author doubled as Director of the International Conference of the Former Yugoslavia and as Director of the Office of the Special Representative. In the latter capacity this author continued to be directly involved in future efforts regarding the mass grave site at Ovcara as well as in efforts to get the peacekeeping troops to play a role on human rights issues.

The examination of the mass-grave site at Ovcara required painstaking work over several months. After the site had been opened up it was important to guard it so as to maintain its integrity and to prevent it from being tampered with. At Stoltenberg's request, this author contacted the UN Force Commander to ask him to provide troops to guard the site. This he did. As the forensic examination proceeded, it would require the emplacement of troops at the site over several months. In the circumstances prevailing at the time, with the pressures on the troops, it took the direct involvement of Stoltenberg to secure that the troops would stay to guard the site over the several months involved.

This was, admittedly, a situation in which the roles of peacemaker had been combined with that of peacekeeper and Stoltenberg therefore had considerable leverage on the force. It does bear out, however, that the direct involvement of the peacemaker can, and did in this instance, play an important role in furthering the process of gathering information into possible international crimes committed during a conflict.

4. Cooperation with the Commission of Experts on War Crimes and Crimes Against Humanity

The negotiators and staff of the ICFY supported the establishment of the Commission of Experts and cooperated with them from the outset. Later, Thorvald Stoltenberg, as ICFY Co-Chairman and SRSG, had particularly close relations with a leading member of the Commission, his boyhood friend Professor Torkel Opsahl. Opsahl pressed Stoltenberg for the UN peacekeepers to contribute to the protection of human rights and, as we saw in an earlier chapter, this author, at the request of Stoltenberg, had meetings with the leadership of UNPROFOR that contributed to the development of a human rights role for UNPROFOR.

This author also had a long-standing friendship with Professor Torkel Opsahl and had opportunities to discuss issues of mutual interest with him and his able assistant Morten Bergsmo. The lines of communication between ICFY and the Commission were thus good.

5. The International Criminal Tribunal for the Former Yugoslavia (ICTY)

As we saw earlier in this chapter, Vance and Owen, later joined by Stoltenberg, supported the establishment of the ICTY and encouraged its activities behind the scenes while pressing on with efforts to negotiate peace agreements for Bosnia and Herzegovina and for Croatia. Later on, after ICFY had folded up its operations and Bosnian and Croatian nationals were charged before the Tribunal, former ICFY personnel cooperated with the Prosecutor of the ICTY and even appeared as witnesses in trials before the Tribunal. Lord Owen, Thorvald Stoltenberg, Herbert Okun, and this writer, were interviewed by staff of the Office of the Prosecutor. Lord Owen and Herbert Okun appeared as witnesses in the trial of President Slobodan Milosevic.

Conclusion

For both peacemakers and peacekeepers in UN peace operations in the former Yugoslavia it was a learning experience to tackle issues of human rights and justice. For the peacemakers the most important assignment was to help negotiate peace agreements and thereby stop conflicts. It was therefore understandable that they gave priority to that task. For peacekeepers, the principal task was to help in the delivery of humanitarian assistance and to help contain and prevent conflicts. UN peacekeepers had their traditions since the early days of the United Nations and they attached importance to principles of neutrality and impartiality.

The former Yugoslavia would challenge them all and the negotiators and peacekeepers would have to deal with the stark fact that criminal violations of human rights and humanitarian law were taking place in conflicts in Bosnia and Herzegovina and in Croatia. As this chapter has shown, the peace negotiators and peacekeepers took a principled stance in favour of the establishment of the Commission of Experts and the ICTY and then cooperated with the Prosecutor and staff of the ICTY as well as, in some instances, appearing as witnesses before it.

Biographers of one of the great UN peace negotiators, the late Ralph Bunche, who won the Nobel Peace Prize for his efforts to negotiate an armistice between Arabs and Israelis have written that he felt that information and papers he obtained during the course of the negotiations should always remain protected from public scrutiny. When the issue arose whether UN personnel who had participated in the negotiations should be interviewed by the Office of the Prosecutor of ICTY, views were very much divided within the UN Secretariat. Some argued vehemently that peacemakers should not be expected to speak to Prosecutors or criminal tribunals. The then Secretary-General of the UN, Kofi Annan, ruled that UN personnel should make themselves available to the Office of the Prosecutor. UN personnel duly cooperated.

This is not the place to enter into a discussion of this issue. But there would seem to be an open issue of principle whether people doing their utmost to help facilitate peace in very difficult circumstances should later be expected to open up themselves to Prosecutors and Criminal Tribunals. On the one hand, it has been argued that the cause of justice demands that those with information make it available in the course of criminal prosecutions—especially in a situation such as that in Bosnia and Herzegovina, where ethnic cleansing had been practised by Croats and Serbs especially. On the other hand, it has been argued that if negotiators are to help make peace, those with whom they are negotiating should not have to worry that conversations might later end up in Court. We are of the second view and consider that the decision of Secretary-General Annan to open up UN peace negotiators to the Office of the Prosecutor and to the Tribunal was wrong. On the other hand, we think that it is legitimate and fair for peacekeepers who were witnesses to crimes to testify to those crimes. We would thus make a distinction between peace negotiators and peacekeepers.

CONCLUSION

In writing this book we have sought to present the evidence and let it speak for itself. We have made no claims about the human rights roles of the peacemakers and the peacekeepers. We leave that to the judgment of the reader. Having been integrally involved in peacemaking, peacekeeping, and humanitarian efforts for nearly four years as Director of the International Conference on the Former Yugoslavia and also, for a year, Director in the Office of the SRSG in charge of all UN operations in the former Yugoslavia, we knew first hand of the honourable efforts made to build a broad range of UN strategies on the foundations of human rights.

At the heart of the concept of the UN Protected Areas was the idea of safeguarding human rights. Humanitarian operations sought to provide assistance and protection to innocent victims but needed the peacemakers to negotiate an end to conflicts. Peacekeepers were introduced to the former Yugoslavia to help protect people, then to assist in the delivery of humanitarian assistance, then to fight for the protection of the victims. The Special Rapporteur of the then UN Commission on Human Rights exposed widespread gross violations of human rights and called for the perpetrators to be brought to justice. The efforts of the peacemakers to prevent conflicts, to build peace on the foundations of principle and of international human rights norms, the evolution of the peacekeeping force into a force prepared to defend people, strategies of peacebuilding that centralised human rights and the rights of minorities, and the quest for justice in the face of ethnic cleansing and other crimes against humanity, all show how widespread considerations of human rights and justice were in the efforts of the United Nations for peace in the former Yugoslavia.

That there were multiple human rights strategies in the UN peace operations in the former Yugoslavia is beyond question; and all those who took part deserve the appreciation of the international community. But the question deserves to be asked: what results did the human rights strategies yield? Perhaps it would be fair to say that when, finally, the warring parties were ready to make peace, they were able to draw on the human rights blueprints of the ICFY peacemakers. Human rights in peacebuilding is probably the most valuable legacy of the human rights strategies. The human rights institutions in Bosnia and Herzegovina, the regimes for the protection of groups and minority rights in Croatia, the Former Yugoslav Republic of Macedonia, in Kosovo, and elsewhere built on the foundations laid by Vance, Carrington, Cutileiro, Ogata, Mazowiecki, , Owen, Ahtisaari, Stoltenberg, Ahrens, Szasz, and others. In the International Conference on the Former Yugoslavia, the human rights drafting of the late Paul Szasz deserves particular recognition.

But we have to recognize that human rights strategies by themselves could not, and did not, stop evil men from doing great harm. The Bosnian Serbs and the Bosnian Croats were well armed and determined to cleanse Muslims from areas of Bosnia and Herzegovina that they coveted. And this they did. The Bosnian Muslims, nowadays termed Bosniacs, were determined to fight back, and this they did, with covert arms supplies from Iran, Turkey, the United States, Saudi Arabia, and elsewhere. Foreign Mujahideens came to their aid and without a doubt perpetrated their share of atrocities. The Croatian government used the first opportunity it had, with intelligence support from the USA, to expel its Serb population, *en masse*.

Vance and Owen, and then Stoltenberg and Owen, had good peace plans that one side or another scuttled, or which the USA failed to support. In the end, the wars in Bosnia and Croatia continued and peace was made in Dayton only after the USA had marshalled its military and intelligence assets to force the parties into making peace. It was in the interests of the re-election campaign of President Clinton to bring the Bosnian conflict to an end before the electoral campaign of 1996.

Two questions arise for reflection: first, should major powers, especially the USA, have used their leverage with the parties to help bring about an honourable peace agreement earlier so as to spare the tens of thousands of lives that were lost between the Vance-Owen peace plan of May, 1993 and the Dayton Accords of November, 1995? We think they should have put their weight behind peace efforts and behind effective regimes for the protection of human rights advanced by Vance, Owen and Stoltenberg.

Second, when the Clinton Administration, in the spring of 1993, called for the lifting of arms embargo so as to enable the Bosniacs to obtain arms and ammunitions to defend themselves and avenge their losses were they foolhardy and unwise? Whether lifting the arms embargo would have changed situation is doubtful. At one stage in the spring of 1994, Secretary-General Boutros Boutros-Ghali asked his

Special Representative, Thorvald Stoltenberg to go to the Bosnian Serb capital, Pale, to urge Radovan Karadzic to accept the Contact Group plan for Bosnia and Herzegovina then on offer. "Radovan", Stoltenberg told Karadzic, "if you do not accept the Contact Group plan you could find yourself in a situation in which the arms embargo would be lifted and you would then have to fight in a new situation". Karadzic was non-plussed. He replied, laughing in the process "Let them lift the arms embargo and then we shall all buy arms from the Israelis"! He was unfazed at the prospect of the arms embargo being lifted.This author was at the table, beside Stoltenberg. Karadzic had his entire senior team with him, including Biljana Plavsic, who came across even more hard-line than he did. What would have been the consequences of lifting the arms embargo?

Vance and Owen, and then Stoltenberg and Owen, were convinced, as were many Governments, that lifting the arms embargo would have carried risks of prolonging and extending the conflicts in the former-Yugoslavia and could have drawn in neighbouring powers such as Greece and Turkey. As a senior aide to the Co-Chairmen at the time, we shared this view.

Perhaps the right conclusion to be drawn from the foregoing is that peacemakers seeking to build peace agreements on human rights foundations must have the backing of the major powers if they are to succeed. In the former Yugoslavia the ICFY peacemakers did not have the backing, crucially, of the USA. Another conclusion is that when the Security Council proclaims 'Safe Areas' it must be ready to protect them on the ground. This the Security Council did not do in the former Yugoslavia with dreadful consequences.

We came away from almost four years of intensive involvement in peacemaking, peacekeeping, humanitarian and human rights efforts in the former Yugoslavia feeling that there is a distinction to be drawn between international mediators and governmental mediators. The former use reason and diplomacy. The latter may use writ and force—especially if they come from a powerful State like the USA. We were at Dayton and witnessed the signing of the Dayton peace accords. We felt within our being that the ICFY, three years earlier, had put forward a better peace plan, the Vance-Owen plan. It had again done so six months later, the Stoltenberg-Owen plan, which Izetbegovic and Siladzjic enthusiastically embraced on HMS Invincible in the Adriatic Sea and then repudiated under pressure from the USA. The honourable efforts of Vance, Owen, Stoltenberg, could not succeed, notwithstanding their historic human rights components, because the writ of the USA was that the Bosniacs should fight. When it suited the interests of the USA to bring about a peace, it marshalled its intelligence, military and diplomatic assets and made the peace happen.

But the human rights blueprints of the Dayton Accords were the fruits of the human rights work of ICFY. This author is a witness to this; for it was this author who, as Director of the International Conference on the Former Yugoslavia, assembled the ICFY papers on human rights and transmitted them to the US State Department on the eve of the Dayton talks. This author was also present at Dayton and witnessed, with respect, the efforts of the US State Department lawyers who built upon the ICFY drafts and put forward even stronger blueprints for human rights protection. The parties, predictably, whittled down these ambitious drafts of the State Department lawyers and what was left was pretty close to what the ICFY peacemakers had striven for exactly three years earlier.

And therein lies the lasting human rights legacy of the ICFY in the former Yugoslavia. For the human rights regimes that came out of the Dayton Accords and the Eastern Slavonia agreement were those of the International Conference on the Former Yugoslavia. Particular credit must go to the lead drafter, the late Paul Szasz, who brought vision, energy and dynamism to his efforts. But he could craft dynamic human rights accords because, first, Vance, Owen, Ahtisaari, Ahrens, and Ogata, then Owen, Stoltenberg, Ahtisaari, Ahrens and Ogata, wanted and encourage him to do so. And we must also recognize the leadership of Stoltenberg as SRSG in charge of all UN peace and humanitarians in the former Yugoslavia during 1993. For it was under his leadership that UN peacekeepers first began to play an active human rights role as part of their peacekeeping efforts.

We must also acknowledge the courageous leadership of Sadako Ogata who, from the beginning, pleaded for the centrality of human rights in the search for solutions in the former Yugoslavia. And Tadeusz Mazowiecki, Special Rapporteur of the then Commission on Human Rights, was a spirited flag-bearer for human rights in the midst of ethnic cleansing and crimes against humanity. The Commission of Experts that gathered evidence of war crimes and crimes against humanity, and the ICTY, were conceived in the ICFY and Vance and Owen waged a diplomatic campaign to get them established. Vance personally led the efforts to get the mass—grave site at Ovcara near Vukovar exhumed, and Stoltenberg, as SRSG in charge of UNPROFOR, saw to it that UN peacekeepers stood guard over the site for many months. Even in the midst of peacemaking and peacekeeping, the foundations stones were being laid to bring to justice those responsible for crimes against humanity in the former Yugoslavia. And people are now serving sentences in the Hague for their crimes in the former Yugoslavia thanks to the efforts, among others, of the leaders of the International Conference on the Former Yugoslavia.

REFERENCE DOCUMENTS

Note on the documentary references

The text of this book relies heavily on the documentation of the International Conference on the Former Yugoslavia most of which are in the possession of the author.

In the documentary references that follow we have selected some materials that will hopefully enable the reader to see the centrality of human rights in practice in the peacemaking and peacekeeping processes. We have made a selection from a much larger pool of documents on human rights issues.

The speaking notes of Mr Vance on 4 September, 1992 show the humanitarian concerns at the start of ICFY.

The note of 16 September, 1992 on the Human Rights Committee's consideration of a report from the Federal Republic of Yugoslavia shows ICFY zeroing in on human rights issues from early on.

Paul Szasz's Memorandum of 21 September, 1992 drew attention to problems in basing political institutions on national or ethnic status.

The Press Statement of 24 September, 1992 shows Vance and Owen registering their revulsion at the practice of ethnic cleansing.

Paul Szasz's note of 29 September, 1992 shows that attention was given to the establishment of an International Criminal Court for the former Yugoslavia almost from the outset of ICFY.

The Note of a meeting with ICRC Officials on 2 October, 1992 shows Vance and Owen warning of the dangers of humanitarian agencies unwittingly being seen to be taking part in ethnic cleansing.

Paul Szasz's Memorandum of 5 October, 1992, and other Memoranda in the collection, of 13 October, 1992 and 12 January, 1993, show ICFY being the initiator of the idea of a Human Rights Court for Bosnia and Herzegovina.

The Note of a Meeting with Dr Karadzic on 8 October, 1992 shows Vance and Owen protesting seriously to Karadzic about ethnic cleansing taking place.

The Note of 23 October, 1992 on a Press Conference by Special Rapporteur Mazowiecki shows ICFY following the work of the Special Rapporteur closely.

Mrs Ogata's statement of 27 October, 1992 gives a snapshot of the evolving humanitarian situation.

The Memorandum of 27 October, 1992 shows ICFY's Ethnic and National Communities and Minorities Working Group in Action on issues of human and minority rights.

The Notes of 4 and 5 November, 1992 show ICFY following up on Lord Owen's initiative to have the Human Rights Committee examine urgent reports from the successor republics.

UNHCR's Memorandum of 14 December, 1992 shows that Organization warning about the idea of safe areas possibly contributing to ethnic cleansing.

Vance and Owen's Message of 30 November, 1992 to the UN Commission on Human Rights shows them asking for the advice of the Commission on issues of minority and group rights.

The Note of 11 March, 1993 gives highlights of a meeting ICFY convened to discuss the idea of a Human Rights Monitoring Mission.

The UN Department of Public Informations' Note on a Press Briefing of 17 March, 1993 on Human Rights Aspects of the Vance-Owen Plan for Bosnia and Herzegovina shows the attentiveness of ICFY to human rights issues.

Paul Szasz's presentation of 24 March, 1993 on ICFY and the War Crimes Issue is a historical document in its own right.

The ECMM Memorandum of 1 June, 1993 shows an ICFY partner sharing its recommendations on how to intensify human rights monitoring in the midst of war.

The next document appended is from January, 1995. Materials from the intervening period are discussed in the text of the book. For reasons of space limitation we have not incuded any documents from 1994.

The UNPROFOR Note of 31 January, 1995 shows that Organization mobilizing on human rights issues.

The document of 27 March, 2003, shows Jose Cutileiro, former negotiator and then Special Rapporteur of the Commission on Human Rights, giving his assessment of the prevailing human rights situation.

The Views of the Human Rights Chamber of Bosnia and Herzegovina dated 31 December, 2003 confirm how important this human rights court was for Bosnia and Herzegovina and indicate how short-sighted European leaders were in disbanding the court.

In the final document we reproduce for historical and comparative purposes the text of Lord Carrington's draft comprehensive convention with its elaborate human rights provisions.

There is much more human rights material we could have included in this collection but space considerations did not make this possible. Hopefully, from the text of the book and from the above pieces, the reader will be able to grasp how central human rights were to the UN peacemaking, peacekeeping and humanitarian processes in the former Yugoslavia.

ICFY

MR. VANCE: TALKING POINTS
FOR
SECOND FOLLOW-UP COMMITTEE MEETING
ON THE
"COMPREHENSIVE RESPONSE TO THE HUMANITARIAN CRISIS
IN EX-YUGOSLAVIA"

CRV
4 September 1992

- Thank you, Mrs. Ogata.
- This meeting is both timely and very necessary:
  - The war in former Yugoslavia grinds on; and
  - Massive human suffering continues and even worsens.
- The United Nations High Commission for Refugees and its associates, both governmental and non-governmental, are performing heroically.
- Over the past eleven months I have observed the activities of you and your colleagues with great admiration. It is difficult to find words to adequately express our gratitude to the men and women of the HCR for their noble work. We all must work together to bring this horror to an end.
- As you know, the Conference on Yugoslavia has just moved its Headquarters to Geneva and a new chapter has opened in our efforts to bring this tragic conflict to an end.
- Lord Owen and I will be co-chairing the Conference and we will be working in continuous session here at our base in Geneva, as well as in the former Yugoslav lands. Your humanitarian efforts are a vital element in almost every aspect of our work.
- We are under no illusions. We know that our task will be complex and difficult, but I pledge to you our unceasing efforts and close and daily co-operation.
- I salute Mrs. Ogata and her colleagues for their magnificent past and present work.
- **Let us all work together to bring the day nearer when we may never more hear expressions such as "ethnic cleansing", or see the daily suffering of hundreds of thousands of displaced persons.**
- I very much hope that this afternoon's appeal for greatly-needed assistance will meet with your generous response and support.
- I thank you again for giving me this opportunity to speak.

ICFY

BGR
September 16, 1992

NOTE
THE HUMAN RIGHTS COMMITTEE (ICCPR) AND THE SITUATION IN THE FORMER YUGOSLAVIA

1. The International Covenant on Civil and Political Rights was ratified by the Socialist Federal Republic of Yugoslavia. Since the break-up of the country, Slovenia has made a declaration of (succession) to the Covenant.
2. Croatia, Slovenia and Bosnia and Herzegovina, are now Members of the United Nations. Macedonia is not yet a Member. Serbia and Montenegro constitute the Federal Republic of Yugoslavia, whose membership in the United Nations is now the subject of disagreement.
3. There are possible legal and diplomatic implications of an invitation to the current Federal Republic of Yugoslavia (Serbia and Montenegro) to submit a special report to the Human Rights Committee. One would need to avoid the pitfall of implicit recognition of the current Federal Republic of Yugoslavia as the continuation of, or successor to, the former Socialist Federal Republic of Yugoslavia.
4. Leaving such implications aside, and assuming that an acceptable formula is used to invite a report from the Federal Republic of Yugoslavia (Serbia and Montenegro), the following background information might be kept in mind:
5. The Socialist Federal Republic of Yugoslavia submitted its third Report to the Human Rights Committee, which functions under the International Covenant on Civil and Political Rights, on March 10, 1992 (CCPR/C/52/Add.9). The Committee considered this report on April 8 and 9, 1992 (CCPR/C/SR.1144–1147). The Report consisted of an introductory section followed by information under Articles 1, 2, 4, 6, 7, 9, 17, 18, 19, 22, 24, 25.
6. In introducing the report to the Human Rights Committee on April 8, 1992, the Yugoslav representative referred to the secession of Croatia and Slovenia and the resulting difficulties of reporting on developments in all parts of the former Yugoslavia. The questions put by the Members of the Human Rights Committee fell under the following categories:
   - Constitutional and legal framework within which the Covenant is implemented, state of emergency and self-determination
   - Freedom of movement and expulsion of aliens, right to privacy, freedom of religion, expression, assembly and association, right to participate in the conduct of public affairs, non-discrimination, equality of the sexes and rights of persons belonging to minorities
7. Among the issues which arose in the questions of Members of the Committee, the following may be flagged:
   - The effect of the crisis on the constitutional order in Yugoslavia
   - Rights which had been derogated from during the recent events; why had Yugoslavia not declared a state of emergency under Article 4 of the Covenant

- What was being done to protect the rights of minorities
- What had been the nature and extent of the flagrant violations of human rights that had occurred during military operations

8. Members of the Human Rights Committee noted that while the Covenant applied to the entire territory of the former Yugoslavia, the Federal Government could protect civil and political rights only in Serbia and Montenegro. The Government was, however, to be considered responsible for the actions of its troops wherever they operated.
9. The representative of the State Party admitted that the Government was no longer in control of the whole territory of the former Yugoslavia. He added that, although the Government did not, at that stage, recognize the secession of the breakaway Republics, it was endeavouring to co-operate with them in finding a solution to problems of day-to-day existence, which included human rights issues. (An issue which the Members of the Human Rights Committee could raise with the representative of the current Yugoslavia in any future discussions would seem to be: What efforts had the Government made to co-operate with the breakaway republics in order to prevent, reduce or stop violations of human rights?)
10. The Members of the Human Rights Committee asked whether investigations had been carried out in respect of gross violations of human rights. The Members commented that the lack of proper Government control over the Serbian army had contributed to the deteriorating situation and, hence, the violations of human rights in the country. The representative of the State Party admitted that the Yugoslav Parliament had not always been able to control its own units. He agreed that those responsible should be punished. The Government was thus prepared to punish all those responsible for crimes against civilians. A Special Commission had been established to investigate all reported violations of international humanitarian law. Thirty members of the Army or paramilitary groups were under investigation. (Other issues which the Members of the Human Rights Committee could raise in a future discussion with the representative of the current Yugoslavia, are: What were the results of the investigations of the Special Commission and how many persons had been tried and punished?)
11. The representative of the State Party informed the Human Rights Committee in April that in the territory under Federal Government control, all interested groups, including non-governmental organizations and the International Committee of the Red Cross, had been invited to inspect places of detention. An impartial procedure for handling complaints of ill-treatment in the courts and the special investigation committee existed. (The Members of the Human Rights Committee could probe the issue of the treatment of detainees held by members of the Army).
12. On the issue of minorities existing in what is now the current Yugoslavia (Serbia and Montenegro) Members of the Committee asked detailed questions about the situations in Kosovo and Vojvodina. (An issue which the Members of the Human Rights Committee could pose to the

representative of the current Yugoslavia is: What measures are being taken to prevent the break out of conflict in these areas?)

13. In commenting upon the discussion with the representative of the State Party, Members regretted that the crisis had prevented the Committee from supervising the application of the Covenant throughout the territory of the former Yugoslavia. They expressed their gravest concern about the atrocities committed during the inter-ethnic conflicts and the many violations of human rights that had resulted. They also expressed concern over conditions in detention centres. The deterioration of the situation of ethnic, religious and linguistic minorities, particularly those of Albanian and Hungarian origin was of grave concern to the Members of the Human Rights Committee as was the situation of population groups which had become de facto minorities as a result of recent inter-ethnic conflicts.
14. The Human Rights Committee adopted a set of comments after its consideration of the report. The following were some of the main points covered:

- The Committee noted that a Commission had been set up to inquire into allegations of genocide and violations of human rights during the armed conflicts
- The Committee noted that difficulties had arisen in the Province of Kosovo, which had led to the proclamation of several successive States of emergency
- The following principal subjects of concern were mentioned by the Committee:

The Committee regretted the fact that under the State of emergency proclaimed in the Province of Kosovo, excessive steps had been taken to limit the rights and freedoms guaranteed by the Covenant.

The Committee expressed its gravest concern with regard to the atrocities committed during the inter-ethnic conflicts. It was disturbed by the many violations of human rights protected by the Covenant, especially rights from which no derogation was possible in any circumstances.

The Committee greatly regretted the many cases of summary and arbitrary execution, forced or involuntary disappearances, torture, rape and pillage committed by members of the Federal Army. Paramilitary groups and militias had also been guilty of similar abuses.

The Committee regretted the extremely low number of inquiries made into these violations. The failure to take measures to punish the guilty and prevent any recurrence of such acts, and the consequent impunity of those responsible.

The Committee expressed its concern over conditions in detention centres.

The Committee expressed its concern over the deterioration in the situation of ethnic, religious and linguistic minorities, particularly those of Albanian and Hungarian origin, and the population groups that had become de facto minorities as a result of recent inter-ethnic conflicts.

15. The Committee adopted the following suggestions and recommendations to the State Party:

"In view of the serious situation prevailing in the State party, the Committee recommends the Government to take all necessary measures to stop violations of human rights, particularly those relating to the right to life and the prohibition of torture. These measures should include re-establishment of control over the army, dissolution of paramilitary militias and groups, punishment of those guilty of violations and adoption of measures to prevent a recurrence of such abuses. The Committee also recommends full application of Article 27 of the Covenant, which recognizes that the right of persons belonging to ethnic, religious or linguistic minorities to enjoy their own culture, to profess and practice their own religion and to use their own language."

16. In the light of the foregoing account of the Human Rights Committee's examination of the third Report of the State Party in April, 1992, and bearing in mind developments since then, the following questions may be considered to be put to the State Party:

(a) Prevention. What measures has the Government taken to prevent violations of human rights in areas under its jurisdiction or under the control of the Yugoslav Army.

(b) Volatile situations. What measures has the Government taken in order to prevent or stop violations of the human rights of minorities and to prevent the break out of conflict in places such as Kosovo.

(c) Investigations and prosecutions. What has been the result of the investigations of the Special Committee set up to examine atrocities and how many persons have been prosecuted and punished.

(d) Rights of Detainees. What measures have been, or are being taken, by the Government to ensure respect for the human rights of persons detained.

(e) Co-operation. What measures has the Government taken to co-operate with the Governments of Bosnia and Herzegovina, Croatia and Slovenia so as to prevent or stop gross violations of human rights.

(f) Restitution/reparation/compensation. What measures does the Government envisage to provide restitution, reparation or compensation for the victims of gross violations of human rights perpetrated by its agents.

ICFY

21 September 1992
PCSzasz

INTERNATIONAL CONFERENCE ON THE FORMER YUGOSLAVIA
WORKING GROUP ON BOSNIA-HERZEGOVINA

Problems in Basing Political Institutions on National or Ethnic Status

1. This note will discuss some of the technical difficulties that might be anticipated in including any provisions relating to ethnic or national or similar groupings in the institutional provisions of the proposed BiH constitution (as distinguished from those relating to human rights – though even there, general principles on minority rights would be much easier than any that refer to specific groupings). These considerations are aside from any relating to the anomaly of introducing such provisions into an internationally brokered instrument in the last decade of the 20th Century, against the entire trend of international human rights developments of the past several decades (e.g., in particular, the firm rejection of apartheid).
2. If any institutional political rights are to be based on any group (national, ethnic or other) identification (i.e., in BiH: Muslim, Serb, Croat), for example, if one of the houses of the legislature is to be composed of a particular number of members of each group and/or if the executive is to have a multi-group composition, it will be necessary to define in some way how the group representatives in the legislature/ executive are to be chosen, i.e. how they are to be elected. For this, there would seem to be two, possible approaches (which are analyzed in turn in paras. 3 and 4):
   (a) geographic – based on the assumption that identifiable regions have a pure enough group composition that representatives elected from those regions are, in effect, representatives of that group;
   (b) personal – which would require classifying citizens to determine which of them may vote for which group representatives.
3. In order to create geographically sufficiently pure regions in a country whose ethnic/national composition is as patchwork as that of 1991 Bosnia and Herzegovina, there would seem to be the following two possibilities:
   (a) It may be possible to negotiate the boundaries of such areas among the representatives of the three groups in question – perhaps following more or less forced regroupings (see (b)) and/or referenda (see (c)).
   (b) To create "pure" group areas (i.e. ones in which one group is sufficiently predominant that in the normal course (i.e., barring a split in the group) its candidates will win any election and which are of sufficient size to entitle them to at least one representative), it will probably be necessary to resort to (or to allow the continuation and to accept the results of) "ethnic cleansing", i.e. the forced transfer of individuals from one area to another; at the minimum, it must be permitted to

exert strong pressures (which would probably be inconsistent with accepted minority rights) on individuals of other groups to leave.

(b) Another possibility would be to identify, without any forced shifting of populations, sufficiently pure group areas (which would naturally constitute a very small-grained patchwork in 1991 Bosnia and Herzegovina); such identification would presumably be done by means of referenda. The major difficulty in conducting such referenda is to decide on the boundaries of each area, for evidently the placement of the boundaries may influence, indeed determine, the outcome. The negotiations for drawing these boundaries are likely to be most difficult, and could probably not be carried out without predominant international intervention – i.e., some international body may have to draw the area boundaries.

It should be noted that in either case it would be practically necessary to define the areas in such a way that they have sufficient size and integrity that they can function as some sort of governmental units, responsible for education, sanitation, health, etc.

4. In order to classify individual citizens as belonging to one or another voting group, it will first be necessary to define these. Presumably in Bosnia and Herzegovina these would be Muslims, Serbs, Croatians and Others (e.g., Slovenians, Hungarians, Albanians, Macedonians, Jews, Gypsies), and possibly some who do not wish to be classified at all. It will also be necessary to determine what other rights (e.g. to education in particular schools) will depend on classification, to establish a system of personal identification cards showing the classification (as was done in the former Soviet Union) and to maintain registers. The principal methods of classification would seem to be the following:

(a) Self-Classification – i.e., every citizen can choose, either at one time or at any time, which group to belong to. (This, essentially, is what citizens of the former Austro-Hungarian state were permitted to do after its dissolution.) If the choice can be changed at any time (e.g., as party registrations in most democracies), then there would be the danger that for a particular election sufficient members of one group might choose to vote in another group (e.g., Muslims as Croats) to distort the results of that election; on the other hand, to permit no possibility of changing at all would be troublesome (e.g., a half Croatian half Serb person who initially chose to be classified as a Serb, might like to change on marrying a Croat.)

(b) Objective Classification – this would require first the specification of particular criteria, e.g., parentage, language, religion, and second the establishment of a governmental authority (reminiscent of South African racial boards) to make the determination – presumably subject to some appeal, probably to the courts.

(c) Subjective Classification – this would permit each group to establish organs to decide on the admission of individuals (much like most churches have admission procedures, or as American Indian tribes now have some mechanism for determining who belongs to the tribe and thus can share in any tribal assets); here, too, it may be necessary to introduce an appeals procedure.

(d) Mixed Classification Systems – For example, to permit an initial basically free choice, only subject to meeting some minimum objective criteria or to admission by the group leadership, while any change would have to be approved by either a governmental authority or by the leadership of the group to which the change is desired. In general, whenever objective criteria are to be taken into account, the process must be subject to at least potential governmental supervision (i.e., at the request of either the individual or of the leadership of the group concerned).

ICFY PRESS STATEMENT

24 September 1992

The Co-Chairmen are deeply concerned about reports which have just reached them from the Banja Luka region indicating a build-up of tension, bomb incidents, and intimidation with the potential threat of violence and the development of an ethnic-cleansing campaign.

This morning the Co-Chairmen called in Ambassador Pavicevic of the Federal Republic of Yugoslavia, and Dr. Koljevic, the Bosnian Serb representative, and urged that immediate steps be taken to reduce tensions in the area.

In view of the urgency of the situation, the Co-Chairmen have decided to fly to Banja Luka tomorrow. There they will assess the situation on the ground, and speak to representatives of the local communities and humanitarian agencies.

INTERNATIONAL CONFERENCE ON THE FORMER YUGOSLAVIA

29 September 1992

To: D. Owen
cc*: P. Hall
H. Okun
B. Ramcharan
*

From: P. Szasz
Subject: Establishment of an International Criminal Court for Yugoslavia

1. By your memorandum of 18 September to Secretary Vance you called attention to the commitment of the ICFY Co-Chairmen to "carry forward a study of the creation of an international criminal court"[1] and indicated the interest of certain EC Governments in proceeding with this and related matters. This note is intended to give some background information relevant to the possible establishment of such a court (ICC).
2. The establishment of an ICC has long been suggested and over the years a dozen drafts have been prepared by various official organs and private institutions for either a court with general jurisdiction in relation to international crimes or one dealing with particular types of offenses[2]. However, over the years, the only such tribunals actually established were the ad hoc ones after WWII to conduct the principal Nürnberg and Tokyo War Crimes trials (the subsidiary ones being conducted by national military commissions). The UN General Assembly itself has considered the matter in various contexts and recently, on the basis of a 1989 proposal by Trinidad and Tobago, asked the International Law Commission (ILC) for a report. The latter considered the question as part of its long-standing study of a Draft Code of Crimes against the Peace and Security of Mankind and, having last year completed its first draft of such a Code, at its May-July session this year gave thorough consideration to creating an "international criminal jurisdiction" (i.e., an ICC and related organs) and is reporting thereon to the General Assembly[3]. That report makes rather heavy weather on this subject, which partly reflects the usual pattern of the Commission's studies but also the difficulties in dealing with this subject in the abstract and in relation to an indefinite number of very disparate international crimes (at this time already numbering about two dozen, and potentially many more[4]). In any event, the ILC study does not set out any draft statute for an ICC, and even if the General Assembly should react positively and give a

[1] Specific Decisions of the London Conference (LC/C7 (FINAL)), para. 8.
[2] See the Appendix, pp. 65–68, of ILC document A/CN.4/L.475/Rev.1 – attached hereto. In the definitive version of the ILC Report (A/47/10), this Appendix appears on pp. 199–203.
[3] A/CN.4/L.475/Rev. 1 – attached – the most significant part of which is the report of an ad hoc Working Group on this subject (part D). The definitive version of
[4] See the list in Annex 1 (p. 174) to Bassiouni's study cited at note 5 below.

further mandate to the Commission to develop one, it is likely to take some years before such a draft emerges.

3. Just a few months ago Professor M. Cherif Bassiouni, recognized as the leading expert in this field and whose thoughts are also reflected in some of the ILC's work, published a Draft Statute: International Criminal Tribunal[5]. This study sets out a detailed, fully annotated draft of a possible basic instrument of an ICC, to be established by an international treaty. This draft, which like the ILC study noted above, deals with a tribunal that is to be competent for an indefinite category of international crimes, is consequently far more complicated than would be necessary for a tribunal that is to have a strictly circumscribed competence in respect of a restricted group of international crimes carried out within a small territory during a relatively short period. Consequently any draft ICC for Former Yugoslavia (ICCFY) statute based on the cited model could be considerably simpler; further simplification would arise from the likelihood that the proposed court would be established by a Security Council resolution rather than by a treaty.
4. The Dutch proposal referred to in your memorandum would have the ICCFY statute prepared, as part of its terms of reference to be established by the Security Council, by an ad hoc UN War Crimes Commission for Former Yugoslavia (WCC). This would, in effect, remove this task from the ICFY Co-Chairmen. The Co-Chairmen may therefore wish to express their views on this to the governments concerned, or even through the Secretary-General to the Security Council, and if they are content to have the WCC undertake this task they might request merely to be consulted in due course. If, however, the Co-Chairmen consider that this work should be done under their auspices, as apparently foreseen by the London Conference, it could be done here, though in that case it might be useful to engage the assistance of Professor Bassiouni as a consultant to at least comment on any internal draft before it is widely circulated.

[5] Association Internationale de Droit Pénal, 1992.

ICFY

NOTES OF A MEETING WITH REPRESENTATIVES OF THE INTERNATIONAL COMMITTEE OF THE RED CROSS

Friday, 2 October 1992, 4.15 – 5.20

Attendance:	Mr. Vance	Mr. Jean de Courten
	Lord Owen	Director of Operations
	Ambassador Okun	ICRC
	Ambassador Hall	Mr. Thierry Germond
	Mr. Ahtisaari	Delegate General for Europe
	Mr. Ramcharan	

Mr. Jean De Courten stated that 1,560 detainees had been transferred to Croatia from Trnopolje Camp. They had been impressed by the security provided by the Bosnian Serbs. The ECMM had been present during the BiH position of the journey. The problem was now the resettlement of these people. Croatia's position was that they should not be there for more than 14 days. At that very moment a meeting on the issue was taking place at UNHCR with Permanent Representatives in Geneva. Efforts were also underway to trace family members of the released persons.

Mr. De Courten continued that, during the plenipotentiary meetings held at the ICRC with representatives of the three sides in Bosnia and Herzegovina, an Agreement had been signed on modalities for the further release of prisoners. The ICRC hoped that by 31 October all the camps would have been emptied. One of the priorities of ICRC in the coming days was to release Serb detainees from Croat or Muslim camps, since they had the impression that the Serbs were expecting this.

Mr. De Courten stated, further, that during the meetings with the plenipotentiaries, another issue had arisen; he asked Mr. Germond to report on that issue. Mr. Thierry Germond then stated that the main topic of the last three days had been the implementation of the London Agreements. The Serb side had insisted that there were categories of civilians being held by the other sides who were de facto prisoners or detainees. The Serb side had insisted that this be included in the Agreement on prisoners. The Serb side had referred, in this regard, to the 19 September Understanding that the three sides had signed under the auspices of UNHCR. Paragraph 3 of that Understanding had pledged the parties to the conflict to co-operate fully with the International Committee of the Red Cross and, as applicable, UNPROFOR to ensure safe passage for convoys of released detainees where necessary. The parties had also agreed to co-operate fully in allowing and being responsible for the free movement of persons. Mr. Germond stated that ICRC had not been a party to that agreement and was concerned with the release of prisoners rather than with issues of freedom of movement. It had therefore suggested that the issue of freedom of movement be dealt with outside the Agreement on release of prisoners. That had led to the conclusion of another document, which was not an Agreement but a Recommendation that the three sides had signed, on the movement of people.

Mr. Vance stated that the Recommendation raised a number of problems: How did it fit in with General Morillon's plans? How did it fit in with the mandate of UNPROFOR? How did it fit in with the role of UNHCR? Mrs. Ogata was concerned that UNHCR would now have to be dealing with civilians generally as opposed to people in camps. Considerably more people would thus be involved. She had also raised the question of whether UNHCR should not be given an opportunity to establish a working group on this matter.

Mr. De Courten stated that he shared Mr. Vance's concern. He then gave ICRC's assessment of the situation: According to ICRC delegates, there were different groups of civilians living in a totally unsecured situation. Humanitarian organizations could not provide them with the necessary protection. The ICRC was very concerned that with the approach of winter these people would be without protection or subsistence. Based on this assessment, which was shared by all of the ICRC delegates in the field, the ICRC as a humanitarian organization had to consider how it could help the people involved. That was why it had taken the position that it would have to take immediate steps to move the people involved to areas where they would have natural protection and to start soon a huge plan of action to help them face a very difficult situation during the winter. The ICRC was aware - and had taken into account - that it could be accused when it came to the issue of ethnic cleansing but it had nevertheless felt that it had to take this risk. The ICRC was ready to undertake the supervisory role involved in checking upon the wishes of the people affected. Even the plenipotentiaries of the three sides participating in the talks had come to the same conclusion and President Izetbegovic himself had personally supported the Recommendation.

Mr. De Courten stated that the President of the ICRC intended to share their assessment with Permanent Representatives and the press on Saturday, 3 October. The ICRC was moved by purely humanitarian concerns.

Lord Owen stated that if the ICRC President went very far he would find it necessary to state publicly that the document came very close to ethnic cleansing. The document raised formidable difficulties on grounds of principle as well as on grounds of practicalities. The Co-Chairmen were working very hard to get Canadian forces to Banja Luka and to try to get a monitored corridor along the road to Travnik. The ICRC was free to go ahead and publicize the document, but he would feel obliged to express his views on it. A danger of the document was that people would think that all they had to do was to get on the road and that they would be safe. Mr. De Courten stated that the ICRC did not intend to publicize the document as such. It would, rather, issue a statement concerning it.

Mr. Germond stated that even if the task appeared difficult and hopeless it was obvious that in humanitarian terms it would be preferable to take people to where they could be protected. The alternative was to provide protection to people where they were. Unfortunately this was lacking. In fact people were paying up to 500 DM to get into Trnopolje Camp. Since there was no protection for these innocent people, there was no alternative but to try something else. In humanitarian terms that was a huge responsibility. The document was not an agreement as such. It was the conclusion of the parties, which they had signed. It should be noted, he added, that the side which had been most vehement that the document should be concluded and signed was that of the Government of Bosnia and Herzegovina. The delegation had specifically consulted President Izetbegovic.

Mr. Vance asked who would be responsible for supervising the process and where the people would go. Mr. Germond replied that there was a big question mark over that issue. Mr. Vance stated that it encouraged ethnic cleansing. What worried him was to suddenly find a document which some well-meaning people had concluded but without thinking the issues through. He hoped that there would not be a press conference about the document on Saturday. Mr. De Courten replied that the press conference would not be on the document, but rather on the tragic humanitarian situation in Bosnia and Herzegovina and the need to take urgent action on it. The ICRC was convinced that something had to be done urgently to save the lives of the Bosnians. Lord Owen referred to the second paragraph of the document and stated that the language used, "can only be saved ..." was an invitation to people to continue what they had been doing; that could lead to a complete eradication of Muslims from the area. It gave the unfortunate impression as if one had given up on holding the line against ethnic cleansing - at the very time when the Co-Chairmen had just succeeded in obtaining clear statements out of Belgrade against ethnic cleansing.

Mr. Germond stated that for the last week, starting on the very day after the Co-Chairmen had left the area, harassment had increased according to the reports the ICRC had been receiving from its delegates in the field. Mr. Vance stated that everyone shared the anguish about the situation. However, to bring the people out, and not to provide protection – and not to know where the people would be going – raised serious difficulties. Mrs. Ogata, whose agency had the lead responsibility on humanitarian issues had to be brought into the process.

Lord Owen stated that the Co-Chairmen recognized that the moral and ethical problems were formidable. However, one had to resist ethnic cleansing. There were dangers in taking people out in an uncontrolled situation. Mr. Vance said that if the question entered the public domain, he would have to say that the document was premature; that the alternatives were not considered; that there ought to be an opportunity for Mrs. Ogata to sit down and talk about these issues; and that the Co-Chairmen also had to be given an opportunity to participate in the discussion.

Mr. De Courten stated that ICRC had sincere appreciation for the Co-Chairmen's efforts. It would not make any public statement on the document. The ICRC had not signed the paper. The ICRC did, however, have around 40 delegates in Bosnia and Herzegovina who were confronted daily with the acute humanitarian situation. The ICRC was feeling very alone on these issues. It felt that it had reached the point where it might have to consider withdrawing from Bosnia and Herzegovina. Prisoners had been killed in places where ICRC delegates had visited. That was unusual in the experience of the Red Cross.

Mr. De Courten added that Mrs. Ogata will be at the press conference to be given by the President of the ICRC who, he reiterated, would not make any statement about the paper under discussion.

Mr. Germond stated that what the ICRC had done was in response to a serious problem. It had sought to put the problem on the table. It was an embarrassing issue for the international community but the humanitarian dimensions nevertheless remained. Lord Owen suggested that the ICRC could add a rider to the document that no convoys would go out unless military commanders on the ground or senior political leadership gave signed guarantees about the safety of the people involved. Such an approach would gain some time and would enable Mrs. Ogata to see how she could deal with the situation.

Mr. Germond reiterated that the document was not an Agreement but could perhaps be turned into an Agreement. Lord Owen commented that the ICRC could put out an edict that the process could only be carried out under international auspices and that follow-up agreements would need to be signed. Such a procedure could in fact make the document the start of something useful.

Mr. De Courten commented that there was not a big difference in the positions being expressed. What was different was that ICRC delegates, who had been instructed until now that they should not get involved in transfers of people, would now get new instructions. The ICRC had clear procedures for dealing with such situations. Its delegates would be able to deal with the most dramatic cases.

Mr. Vance suggested that a meeting take place on Saturday, 3 October, involving ICRC, UNHCR and the Co-Chairmen. It was agreed that the meeting would take place at 2 p.m. at the ICRC. The ICRC undertook to inform Mrs. Ogata.

Ambassador Okun noted that the ICRC representatives had said that the Recommendation would not be publicized. He asked whether Dr. Karadzic understood that. Mr. Germond replied that the ICRC had undertaken to transmit the Recommendation to the Co-Chairmen and that the signatories had been given copies to transmit to their political leadership.

Ambassador Okun commented that the line between ethnic cleansing and safe havens was a thin one. One would have to think about where the people would go. Mr. Germond replied that the ICRC had a number of ideas about this. Mr. Vance commented that somebody ought to be giving thought about which international body would be responsible to check the will of the people.

BGR 2 October 1992 0023BR

INTERNATIONAL CONFERENCE ON THE FORMER YUGOSLAVIA

5 October 1992

To: D. Owen

cc: C. Vance
M. Ahtisaari
P. Hall
H. Okun
B. Ramcharan

From: P. Szasz

Subject: Discussions with Council of Europe Secretariat on a possible C/E Mechanism to facilitate the establishment of a Human Rights Court for Bosnia and Herzegovina

---

1. After the luncheon at C/E headquarters on Saturday afternoon, 3 October, I met with the following C/E Secretariat officials:

   Mr. Hans-Peter Furrer
   Director of Political Affairs

   Mr. E. Harremoes
   Director of Legal Affairs

   Mr. P. Leuprecht
   Director of Human Rights

   Mr. M Scheuer
   Deputy Director of the Secretary-General's Private Office

2. I distributed, on a confidential basis, copies of the three human rights papers we had handed to the parties participating in the ICFY Bosnia-Herzegovina Working Group on 25 September (Revised Checklist of International Human Rights Instruments; List of Human Rights; Preliminary thoughts on Implementation, Enforcement and Guarantees), and invited special attention to paragraph 2.1 of the latter, which foresees the establishment by the BiH constitution of a special human rights court to consist of a majority of European judges and that might constitute an "extension of the European Court of Human Rights". I pointed out that your proposal to the C/E Parliamentary Assembly that morning (Annex I) (which of course reflected the proposal that Mr. Furrer had mailed to me on 23 September – copy attached to my memorandum of 29 September), which was then endorsed by the antepenultimate paragraph of the Declaration approved by the Assembly at the end of the debate (Annex II), was designed to establish a mechanism for implementing that proposed constitutional provision. Finally, I distributed a very preliminary draft of such a provision (Annex III) to illustrate how the BiH constitution could take account of the proposed C/E mechanism.
3. A most useful discussion followed about various aspects of the proposed mechanism, in which great appreciation was expressed for your

initiative in presenting this proposal to the Assembly. The following points emerged:

(a) The proposed mechanism had been elaborated within the C/E Secretariat a number of months ago, but no opportune occasion had arisen to present it to the inter-governmental organs. Consequently, the mechanism had not been designed especially with BiH or even Yugoslavia in mind, and it was considered desirable to establish it in quite general terms – which I confirmed would also be the our preference.
(b) The reason why it was proposed to select judges from both the European Court of Human Rights and the European Commission of Human Rights was both to increase the pool of candidates from two already heavily burdened bodies, and to draw on the experience of the Commission, which is mostly in fact-finding, and on those of the Court, which is mostly in legal interpretation. It was confirmed that the members of the Commission act in a fully judicial capacity and would thus be appropriate judges on a BiH human rights court. It was also confirmed that once appointed to that court, the same European judges would continue to serve, until there was a special reason for requiring a replacement.
(c) With respect to the law that this special BiH court would apply, I explained that it should in principle be that of the BiH constitution, but that constitution would incorporate by reference the applicable international human rights instruments, including the European Convention on Human Rights and its Protocols. Should there be any discrepancy in the provisions of several applicable instruments, presumably the court would apply the higher applicable standard; in any event, it would develop a jurisprudence for dealing with such conflicts.
(d) The question was raised whether the special BiH court could also respond to questions addressed to it by other BiH courts in respect of pending proceeding (instead of requiring an appeal to be taken from a final judgment in such a proceeding), similar to the powers of the European Court of Justice under Article 77 of the EEC Treaty. I indicated that I would include such an option in a revised draft of the proposed BiH constitutional provision (see Annex IV, para. 4).
(e) With respect to miscellaneous matters such as the number of European judges to be appointed, the languages of the proceedings, the allocation of costs, etc., it was considered that these would not have to be resolved in the general statute of the mechanism that the C/E would now proceed to formulate and adopt, since these matters could be regulated by the declarations of acceptance of the mechanism that the BiH government would, after the entry into force of the constitution, file with the C/E and by the decision of the C/E Committee of Ministers accepting such declaration.
(f) As to timing, the adoption of the proposed mechanism would require a series of consultations with the Committee of Ministers or of their

Deputies, as well as with the Court and the Commission. Although the text of the instrument expressing the proposed mechanism could be developed by November, it might be difficult to get final approval before early in 1993. I indicated that this would probably be satisfactory for us. Mr. Furrer undertook to keep me informed by fax of the progress of their drafts, and it was anticipated that further thoughts might also be exchanged on the occasion of the C/E Secretary-General's visit to Geneva, tentatively planned for the end of the current week. Finally, it was suggested that it might be useful if at some stage I returned to Strasbourg to explain to the Committee of Ministers or Deputies the possible application of the proposed mechanism to BiH.

4. I was asked whether the C/E Secretariat could assist us in any way in our negotiation of the human rights provisions of the BiH constitution, in particular by sending an expert. I indicated that there might be a time when that could be useful, but for the moment requested the following:
   (a) Comments on the human rights papers that we had presented to the parties in the B-H Working Group, in particular on the List of Human Rights and on the Preliminary thoughts on Implementation, Enforcement and Guarantees;
   (b) English texts of the human rights and judicial review provisions of recent European constitutions, particularly those of the other ex-Yugoslav and other Central and Eastern European states, of which the C/E apparently has a good up-to-date collection.

ATTACHMENT

EXTRACT FROM A SPEECH BY THE RT HON LORD OWEN, CO-CHAIRMAN OF THE STEERING COMMITTEE OF THE INTERNATIONAL CONFERENCE ON FORMER YUGOSLAVIA TO THE COUNCIL OF EUROPE ASSEMBLY, 3 OCTOBER 1992

The International Conference on the former Yugoslavia are very interested in developing a transitional ad-hoc mechanism for the judicial protection of human rights in European States which are not yet member States of the Council of Europe. For new States the criteria for entry are rightly demanding and not easy to fulfil immediately when transfering from a Communist to a democratic State.

One interesting proposal which we are studying and are likely to put before the parties to the Bosnia and Herzegovina Working Party is for the Council of Europe to create an ad-hoc mechanism whose task would be to ensure the protection of human rights in European States which are not yet members of the Council of Europe ("subscribing" states). I have in mind in particular Bosnia and Herzegovina whose new constitution is currently under discussion and could not expect to be a full member for some years.

A non-member State could subscribe to the Council of Europe ad-hoc mechanism by means of a unilateral declaration which would have to be accepted by the Committee of Ministers of the Council of Europe.

The mechanism would consist of a body which would be set up for a transitional period pending the accession of the "subscribing" State to the Council of Europe and to the European Convention on Human Rights.

The body could be composed of -

- judges of the European Court of Human Rights
- members of the European Commisson of Human Rights
- persons from the "subscribing" States.

The body could receive communications from any "subscribing" State, individual, group of individuals or non-governmental organisation alleging violations of human rights in a "subscribing" State.

The body would be able to examine the admissibility and merits of the allegations received. It could make findings of fact and state its opinion, in the first place by reference to the European Convention on Human Rights and the case law developed under it, but also by reference to other international human rights treaties and agreements to which the "subscribing" State was already a Contracting Party (eg UN Covenants) and other legal instruments relating to human rights.

The opinion of the body could be made binding on the "subscribing" State. I hope they would not choose it to be only an advisory opinion. They could entrench this body in their constitution until such time as they were able to become members of the Council of Europe.

END

ATTACHMENT

DECLARATION

sur la crise dans l'ancienne Yougoslavie

L'Assemblée Parlementaire du Conseil de l'Europe a entendu aujourd'hui un exposé de Lord Owen, Co-Président du Comité Directeur de la Conférence sur la paix dans l'ex-Yougoslavie.

Elle est profondément bouleversée et choquée par les violations massives, flagrantes, particulièrement brutales et cruelles des droits de l'homme dans le territoire de l'ancienne Yougoslavie qui constituent un inacceptable retour à la barbarie.

Elle condamne avec force ces exactions, tortures, meurtres de civils, prises d'otages, déplacements de population et l'existence de camps de concentration qui sont autant de crimes contre l'humanité dont les auteurs devront être jugés.

Elle rejette avec la plus grande fermeté tout projet et toute action visant la purification ethnique qu'elle considère comme un crime contre l'humanité et étant contraire à tous les principes du Conseil de l'Europe. Elle refuse par conséquent tout partage de territoire basé sur des critères ethniques.

Elle rappelle les engagements signés par les Etats participants à la Conférence sur la sécurité et la coopération en Europe en matière de frontières qui ne peuvent être modifiées qu'avec l'accord de toutes les parties concernées.

L'Assemblée demande aux gouvernements de se mobiliser d'urgence pour apporter aux populations éprouvées l'aide nécessaire pour leur survie au seuil d'un hiver qui, faute d'action concrète, provoquera la mort de centaines de milliers de personnes.

L'Assemblée estime que, compte tenu des circonstances, il est devenu indispensable, d'assurer une protection efficace, y inclus par les armes, des convois d'aide humanitaire et approuve pleinement la création d'une zone d'interdiction de survol aérien du territoire de la Bosnie-Herzégovine.

L'Assemblée appuie la demande du Comité des Ministres que toutes les mesures soient prises pour imposer le respect des décisions du Conseil de Sécurité de l'ONU par les parties qui continuent à faire obstruction à une solution du conflit.

L'Assemblée appuie pleinement la proposition de Lord Owen de créer, dans le cadre du Conseil de l'Europe, un mécanisme ad hoc de protection des droits de l'homme au bénéfice des ressortissants des pays européens non membres de l'Organisation.

L'Assemblée demande aux gouvernements de partager la charge que représente l'octroi de l'asile aux personnes qui fuient la guerre, et de faire pleinement usage des possibilités offertes par le Fonds de développement social pour améliorer la situation des personnes déplacées accueillies sur leur territoire.

L'Assemblée en appelle aux parlements nationaux pour qu'ils utilisent tous les moyens à leur disposition pour sensibiliser l'opinion publique et veillent à ce que les gouvemements mettent en oeuvre rigoureusement tous les engagements souscrits dans le cadre des Nations Unies ou résultant de la Conférence de Londres.

ATTACHMENT

INTERNATIONAL CONFERENCE ON THE FORMER YUGOSLAVIA

2.1 Appeals to the Council of Europe Mechanism

1. Any person and the official representative of any recognized group shall have a right to appeal from the final judgment of any court established under this Constitution in a proceeding to which it was a party, provided such judgment is not subject to appeal to any other such court for a reason other than the lapse of time limits and provided that the appeal is grounded on a provision of Chapter [human, civil and political rights] or [group or minority rights] of this Constitution, to the Mechanism established by the Council of Europe by its Resolution _____, and the decision of such Mechanism shall be binding [on all organs of the government].
2. An appeal in accordance with paragraph 1 may also be taken to the specified Mechanism if a proceeding is pending in a court established by this Constitution for a period which the Mechanism decides, after a preliminary consideration of the appeal, is unduly long.
3. The present Article shall remain in force [for a period of _____ years or] until Bosnia and Herzegovina becomes a party to the European Convention on Human Rights.

ATTACHMENT

5 October 1992
PCSzasz

INTERNATIONAL CONFERENCE ON THE FORMER YUGOSLAVIA

Draft Provision for proposed Bosnia-Herzegovina Constitution

Article X Human Rights Court

1. There shall be established a Human Rights Court operating within the framework of the Mechanism established by the Council of Europe by its Resolution _____ [as it may be amended from time to time]. The Court shall consist of three/four judges appointed by the Presidency in accordance with [the provision of the Constitution providing for high judicial appointments], of which one each shall be from each of the three groups referred to in _____ [and one shall be a person not affiliated with any such group], all of whom shall enjoy tenure in accordance with that provision, and of four/five judges appointed by the _____ of the Council of Europe. The Court shall regulate its own procedures and adopt rules for that purpose, provided that such rules shall allow every party to a proceeding in respect of which an appeal is taken or a question is addressed pursuant to paragraphs 2-4 below, to address the Court, in writing or orally, on the basis of equality.
2. Any party[1] to a proceeding in which another court established under this Constitution has pronounced a judgment that is not subject to appeal to any other such court, for a reason other than the lapse of a time limit for which the moving party is responsible, may appeal such judgment to the Human Rights Court on the basis of any provision of Chapter [human, civil and political rights] or [group or minority rights] of this Constitution, and the decision of the Court on such an appeal shall be final and binding with respect to any matter within its competence.
3. An appeal in accordance with paragraph 2 may also be taken to the Human Rights Court if a proceeding is pending in any other court established under this Constitution for a period which the Court decides, after a preliminary consideration of the appeal, is unduly long.
4. Any [appellate] court established under this Constitution may, at the request of any party to a proceeding before it or on its own motion, address to the Human Rights Court a question arising out of such proceeding and relating to a provision of Chapter [human, civil and political rights] or

---

[1] As here formulated, an appeal can be taken by any party to a proceeding, i.e., not only by the "victim" but also by the government. If this is not desired, this provision would have to be changed to start: "Any person or the official representative of any group recognized pursuant to _____ or an Ombudsman shall have a right to appeal ...", with some minor changes in the rest of the text.

[group or minority rights] of this Constitution, and the response of the Court to such question shall be final and binding.

5. This Article shall remain in force [until Bosnia and Herzegovina becomes a party to the European Convention on Human Rights]/[unless modified by an amendment to the Constitution adopted in accordance with [the special procedure for amending the human rights provisions of the Constitution]], unless the Council of Europe Mechanism referred to in paragraph 1 ceases to be in force in respect of Bosnia and Herzegovina.

INTERNATIONAL CONFERENCE ON THE FORMER YUGOSLAVIA

NOTES OF A MEETING WITH DELEGATION OF BOSNIAN SERBS

Thursday, 8 October 1992, 2–3 p.m.

Attendance:	Mr. Vance	Dr. Karadzic
	Lord Owen	Mr. Buha
	Mr. Ahtisaari	
	Mr. Szasz	

Mr. Vance: First of all, ethnic cleansing is getting worse.

Dr. Karadzic: Need details.

Mr. Vance: We know that yesterday there had been a meeting of the BH Serb Parliament in Banja Luka at which the local administration had come under heavy attack because ethnic cleansing was not going fast enough; that was a totally unacceptable reaction to the Co-Chairmen's visit the previous week. Furthermore, the Muslim leaders who had talked to the Co-Chairmen during that visit had been called to the Serbian party headquarters for questioning; that too was entirely unacceptable. Finally, reports had reached us that in Kator Varos the entire Muslim population had been arrested.

Dr. Karadzic: The radicals, i.e. the extreme rightists, in Parliament were not representative of the whole; it was they who had conducted the attack. My party was more moderate.

Mr. Vance: Did the moderates speak up?

Dr. Karadzic: The majority in Parliament is opposed to the extreme rightists; however, the radicals are getting more and more influential. I guarantee that the Muslim leaders would be protected. In any event, what is happening to the Serbs in Sarajevo is much worse than anything in Banja Luka. The Muslims had just announced that they had killed some 250 Serbs.

Mr. Vance: This cannot justify what is happening in Banja Luka. It was not acceptable to harass those who had spoken to the Co-Chairmen.

Dr. Karadzic: Mr. Vance is right. If something like that should happen again, Dr. Karadzic would replace the local party leader. But his moderates were loosing influence to the radicals.

Mr. Vance: It wasn't apparent that Dr. Karadzic was loosing influence.

Dr. Karadzic: Showed pictures from a local magazine of foreign Muslims holding heads of slain Serbs.

As of midnight, there would be a ceasefire with the Croats.

Vance: How does Dr. Karadzic see the situation?

Dr. Karadzic: If the Muslims should stop fighting in Sarajevo, the Serbs will too. Trade is now flowing between Serbs and Croats. It was a great thing that along 65% (later said 75%) of front the fighting would stop.

Vance: Are negotiations continuing, or have they been put off until tomorrow?

Dr. Karadzic: Don't know.

Mr. Vance: What is situation as to water and electricity in Sarajevo?

Dr. Karadzic: There is neither water nor electricity. The Serbs have never shut off the main power line, but the Muslims have repeatedly shut off subsidiary lines leading to certain districts, principally Serb. His people have never shut off water – as a doctor, he would never allow that.

Lord Owen: You have about two weeks. A War Crimes Tribunal is likely to be established. So much anger has built up in the UN and the EEC, the moderates cannot contain it. While the Conference will not particularly be helped by War Crimes trials, these will come. Similarly, while the imposition of a no-fly zone won't help the Conference, it is now inevitable because of the general frustration with the current situation.

It should be realized that there was a change of mood in Belgrade. Not only Prime Minister Panic, but even President Milosevic. Similarly, in the world community, Croatia was likely to benefit from assistance, will be welcomed to all the international institutions. Serbia, however, will be excluded – and people won't forget what is now happening, not for 20 years. It must be recognized that there is no chance of a BH Serbian Republic ever being accepted. It just won't happen.

However, there were some hopeful signs. If there was an end to hostilities, all sorts of problems could be negotiated.

Meanwhile, however, more enforcement was on the way. There would be a no-fly zone as of Friday.

Dr. Karadzic: What about helicopters carrying wounded?

Lord Owen: They will be permitted if the plan to fly them is first reported to UNPROFOR and the helicopters are then inspected and accompanied by a UN person. These things can be worked out.

Dr. Karadzic: This is not acceptable. It would be a measure against Serbs.

Lord Owen: Majority of the EEC Foreign Ministers are for a War Crimes Tribunal.

What about the reported arrest of Muslims in Kator Varos?

Dr. Karadzic: There is fighting going on around there.

Mr. Vance/Lord Owen: The horror there is unacceptable to the world community.

Dr. Karadzic: The world doesn't quite understand what is going on. Serbia is not supporting the Bosnian Serbs. They would like to get rid of them, but cannot say so.

The European Community shares responsibility for what happened, for everyone knew the consequences of recognizing Bosnia and Herzegovina prematurely. It must not be forgotten that 50 years ago, 750,000 Serbs were killed. Now his party was preparing a White Book on Muslim war crimes; there are already hundreds of names.

Lord Owen: History is not the point – the issue is what is happening at present. Right now there is an opportunity to negotiate.

Dr. Karadzic: I have never committed a war crime. I have publicly condemned those (Serbs) who have committed any; we will try them ourselves.

Lord Owen: What could be done at the military talks?

Dr. Karadzic: Just don't push. This process cannot go too fast. And use no threats – they will not work.

Lord Owen: Neither of the Co-Chairmen want to enforce a no-fly zone, but at this stage the Security Council resolution cannot be stopped. You have until tomorrow to come up with an acceptable proposal to implement such a rule. It might be best for you to put something on this on the table at the joint military meetings in Sarajevo.

Dr. Karadzic: We will never enter Slavonia.

Mr. Vance: You are a key leader. You are now in a position to turn the no-fly rule into something positive – make a positive contribution.

Mr. Ahtisaari: He had talked to Boban. He has sent papers responding to the questionnaires on human rights and on the distribution of governmental powers, but hasn't yet said whether these could be released to the other parties. We are circulating to each party the papers received from the others, with the author's approval.

Lord Owen: Who is the general who should be attending the Sarajevo talks on behalf of the Bosnian Serbs? Who could make the arrangements for a major ceasefire.?

Dr. Karadzic: General Mladic. But, please don't push too fast.

Lord Owen: Both Co-Chairmen or either one of them are prepared to come to the Sarajevo talks if that should be useful.

Dr. Karadzic: Better to wait until there is some progress.

Lord Owen: OK. Please put your proposals for implementation of no-fly rule on table in Sarajevo. These matters can be negotiated.

The negotiations should be carried out intensely, so that the Serbian generals will see that they are leading somewhere.

Dr. Karadzic: We have already announced that we won't fly, except if attacked.

Lord Owen: You must understand that if you should fly on two consecutive days, say on next Monday and Tuesday, then the Security Council will promptly adopt a Chapter 7 resolution. The pressure therefor will become irresistible.

Dr. Karadzic: If Muslims attack, the Serbs must fly.

Lord Owen: That will lead to a Chapter 7 resolution.

Mr. Ahtisaari: It won't be difficult to determine who is co-operating in the negotiations. So, please be cooperative.

Lord Owen: Would be best to discuss the no-fly zone, in the military working group. This won't stop the Friday resolution, but it may prevent a later resolution specifying enforcement.

Also, the Sarajevo cease-fire should be pressed in the military group. Once that is successful, it may spread to other regions.

Dr. Karadzic: What should we be doing in the military working group?

Mr. Vance: Start by settling the water and electricity issues; go on from there.

Mr. Ahtisaari: The repair crews have been fired upon.

Mr. Vance: Professor Koljevic must have a telephone in order to be able to negotiate effectively.

Dr. Karadzic: Will immediately order that we do our best to have electric, water and telephone service restored.

Mr. Ahtisaari: All of the parties are taking too hard a line.

Dr. Karadzic: True. But we have to go slow. We have to get used to each other.

It would help me if the Conference could arrange to have the Serbian "prisoners" in Sarajevo released. We can't do anything unless these people are released.

Vance: First stop the fighting. You should send high level representatives to the military meeting. General Mladic should be sent.

Who are the snipers in Sarajevo?

Dr. Karadzic: The Serbs have no snipers. Those are the "green berets", who are commanded by criminals.

Lord Owen: How long are you staying?

Dr. Karadzic: Until Monday. Would like to meet Boban here.

Mr. Ahtisaari: Boban isn't coming unless we call him specially.

Dr. Karadzic: The Bosnian Serb delegation wishes to be included in the other Conference Working Groups.

Mr. Ahtisaari: The Minorities Working Group does not deal with Bosnia and Herzegovina.

Lord Owen: Presumably you are participating in Mrs. Ogasa's expanded Humanitarian Working Group.

Dr. Karadzic: How about the Economic Issues Working Group?

Lord Owen: That one is not meeting just now.

Dr. Karadzic: Everything would be easier if there were a ceasefire.

Mr. Ahtisaari: Important that the time be used before people start dying in the winter. The political leaders will be blamed.

Lord Owen: Time is running out. The no-fly resolution will be adopted on Monday.

Dr. Karadzic: Please arrange for implementation to be flexible.

Lord Owen: All the necessary flexibility can be arranged through UNPROFOR.

Mr. Vance: It is too late to change the language of the resolution.

Lord Owen: The language does allow sufficient flexibility.

Mr. Vance: Progress on achieving flexibility can be made as time goes on.

Dr. Karadzic: The resolution will cause more fighting.

Lord Owen: Put all these questions on the agenda of the military working group. Also the questions of the frequency, time and place of the meetings. All these matters are properly part of the agenda and can be negotiated there.

PCS, 09/10/92

INTERNATIONAL CONFERENCE ON THE FORMER YUGOSLAVIA

13 October 1992

To: D. Owen
H. Okun
cc: M Ahtisaari

From: P. Szasz

Subject: Recent developments concerning the proposed Council of Europe Mechanism for Resolving Human Rights Disputes in Bosnia and Herzegovina and other Non-Members States.

---

1. In connection with Judge Badinter's visit tomorrow (who has apparently expressed interest in this subject), I am attaching some updating information concerning developments following those reported in my memorandum of the 5th on the negotiations in Strasbourg immediately following Lord Owen's visit to the Council of Europe.
2. Attached are the following papers:
   (a) Draft of a memorandum on "PROTECTION OF HUMAN RIGHTS IN EUROPEAN STATES WHICH ARE NOT YET MEMBERS OF THE COUNCIL OF EUROPE: Creation of a transitional ad hoc judicial mechanism (for possible first use in favour of Bosnia-Herzegovina)", which was circulated by the C/E Secretariat to the Ambassadors Permanent Representatives of Member Countries on 8 October.
   (b) "Draft Provision for proposed Bosnia-Herzegovina Constitution" on a "Human Rights Court" that I sent to the C/E Secretariat on 6 October, after receiving the above mentioned draft memorandum.
   (c) Mr. Furrer's account of the meeting of Ambassadors of C/E Member Countries on 8 October.
3. As appears from (c), the C.E consideration of this matter is well on track, and the mechanism that the Council is likely to adopt will be flexible enough to accommodate any reasonable variant of our current thinking concerning a BiH Human Rights Court.

ATTACHMENT

PROTECTION OF HUMAN RIGHTS IN EUROPEAN STATES WHICH ARE NOT YET MEMBERS OF THE COUNCIL OF EUROPE

Creation of a transitional ad hoc judicial mechanism (for possible first use in favour of Bosnia-Herzegovina)

INTRODUCTION

1. In his address to the Parliamentary Assembly on 3 October 1992, Lord Owen, Co-Chairman of the International Conference on the Former Yugoslavia (ICFY), made a proposal for Council of Europe involvement in a scheme for judicial protection of human rights under a future Constitution for Bosnia-Herzegovina (text attached).
2. This proposal is to be understood on the background of discussions in the context of the CSCE (Conference on the Human Dimension of the CSCE held in Moscow in autumn 1991 in particular) on whether Council of Europe mechanisms and control procedures in the human rights field could be put at the disposal of European States which are not yet members of the Council of Europe. In this context reference was made to the bodies and procedures established under the European Convention of Human Rights, whilst recognising that this Convention itself was open to accession by Council of Europe Member States only and that this should not be changed, for institutional and legal as well as political reasons.
3. The Parliamentary Assembly (Recommendation 1183(1992)) has indicated an interest in the approach underlying such suggestions, referring in particular to the possibility of making use of the experience and the standing of Members of the European Court and Commission for the purpose of providing European non member countries which so wish with appropriate international control on their human rights performance. It was stressed in this context that such schemes should be of a transitional character, the aim being that all European countries sooneer or later be integrated into the Council of Europe and be fully bound by the European Convention of Human Rights control mechanism.
4. Lord Owen's proposal refers to the question of the future Constitution of Bosnia-Herzegovina, but it is understood that the scheme proposed should be of a general nature applicable to other possible subscribing States, with the proviso that each interested State implement the proposal, taking into account specific features required by the situation and conditions prevailing in that country and agreed to by both sides. This would in particular apply to the appointment of members of the body by each State concerned.

A GENERAL SCHEME TO BE ESTABLISHED BY THE COUNCIL OF EUROPE

5. The general feature for the scheme would consist of the setting up of a judicial control mechanism for each country which so wished

("subscribing State") composed of judges of the European Court of Human Rights, members of the European Commission of Human Rights as well as independent persons coming from and appointed by the subscribing State. The body would be operational as soon as the scheme would have been accepted by a given subscribing State, with a composition of the body as agreed to with that State. In that composition it would have jurisdiction over all cases which would be referred to it under the agreement making the scheme operational for that State.

6. The scope of jurisdiction would have to be determined for each subscribing State but it should comprise at least the right of individual application and reference to the normative contents of the European Convention of Human Rights and the case law developed under it as the applicable law.
7. Additional elements of jurisdiction could be added dependent on the agreement with the subscribing State, i.e. the right of groups of individuals or non governmental organisations to bring applications before the body, reference to legal instruments other than the European Convention of Human Rights, etc…

The decisions of the body should normally be recognised as compulsory with a promise of execution within the State concerned. However, if the subscribing State so prefers, these decisions could take the form of advisory opinions.

PARTICULARITIES FOR THE CASE OF BOSNIA-HERZEGOVINA

8. According to Lord Owen's proposal for Bosnia-Herzegovina, the following particularities may have to be taken into consideration:

   - The jurisdiction to be established would be based, as far as Bosnia-Herzegovina is concerned, on specific provisions to be inserted in the Constitution of Bosnia-Herzegovina. Under the relevant constitutional provisions, human rights and fundamental freedoms to be guaranteed would be expressly listed, as would also international human rights instruments, including the European Convention of Human Rights. These instruments would be declared directly applicable in the internal legal order of the country, so that they could be invoked by parties in internal court proceedings and applied by the courts in their decisions. In addition, these constitutional provisions would provide for the right of application to the European body being established in agreement with the Council of Europe, with the Government being obliged to subscribe to the Council's scheme.
     - For Bosnia-Herzegovina, the judicial body could be composed of two judges of the European Court, two members of the European Commission of Human Rights, and three members to be appointed by Bosnia-Herzegovina.
   - The body would have the right to decide on the admissibility as well as on the merits of the applications received. It would make findings of facts and declare the law by reference to the European Convention of Human Rights and the Strasbourg case law, the UN Covenants on Human Rights and other international legal instruments relating to human rights that may be applicable in Bosnia-Herzegovina.

- The findings of the body would be compulsory for Bosnia-Herzegovina.

COUNCIL OF EUROPE ACTION

9. As stated above, the Council of Europe's response to such suggestions, if it were to be positive, might be in two stages:
   1. The creation of the general scheme to be offered to European non member countries for implementation on the basis of specific agreements to be concluded with each of those States which might wish to submit themselves to the scheme.
   2. Negotiations and agreement with Bosnia-Herzegovina for the implementation of the scheme.

10. As regards the creation of the general scheme, it is suggested that this could be established by a Resolution of the Committee of Ministers, to be adopted after contacts and with the consent of both the European Court and the European Commission of Human Rights. Such a Resolution would contain provisions for the creation of a special judicial control body for interested European non member countries, the composition of which would comprise members of the Court and Commission (to be appointed by these organs under specific rules to be adopted for that purpose) and for each subscribing State, a member or members appointed by that State, and which would have jurisdiction applying inter alia the substantive law of the European Convention of Human Rights.
11. As regards Bosnia-Herzegovina, the use of the scheme would have to be negotiated with the representatives of the parties in that country. Under the present circumstances, these representatives meet within the framework of the International Conference on the Former Yugoslavia (ICFY). The Co-Chairmen of the Conference, as indicated by Lord Owen, are prepared to introduce the possibility of making use of the Council of Europe scheme into the preparations of the future Constitution of Bosnia-Herzegovina. In due course they might wish to appeal to the Council of Europe for expert advice on this. However, the main question at present is for them to know whether or not the Council of Europe is prepared to create such a scheme.

...

12. In the light of the above, the Committee of Ministers is invited to give urgent consideration to the proposal to create a scheme for judicial control of human rights in European countries which are not yet members of the Council of Europe. The urgency of this proposal lies in the fact that such a scheme might be put to use immediately within the framework of a future Constitution of Bosnia-Herzegovina. The Geneva Conference, for obvious reasons, is urging for rapid progress in the talks among the parties in Bosnia-Herzegovina for the preparation and adoption of a new Constitution for that country. For reasons of timing of these talks, a positive signal in response to Lord Owen's proposal would have to come out of the Ministerial Session of the Committee of Ministers on 5 November 1992.

ATTACHMENT

5 October 1992
PCSzasz

INTERNATIONAL CONFERENCE ON THE FORMER YUGOSLAVIA

Draft Provision for proposed Bosnia-Herzegovina Constitution

Article X Human Rights Court

1. There shall be established a Human Rights Court operating within the framework of the Mechanism established by the Council of Europe by its Resolution _____ [as it may be amended from time to time]. The Court shall consist of three/four judges appointed by the Presidency in accordance with [the provision of the Constitution providing for high judicial appointments], of which one each shall be from each of the three groups referred to in _____ [and one shall be a person not affiliated with any such group], all of whom shall enjoy tenure in accordance with that provision, and of four/five judges appointed by the _____ of the Council of Europe. The Court shall regulate its own procedures and adopt rules for that purpose, provided that such rules shall allow every party to a proceeding in respect of which an appeal is taken or a question is addressed pursuant to paragraphs 2-4 below, to address the Court, in writing or orally, on the basis of equality.
2. Any party[1] to a proceeding in which another court established under this Constitution has pronounced a judgment that is not subject to appeal to any other such court, for a reason other than the lapse of a time limit for which the moving party is responsible, may appeal such judgment to the Human Rights Court on the basis of any provision of Chapter [human, civil and political rights] or [group or minority rights] of this Constitution, and the decision of the Court on such an appeal shall be final and binding with respect to any matter within its competence.
3. An appeal in accordance with paragraph 2 may also be taken to the Human Rights Court if a proceeding is pending in any other court established under this Constitution for a period which the Court decides, after a preliminary consideration of the appeal, is unduly long.
4. Any [appellate] court established under this Constitution may, at the request of any party to a proceeding before it or on its own motion, address to the Human Rights Court a question arising out of such proceeding and relating to a provision of Chapter [human, civil and political rights] or

[1] As here formulated, an appeal can be taken by any party to a proceeding, i.e., not only by the "victim" but also by the government. If this is not desired, this provision would have to be changed to start: "Any person or the official representative of any group recognized pursuant to _____ or an Ombudsman shall have a right to appeal …", with some minor changes in the rest of the text.

[group or minority rights] of this Constitution, and the response of the Court to such question shall be final and binding.

5. This Article shall remain in force [until Bosnia and Herzegovina becomes a party to the European Convention on Human Rights]/[unless modified by an amendment to the Constitution adopted in accordance with [the special procedure for amending the human rights provisions of the Constitution]], unless the Council of Europe Mechanism referred to in paragraph 1 ceases to be in force in respect of Bosnia and Herzegovina.

ATTACHMENT

COUNCIL OF EUROPE

SECRETARIAT GENERAL

Strasbourg, 9 October 1992

Dear Mr Szasz,

Thank you very much for your fax of 6 October which was very useful for our further discussions within the Secretariat and with the Ambassadors of our Member countries.

I am now in a position to inform you that the Ambassadors have generally given a positive response to the initiative and to the proposal to take the preparation of the Council of Europe scheme at hand without delay. They also were generally favourable to the approach we have been advocating, that is the establishment by the Committee of Ministers of the judicial mechanism and the attempt to make it operational for Bosnia-Herzegovina under provisions of the Constitution of the country.

On the basis of such favourable approach, we are now preparing, in contact with the Ambassadors, draft decisions to be adopted by the Committee of Ministers at Ministerial level on 5 November next in Strasbourg.

These decisions will hopefully confirm the willingness of the Committee to establish the scheme as soon as necessary for an early implementation in respect of Bosnia-Herzegovina. In addition, the Ministers would give instructions to the Secretariat and the Ambassadors to prepare, before the end of 1993, texts embodying the Council of Europe's Resolution, in contact with the bodies of the Human Rights Convention.

There was an understanding that the scheme to be adopted by the Council of Europe should be in very general terms, leaving details to be sorted out and agreed to in discussions with each country concerned, starting with Bosnia-Herzegovina, so as to allow specific features to be worked out and agreed to for that country.

The additional information you have given us in your fax of 6 October is perfectly in line with this approach.

Mr Paul C. SZASZ
Legal Adviser
ICFY
Palais des Nations
Room A-650
CH - 1211 GENEVA

At the beginning of next week we shall prepare draft preliminary decisions to be submitted to the Committee of Ministers on 5 November. Of course, I will keep you informed of our drafting.

We are looking forward to further information on progress you will be able to make in Geneva. As you know we are also ready to come to Geneva as soon as you feel it necessary or useful.

Concerning Mrs Lalumière visit to Geneva, you are certainly informed of the difficulties we have met in choosing an appropriate date. We are in contact with Mr Ludlow. As far as Mrs Lalumière is concerned, we have indicated the following possible dates: 20, 21, 22, 26 or 27 (morning) October, hoping that one of those would allow Mrs Lalumière to meet Mr Cyrus Vance and possibly again Lord Owen or at least Ambassador Peter Hall (and yourself of course).

Please find herewith the text of Recommendation 1183(1992) of the Parliamentary Assembly.

Yours sincerely

Hans-Peter Furrer
Director of Political Affairs

ICFY

NOTE TO THE CO-CHAIRMEN

HIGHLIGHTS OF A PRESS CONFERENCE BY MR. MAZOWIECKI, SPECIAL RAPPORTEUR OF THE UNITED NATIONS COMMISSION ON HUMAN RIGHTS

Friday, October 23, 1992, 11.15–12.25

1. The Human Rights situation in the area of the former Yugoslavia had not improved since his last visit to the area. It had even deteriorated in Bosnia and Herzegovina.
2. The objectives and policies of ethnic cleansing had already been achieved. There had been "dramatic incidents" of gross violations of human rights.
3. He hoped that the three sides to the conflict in Bosnia and Herzegovina would respect their agreement to empty all camps by October 31. During the mission he had spoken with Mr. Boban who had promised to free all detainees held by his side. The crucial question was where the people should go to. He reiterated his appeal to European countries: "It would be a shameful disgrace for all Europe if we would not be able to solve this issue."
4. During his visit he had learned about a village (Vecik) where 70 Muslim families had been encircled by Serbs. He had contacted Dr. Karadzic and had asked him to do his best to save these people. He appealed again that they should not be killed.
5. He had seen the route used for humanitarian convoys – "Salvation road" – and had witnessed the devotion of the truck drivers on humanitarian convoys. In all probability the road will be closed in two weeks.
6. The conditions of Muslim refugees in Travnik were very difficult.
7. He had visited Trnopolje camp: "There exists some misunderstanding, even in UNHCR. It has been said that the camp was empty and new people are coming in. The truth is different." He has a full list of people in the camp. He showed a video cassette of conditions in the camp during his visit. He stated: "I am convinced these people will not survive the Fall in these conditions, much less the winter".

   He replied to a question about this camp as follows: "At present it is a refugee centre. There is a staff trying to take care of the people. These people are afraid of the staff. The village is surrounded by burnt-out houses. The people are afraid that as soon as they leave they will lose their lives".
8. He had visited a refugee centre for Serbs who had fled to Banja Luka. They are also in a difficult situation.
9. The difference between people held in Serb camps and those held in Muslim camps was striking.
10. The situation in Kosovo, Sandzak and Vojvadina was very difficult: "In Pristina we analysed the situation of Kosovo; also the legal aspects and the

problem of schools. All these issues will be mentioned in my report. I do believe there is a great deal of goodwill on the Albanian side. I hope the steps started by Prime Minister Panic will be continued.

11. He and Dr. Snow had been able to visit places where war crimes appear to have been committed. He read out a statement that Dr. Snow had made on Thursday, October 22, about a massacre in the Vukovar area where many people had been killed in November 1991. He had asked the United Nations Secretary-General and UNPROFOR to provide security around the area so as to protect evidence of alleged war crimes from being tampered with: "I do believe that further investigations should be carried out by the Security Council Committee. It is very important that all war crimes committed should be investigated."
12. The most important thing was to help the living. In Sarajevo he had seen that the destruction was "bigger and bigger". Various people had asked him why the shelling had not stopped, notwithstanding the accords reached in London and Geneva: "These people are losing hope in the international efforts."
13. In response to a question about whether the measures that had been agreed upon in Geneva were being implemented, he replied: "Ethnic cleansing is continuing. Sarajevo is being shelled. UNPROFOR is still not in Banja Luka. Many competent observers informed me that ethnic cleansing has been intensified in Banja Luka in order to achieve their objectives before the deployment of UNPROFOR. It does not say anything about the value of the efforts Mr. Vance and Lord Owen are making here but it does say something about the willingness of the parties to implement what they have agreed to. It also says something about the ineffectiveness of the international community in implementing its decisions."
14. His report will be published on Tuesday, October 27. He may meet the press on that day. His report will contain recommendations concerning the situation in the camps and humanitarian aid corridors.

BGR
October 23, 1992

Circulation:

Mr. Vance
Lord Owen
Ambassador Okun
Ambassador Hall
Mr. Ahtisaari
Ambassador Ahrens
Mrs. Ogata
Fred Eckhard

ICFY

STATEMENT MADE BY MRS. OGATA ON 27 OCTOBER 1992 (as delivered)

Distinguished Delegates of the Steering Committee,

As you are all aware, the humanitarian situation in the former Yugoslavia is dramatic. I estimate that within the region of the former Yugoslavia alone some 3 million people - displaced persons, refugees and people in besieged cities and regions - are directly affected by the crisis and are to a large extent dependent on external assistance for their survival. The main theatre of compelled displacement, as a result of fighting, ethnic cleansing and lack of means for survival, continues to be the Republic of Bosnia and Herzegovina. With the onset of winter, the plight of the civilian population, whether already displaced or not yet, is becoming harsher every day.

It is for this reason that in my capacity as Chairperson of the Working Group on Humanitarian Issues I have concentrated on the situation in Bosnia and Herzegovina. There the needs are undoubtedly the highest and the most urgent, and by trying to improve the situation in humanitarian terms, perhaps less people would be compelled to look for safety and assistance in the already over-burdened adjacent States, and beyond.

On 18 and 19 September I met with the Bosnian parties, here in Geneva, and obtained written assurances for the safe resumption of the vital airlift to Sarajevo (which at that time had been suspended due to the shooting down of the Italian aircraft on 3 September), for the safe passage of road convoys, for the release and safe transit of detainees, and for the unhindered supply of basic necessities such as water and electricity to besieged cities, in particular Sarajevo.

Since the September meeting the airlift could be resumed, thanks also to the progress made in Mr Berasategui's Working Group on Confidence and Security Building Measures. Furthermore, UNHCR obtained the names of local authorities responsible for the safe passage of road convoys. Some 1670 detainees (from Trnopolje and Bileca) regained freedom, after obtaining safe passage to Croatia and Montenegro respectively, where they are now temporarily under UNHCR's care.

On 15 and 16 October I convened a second meeting with the Bosnian parties to review the implementation of the September commitments, and to discuss the ever increasing needs of the civilian population and the ways to reach them in the most efficient and safest manner. I confronted the parties with the fact that harassment at checkpoints and other obstacles continue to hamper UNHCR's safe humanitarian access through road convoys. They re-confirmed their commitment to full collaboration in ensuring the safe and unhindered passage of relief convoys. As not all parties were participating in the important negotiations of the Mixed Military Working Group, dealing among other things with the restoration of water and electricity to Sarajevo, I urged them to do so.

In the presence of the ICRC, I reminded the parties of their commitment under the London Programme of Action on Humanitarian Issues to proceed unconditionally with the release of detainees, the majority of whom continue to be in detention. The ICRC inter alia complained to the Serbian side that it had not yet obtained access to all places of detention, whereas the Bosnian authorities had not yet notified all detainees. Positive, however, is the imminent release of some 5000 prisoners from ten different locations. The biggest group consists of 3700 persons of the Muslim faith held in the Manjaca camp. As to their destination upon release, we discussed the need to respect the wishes of this most vulnerable category of people, in accordance with the London agreements.

It is rather ambiguous and unfortunate, that the co-operation of third states in temporarily receiving the detainees has become a crucial factor in implementing their release. As Chairperson of the Working Group on Humanitarian Issues and as UN High Commissioner for Refugees, I count on the understanding of the international community to offer temporary protection to these people. Yesterday the United States have generously offered to accept 1000 persons with their families, bringing the total of secured places outside the region to 2100. However, there are at this point in time some 5370 persons in need of placement. They are those waiting in Karlovac in Croatia, in Sutomore in Montenegro, and - most pressing - the 3700 persons mentioned earlier, who are still suffering in detention in the Manjaca camp in Bosnia. There is therefore a serious shortfall of 3270 places.

You should rest assured that I shall continue to expose the persistent practice of ethnic cleansing, especially in North-West Bosnia. During both the September and October meetings I have reminded all parties of their London commitments to respect international humanitarian law and human rights. The freedom of movement is an important human right, which should be respected on all sides, but it should not be used to facilitate the abhorrent practice of ethnic cleansing, as part of a cruel strategy to compartimentalise Bosnia and Herzegovina. In my Working Group, and elsewhere, I shall continue to insist on the right to stay, in conditions of security, and on the responsibility of everyone to ensure respect for this right. I have asked the Serbian side (Dr Karadzic) in particular to take measures to prevent the outbreak of ethnic cleansing in Banja Luka town, where the harassment of non-Serbs has thus far been less violent than in many surrounding towns and villages.

Despite the commitments of the parties the situation on the ground remains critical. The very day I talked to the parties here in Geneva, a UNHCR convoy on its way to Sarajevo was shelled near Mostar. Last week fighting broke out between the Croatian side and governmental forces in Central-Bosnia, a region which accomodates under very difficult conditions a large and ever rising number of displaced persons. As a result I have been compelled to suspend all land deliveries, from Split to Sarajevo and Central Bosnia, whereas my staff in Vitez had to be evacuated.

Yet, I do not want to despair. I believe that the discussions in my Working Group do serve a purpose. First, they lend support to the practical arrangements which necessarily have to be worked out on the ground, for instance regarding the priorities of assistance, the safe passage of road convoys and the modalities of the release of detainees. Second, these discussions serve to constantly remind the parties of their commitments, to respect the London agreements and to respect humanitarian law and human rights. In so doing, in insisting on the observance of the London accords, I hope that my Working Group is of service to the efforts of the Co-Chairmen and of Mr Ahtissaari to find a peaceful solution for Bosnia and Herzegovina.

I therefore intend to pursue these discussions, through periodic meetings. The next one would probably be more at the humanitarian expert level, and would hopefully permit to evaluate the expansion of UNHCR's road convoys after the deployment of the additional UNPROFOR troops. As you know, we need these troops fast. We need the men, the technical assistance of logisticians and of engineers, and we badly need the the Belgian and Dutch trucks. I also hope that the expanded presence of UNPROFOR can help to contain the appalling human rights abuses, as well as the outbreak of new hostilities. I am deeply worried about the increasing animosity between the Croatian side and governmental forces.

I am not paying exclusive attention to Bosnia and Herzegovina. The meeting of 9 October 1992, which I convened in my capacity as Chairperson of the Working Group on Humanitarian Issues, united all countries of the former Yugoslavia, donor countries and other interested States as well as international agencies. It served to re-examine the various aspects of the humanitarian crisis in the whole region, to highlight the rising needs, and to request support for adequate responses. During that meeting I emphasized that admission to safety and assistance for survival should be more than ever our priorities. With the virtual closure of some international borders and given the risks involved in fleeing inside Bosnia, the admission to safety of those fleeing from war and persecution is seriously at stake.

In the coming weeks I intend to work also on the Quadripartite Mechanism relating to the return of displaced persons on all sides to the UNPA's. As you are aware, the establishment of this Mechanism was proposed by President Cosic and President Tudjman in their Joint Declaration of 30 September. The return of the displaced persons is both a humanitarian and a political endeavour. I see it as an opportunity to "de-cleanse the ethnic cleansing". But it should be viewed also in the overall context of a political settlement between the Serbian population of the UNPA's and the Croatian government. Progress on the issue could moreover further advance relations between Zagreb and Belgrade.

It is therefore important to proceed with this Mechanism, which the Co-Chairmen have asked me to chair. I have asked Ambassador Jonathan Moore to serve as my Special Representative for the Quadripartite Mechanism. It should however be noted that according to UNPROFOR security conditions in the UNPA's do not yet permit the return of non-Serbs in conditions of safety. In fact, recent pressure on the Croatian side has heightened tensions in the UNPA's, thereby hampering the prospects for return.

Let me end this summary by expressing my support for the efforts of the entire International Conference. There is no peace yet, but there have been notable achievements, which some weeks ago were unthinkable.

I thank you for your attention.
Geneva, 27.10.92

INTERNATIONAL CONFERENCE
ON THE FORMER YUGOSLAVIA

Palais des Nations, 1211 Geneva 10

Geert Ahrens Geneva, 27 October 1992

Ethnic and National Communities and Minorities Working Group

1. Under the new London arrangements, the Ethnic and National Communities and Minorities Working Group started its rather wide spread work with a Plenum on September 15, 1992 in which Government delegations from Slovenia, Croatia, Bosnia-Hercegovina, and Macedonia participated. The delegation from Belgrade, comprising Federal, Serbian and Montenegrin Government representatives as well as representatives from Knin did not attend, obviously for technical reasons. In the Plenum all those present reconfirmed their commitment to the Conference principles, particularly to Chapter Two of the Treaty Provisions for the Convention adopted in The Hague. During the same week there were also talks in Geneva with Ethnic and National Communities and Minorities, namely, Albanians from Kosovo, Albanians from Macedonia, Muslims from Serbia, Muslims and Albanians from Montenegro, Hungarians from Vojvodina, Croats from Vojvodina, and Serbs from Croatia. These talks showed, probably with the exception of Macedonia, pictures of continuous and at places dangerous ethnic conflicts that were to be taken up urgently with the Governments concerned. There will be another Working Group Plenum on 2 November in Geneva.

   In order to discuss complaints and to hear the opinion of the Belgrade Government on the subject of the Working Group on 15 September, a Working Group delegation travelled to Belgrade in the following week, 22–24 September. Talks with Federal Ministers showed a general readiness to address critical issues, but also a certain hesitation to accept Conference mediation. Moreover, there has so far not been a clear commitment of the Belgrade Governments, the Federal or the Serbian, to all of Chapter Two of the Treaty Provisions for the Convention. I may remind you that originally President Milosevic was the only of the six Republican Presidents not to accept the Special Status Provisions contained in c) of Chapter Two.
2. The Sub-Group on Macedonia held two meetings between Government representatives and Albanians, in Geneva on 17 September, and in Skopje on 15 October. The very intensive work that had been done in the summer of 1992 was continued. Although some further progress could be achieved, the overall situation of the Republic (economic blockade, as the Government put it, non-recognition, and as a consequence, upsurge of nationalism) – makes it increasingly difficult for the moderate Government to compromise on ethnic questions. A further meeting of the Sub-Group will be held here in Geneva next week. In my opinion, everything has to be done to uphold the so far positive internal development in Macedonia which is in real danger.

3. Sub-Groups on Vojvodina and on Sandzak have not yet been able to start trilateral talks due to some hesitation in Belgrade. There is, however, some reason for hope that this will change soon. The corresponding Sub-Group had talks on Vojvodina in Geneva, Belgrade, and Subotica which was visited on 24 September and where both Hungarians and Croatians were met.
   In the overall situation of the Vojvodina Hungarians there seems not to have been further deterioration, whereas the Croats in Vojvodina are under severe pressure. The situation in Sandzak, which is related to the Bosnian war, is alarming. Large numbers of Muslims have already left. Hopefully, the presence of CSCE observers there will help to defuse the tense situation on the ground which is a serious obstacle to meaningful dialogue.
4. On the Serbs in Croatia, the Working Group had a talk with Mr. Goran Hadzic – in quotation marks – President of the Republic of Krajina, and several meetings with Croatian representatives. In Belgrade on 25 September, Mr. Hadzic said he was quite prepared for talks on human rights, economic and communication issues, but not on any form of Serbian autonomy inside Croatia. The Krajina would rather resort to renewed warfare than become a part of Croatia again. It was not possible so far to convince Mr. Hadzic or any other Knin representative that a solution has to be found on the basis of the London Principles. At a forthcoming Working Group visit to Zagreb, preliminary talks with UNPROFOR and UNHCR on how to proceed and cooperate on the Krajina problem, which have taken place, will be continued. The continuation of contacts with both Croatian and Serbian politicians is envisaged.
5. The most intensive work was done in the Special Group on Kosovo. The basic approach agreed to by both sides is to try a pragmatic breakthrough in one important sector - the Albanians chose education - in order to improve the political atmosphere for talks on more fundamental issues where positions are at present irreconcilable. After difficult and tedious preparations, in which the release of the Chairman of the Albanian Teachers Association from prison could be achieved, the first Conference sponsored talks between the Federal and the Serbian Governments from Belgrade on one side and Albanian representatives from Kosovo on the other took place. In these meetings the Special Group was reinforced by Ambassador Peter Hall, as direct representative of the two Co-Chairmen. On 14 October, all parties agreed to a statement which read:

   > "1. Representatives of the Government of the FRY and Serbia led by the Federal Minister of Education, Mr. Ivic, and representatives of the Albanians met in Pristina on 13/14 October with the participation of the Geneva Conference Special Group on Kosovo, under the Chairmanship of Ambassador Ahrens. A representative of the CSCE mission was also present.
   >
   > 2. After detailed discussion of the problems of education in the Albanian language, the participants agreed that the present situation must be changed. They further agreed on the urgent desirability of

the return to normal working conditions for schools and other educational institutions.

3. It was agreed that, to achieve this, it would be necessary to adopt a pragmatic approach requiring urgent resolution, without prejudice to the positions of the parties on broader political issues.

4. The Albanian representatives agreed to provide a list of schools and other educational institutions to be covered by the measures mentioned in (2); as well as a list of teaching plans and programmes.

5. The Group agreed to meet again in Belgrade on 22 October. At that meeting discussions will be held on all the issues mentioned above and on the equal working status of teaching and educational personnel with the aim of reaching the necessary decisions for immediate action."

These talks were indeed continued accordingly on 22 October in Belgrade, after meetings of the Working Group Chairman and Ambassador Hall with both President Cosic and Mr. Rugova. The participants reaffirmed their commitment to the necessity of changing the existing situation in the field of education, and the urgent need for a return to normal conditions in schools and other educational institutions in Kosovo, as set out in their statement of 14 October. They agreed that this commitment refers to all four levels of education: pre-school, elementary school, secondary school, and higher education. On Albanian insistence, there was agreement that all problems related to education in Albanian at all levels are related and must be treated as a whole. The Serbian and Federal representatives made plain the material and financial constraints affecting their areas of responsibility. Within those constraints, there will be no discrimination as between the support which they will provide for instruction in both the Albanian and the Serbian languages. However, no agreement could be reached so far on conditions under which school buildings should be opened, teachers should be reinstated and entrance examinations should be handled. The Group chose, therefore, not to publish a second statement this time and to resume work after the visit of the two Co-Chairmen to Belgrade and Pristina next week. What the Italian delegate said about Albanian participation in the forthcoming elections is to be supported. On the other hand, it must be seen that it will be extremely difficult for any Albanian politician to agree to this as long as not a single iota has changed on the ground.

6. The Federal Government in Belgrade and other authorities and groups in former Yugoslavia complain about an exaggerated number of foreign mediators belonging to different organizations or countries. This is indeed a problem. The Working Group did its best to come to a proper coordination with the CSCE efforts in the former Yugoslavia. A representative of the CSCE participated in both of the Kosovo talks, in Pristina on 13 October and in Belgrade on 22 October. On 21 October there was also a conversation with the leader of the CSCE mission in Belgrade, Ambassador

Boegh. The activities of the CSCE observers on the ground are a most welcome supplement to the negotiating endeavours of the Yugoslavia Conference. The respective mandates should, taking account of a clear division of labor, be clear. As far as the mission of former Polish Prime Minister Mazowiecki is concerned, a close personal contact between the Working Group Chairman and Mr. Mazowiecki's main assistant could be established which should provide for the necessary co-ordination. Generally speaking, it is absolutely necessary that in the interest of an overall solution to former Yugoslavia's problems all the mediators show goodwill and responsibility in their dealings with respect to coordination.

ICFY

NOTE ON THE HUMAN RIGHTS COMMITTEE'S EXAMINATION OF A REPORT FROM THE GOVERNMENT OF CROATIA

November 4, 1992, 10.00 to 13.00

The report was introduced by Mr. Simac, Assistant Minister for Foreign Affairs. He was assisted by two professors. In his introductory remarks, Mr. Simac highlighted the following points:

- The recent adoption of a new constitution
- The adoption of a law on minorities
- The establishment of an office of ethnic relations
- Croatia's formal indication of acceptance to be bound by the International Covenant on Civil and Political Rights

The questions asked by members of the Committee touched upon the following points:

- The duties of Croatia to respect human rights even during a situation of conflict.
- Preventive measures that the Government had taken to avert violations of human rights.
- Whether there were detention camps in Croatia.
- Whether ethnic cleansing had taken place in Croatia.
- The behaviour of Croatian forces in Bosnia and Herzegovina.
- The existence and numbers of minorities in Croatia.
- The role of the office for ethnic relations.

The Croatian representatives answered these questions by saying that the Government was committed to respecting human rights; some violations had taken place but they were not the result of official policy. Rather excesses had been committed by individuals. The delegation provided figures of persons arrested and charged for breaches of human rights and humanitarian law. More than 1,400 persons had been charged with armed insurrection. 1,880 persons had been charged with war crimes. 412 persons had been charged for crimes against civilian populations. More than 50 persons had been charged with genocide. 423 judgments had been delivered by the courts, of which there had been convictions in 91 per cent of the cases.

On homes destroyed during the conflict, the delegation gave a figure of 5,937 with the following breakdown: 4,014 Serbs; 1,067 Croats; 115 others.

There was some discussion about the role of the Constitutional Court. The delegation was asked whether it envisaged the establishment of a Human Rights Court. Members of the Committee showed particular interest in the protection of minorities. The delegation stated that it expected to host a CSCE seminar on human rights, in May 1993, which would be devoted to an examination of the experiences of countries in dealing with minority situations.

The delegation came across as reasonable and competent. However, the facts cited by the Members of the Committee seemed to leave little doubt that ethnic cleansing had taken place in Croatia and that there were detention centres in the country about which the Government had not been forthcoming.

B.G.Ramcharan
November 4, 1992
ICFY/0069BR

c.c. Mr. Vance
Lord Owen
Ambassador Okun
Ambassador Hall
Mr. Ahtisaari
Mr. Szasz
Fred Eckhard

ICFY

NOTE TO THE CO-CHAIRMEN

THE HUMAN RIGHTS COMMITTEE'S EXAMINATION OF A REPORT FROM THE FEDERAL REPUBLIC OF YUGOSLAVIA (Serbia/Montenegro)

This note summarizes the Human Rights Committee's examination of a report submitted by the FRY.

The Government delegation was led by the Deputy Minister for Human Rights and Minority Affairs, Professor Obradovic. He was substantively very impressive and his tone was reasonable and constructive. His introductory remarks, and the written report he presented, sought to convey the following messages:

- The current Government in the FRY, unlike its predecessor, was doing its utmost to promote respect for human rights.
- Within the territory of the FRY, there had been some excesses but the Government had taken measures to deal with them.
- Not withstanding the Government's efforts to promote human rights, difficulties arose in the implementation of new laws and policies because officials either misunderstood them or old attitudes persisted.
- There were no detention camps in the FRY although there were a few prisoners of war still to be exchanged following the conflict in Croatia.
- There was no policy of ethnic cleansing in the FRY.

The members of the Human Rights Committee were severe in their questions and comments. They thought that it was rather naive and extraordinary of the Government to discuss only the situation in the FRY and not in places where the FRY obviously had an impact and a role, particularly in Bosnia and Herzegovina. The Members of the Committee insisted that the international responsibility of the FRY was engaged in Bosnia and Herzegovina because of the role of the Yugoslav army, the role of Serbian leaders, and the role of other agents whose actions were attributable to the Government. If there is one thing that the Human Rights Committee did in its examination of the report of the FRY, it was to establish in an authoritative form, and with impeccable reasoning, that the Federal Republic of Yugoslavia could not evade international responsibility for events taking place in Bosnia and Herzegovina.

The Members of the Committee were quite caustic in the terms they used to characterize what was taking place in Bosnia and Herzegovina: Genocide, holocaust, unbelievable horrors, atrocious crimes against humanity. The members told the representative of the FRY bluntly that they found it hard to believe that the Government could come before the Committee and pretend that these events were not taking place.

In his reply, Professor Obradovic tried in vain to explain that the written report and his comments had sought to deal with areas under the jurisdiction of the FRY. To this the Members of the Committee riposted that large parts of Bosnia and Herzegovina were under the functional control of agents of FRY.

Professor Obradovic did admit that there were elements in the FRY that had secret links with Serb elements in Bosnia and Herzegovina and he was indirectly asking for understanding on this point. He sought to convey the message that the Government of the Federal Republic was trying its best to deal with a tricky political situation. The Members of the Human Rights Committee were uncompromising in reacting to this. They stated bluntly that the Government of the Federal Republic seemed to be an outward shell, with real power lying with the Governments of Serbia and Montenegro. They expressed some frustration that the Government of the Federal Republic could not establish its authority over the Governments of Serbia and Montenegro.

In the end the Members of the Committee asked Professor Obradovic to report to Belgrade the strength of feelings of the Human Rights Committee. He promised to do so.

From the Human Rights Committee's examination of the reports of Bosnia and Herzegovina, Croatia and the FRY, one could offer the following assessments:

(a) In all three instances the process was valuable. It recorded the international community's concerns over specific human rights problems.
(b) It registered the point clearly that each government was responsible for taking measures to assure protection for human rights in areas under its control. Each government was left in little doubt that it was expected to establish arrangements to prevent violations of human rights and to deal effectively with excesses that took place.
(c) The need for the governments, especially Croatia and Bosnia and Herzegovina, to co-operate with the ICRC came across strongly.
(d) The reports on human rights issued by the CSCE, Mr. Mazowiecki, and Amnesty International, were used repeatedly as sources of information in putting questions to the governments. They served a very useful purpose. The Co-Chairmen may well wish to consider how they could enhance co-operation with Mr. Mazowiecki.
(e) The Human Rights Committee's examination of the report of the Federal Republic of Yugoslavia, has laid down the normative benchmarks on issues such as ethnic cleansing, criminal responsibility for gross violations of human rights, and international responsibility for events taking place in Bosnia and Herzegovina. It confirms that the Co-Chairmen of the International Conference were absolutely correct in taking positions of principle about events taking place in Bosnia and Herzegovina. After the Human Rights Committee's examination of the report of the Federal Republic of Yugoslavia, it may well be that the Co-Chairmen would have to take an even more strident position regarding issues of principle related to gross violations of human rights and international crimes

taking place in Bosnia and Herzegovina. There is no room for ambiguity on these issues.

B.G. Ramcharan
November 5, 1992

cc. Mr. Vance
Lord Owen
Amb. Okun
Amb. Hall
Chairmen of Working Groups
All members of the OCC

UNHCR

"Safe Areas for Humanitarian Assistance" (SC res 787) Position of UNHCR

1. In UNHCR's opinion the overriding principle in Bosnia and Herzegovina should be to bring safety to the people, rather than to bring people to safety. The first priority should remain to improve the level of safety and to provide assistance in situ.
2. To the extent human suffering and displacement are caused primarily by armed conflict, notably in areas and cities under siege or threat, this means that a genuine and durable cessation of hostilities is imperative. UNHCR sees no viable alternative. The establishment of safe areas risks to distract from the necessity to bring all fighting to a halt.
3. In areas where displacement is caused by ethnic persecution, measures should be taken to improve the safety and material conditions of the remaining minority groups. Both assistance and protection mechanisms should be enhanced through a strategy of three complementary elements: deployment of peace keeping forces, human rights monitoring and humanitarian assistance. Such measures should include military protection, and would involve a highly visible and mobile international presence. This approach should be followed without discrimination in all areas where minority groups are subject to harassment, but notably in northern and western Bosnia. UNPROFOR's deployment to this region is crucial. It should be possible to implement this approach based on the consent of all parties to the conflict, which is preferable, either as a "package" or through separate agreements.

   The advantage of this approach would be its implementation in the short term. It would build on the capacity of the current UNPROFOR troops, and a formal extension of the mandate of these troops would perhaps not be necessary.
4. It is recognized that this approach may at best reduce the level and scope of "ethnic cleansing". Failing a cessation of all hostilities, displacement as a result of armed conflict will continue to occur. UNHCR's second priority therefore remains admission to safety, either in neighbouring States or, especially for those unable to gain admission abroad, in relatively secure regions of Bosnia and Herzegovina. The three points strategy referred to above should equally apply to these regions, thereby improving the safety and material conditions of both the displaced and local population, including minority groups. However, the right to seek asylum abroad must be upheld. The burden of the neighbouring States can and should be alleviated by increased international burden-sharing.
5. In UNHCR's opinion the establishment of one or more clearly delineated "safe areas" under international military protection, should only be a last option. When considering this option, the following considerations would justify utmost caution:

a) reaction of the parties
All parties to the conflict have voiced their opposition to the establishment of "safe areas", or want to use the concept to further their own - military - objectives.

b) military considerations
The establishment of militarily protected areas would require local enforcement action (without producing a cessation of hostilities on all fronts, or even risking to lead to intensified fighting on other fronts). This may apply in particular to city areas under siege or direct threat, if the consent of the parties is not forthcoming (see above). The necessary preparation time severely risks to be used to intensify both the current military offensive and the "ethnic cleansing". Once safe areas were established, the complete preservation of security would be doubtful. Terrorist attacks from outside or from within the areas are not to be excluded.

c) political considerations
The establishment of safe areas, especially of regional zones in central Bosnia, could result in the consolidation of front lines and thereby of territorial conquests, with serious political consequences. Non-acceptance of this by individuals or groups belonging to one or two party(ies) in the conflict would increase the risk of insecurity referred to above.

d) human rights and international refugee protection
Admission to and residence in safe areas should not affect freedom of movement nor ipso facto frustrate the right to seek asylum. Denial of asylum and forcible returns of persons having already found refuge abroad would, however, be likely, resulting not only in human drama but also in political dispute and tension.
The establishment of militarily protected, closed areas within ethnic cleansing regions, notably in northern and western Bosnia, would inevitably attract additional "ethnic cleansing" towards such areas.

e) impact on durable solutions
In the absence of a political settlement, protracted camp-like situations would risk being perpetuated, surrounded by enemy forces or territory. The homes of people attracted by the existence of safe areas would risk destruction, so as to frustrate the chances for return. After a certain period of time, demands within the areas concerned for transfer abroad, are likely to produce enormous pressure.

14.12.92

INTERNATIONAL CONFERENCE
ON THE FORMER YUGOSLAVIA

Palais des Nations, 1211 Geneva 10

Office of the Co-Chairmen

November 30, 1992

Mr. Chairman,

We would appreciate it very much if you would convey the attached message to the Commission on Human Rights at the start of your special session on the situation of human rights in the former Yugoslavia.

Unfortunately, we cannot be with you because we are travelling to Jeddah today to attend an Extraordinary Session of the Organization of the Islamic Conference on the situation in Bosnia and Herzegovina.

Please accept, Mr. Chairman, the assurances of our highest consideration.

Cyrus Vance	David Owen
Co-Chairman	Co-Chairman

Mr. Pal Solt,
Chairman, United Nations Commission on Human Rights,
United Nations Centre for Human Rights,
Palais des Nations
1211 Geneve 10

MESSAGE OF THE CO-CHAIRMEN OF THE INTERNATIONAL CONFERENCE ON THE FORMER YUGOSLAVIA TO THE UNITED NATIONS COMMISSION ON HUMAN RIGHTS

Mr. Chairman, Distinguished Members of the Commission on Human Rights,

We welcome your decision to convene in special session to consider the serious situation of human rights in the area of the former Yugoslavia, especially in Bosnia and Herzegovina.

Regrettably the disgraceful practice of ethnic cleansing has not ceased and violations of international norms on human rights and humanitarian law are rampant. We condemn these violations in the most categorical terms.

In our efforts to promote peace with justice in the area of the former Yugoslavia, we have placed emphasis on the provision of humanitarian assistance; the strict application of sanctions; helping to bring about a cessation of hostilities in Bosnia and Herzegovina; and the preparation of a constitution for Bosnia and Herzegovina. We have also sought to promote preventive measures to avoid the spread of the conflict. We would draw your attention to the recent report submitted by the Secretary-General to the Security Council on the activities of the International Conference. It provides detailed information on our activities.

We urge the distinguished members of the Commission on Human Rights, all Member States of the United Nations, and non-governmental organizations, to do everything possible to support and to strengthen the endeavours being undertaken in accordance with decisions of the Security Council of the United Nations.

We hope that your session will help in bringing an end to the violations of human rights and humanitarian law taking place. We also hope that you will give attention to the important question of protecting the rights of minorities. This issue is of great importance to the future stability and security in the area of the former Yugoslavia.

We wish you a successful session.

INTERNATIONAL CONFERENCE
ON THE FORMER YUGOSLAVIA

12 January 1993

To: C. Vance
D. Owen
cc: M. Ahtisaari
H. Okun
P. Hall
From: P. Szasz
Subject: Report on Meeting of Legal Experts on 7 January convened by the Council of Europe on a possible C/E Mechanism to facilitate the establishment of a Human Rights Court for Bosnia and Herzegovina

---

1. I attended the above-mentioned meeting by invitation as the representative of this Conference (see my related memorandum of the 4th). The principal participants were five legal experts from C/E member states (actually the members of the Bureau of the Council's Steering Committee for Human Rights (CDDH), serving in a personal capacity), plus two members each of the European Court of Human Rights and of the European Commission of Human Rights, each assisted by a member of the respective Secretariats; a number of senior members of the Council Secretariat also participated. (I expect that a full list of participants will be attached to the official report on the meeting, which I shall circulate.)
2. At the request of the Chairman I gave a brief oral report on the state of negotiations on the Bosnia-Herzegovina Constitution, indicating that although there were still many uncertainties about its contents and timing, it was reasonable to expect that the proposed Human Rights Court would be included in the Constitution because that was one point on which the three Bosnian parties did not seem to be in disagreement. I indicated our hope that the C/E Committee of Ministers would proceed with their plan to implement Lord Owen's proposal, and would do so in a form that would make the suggested mechanism apply not only to Bosnia and Herzegovina but also to other European non-members of the C/E – and that it would indeed be desirable if some of these would sign up even before BiH did.
3. The Council Secretariat circulated the attached Draft Resolution to facilitate the formulation of a recommendation by the Legal Experts to the Council of Ministers. In the ensuing discussion a number of modifications were proposed, some of which addressed points of concern to us – to which I spoke as appropriate:

   (a) As other states to which the proposed mechanism could apply might not provide for it in their constitutions (as we are proposing in respect of BiH), the references to "constitutional order" and "... bodies" should be deleted from the Preamble and Articles 2 and 3.
   (b) As there was a concern that members of the European Court or Commission, both of which are busy bodies falling further and further behind in their work, might not be able to devote sufficient time to the

proposed BiH Human Rights Court, especially if the same persons might also serve on corresponding institutions of other states, it was suggested that although the appointment of the judges should be made by or on the nomination of the Presidents of the Court and the Commission, they need not restrict the list of candidates to the membership of those bodies.

(c) As it might be useful if the proposed mechanism could also function for a period after BiH or other similarly situated states became members of the C/E (as foreseen as a possibility at the end of para. VI.B.3 of our Constitutional Structures paper), Article 5 of the Secretariat draft should be deleted.

(d) That the European judges appointed through the C/E mechanism should always constitute a majority on the courts to which they would be appointed (as also foreseen in the above-cited paragraph of our paper).

4. Considerable time was devoted to developing an entirely different alternative mechanism obviously preferred by several participants, under which a special C/E organ would merely provide advice to non-member governments on questions relating to the European Convention of Human Rights. I indicated that no such mechanism was foreseen in our current proposals regarding the BiH Constitution, and probably it would not be too useful for our purposes, but that I could not see any objection to adopting this alternative too, as long as the one the Conference needed was also put in place.
5. The meeting lasted all day. No decisions were taken, except to reconvene on Friday, 12 February, to consider new drafts to be prepared by the Secretariat on the basis of the discussion that had taken place. I indicated that I would probably be able to attend, flying in from New York City that morning. I also expressed the hope that at that meeting a recommendation to the Committee of Ministers of the C/E would be formulated and that the latter would be able to act on it fairly soon.
6. It appears probable that the Legal Experts will on 12 February, inter alia, recommend to the C/E Committee of Ministers a text along the lines of the attached draft, as modified in accordance with para. 3 above – which would suffice for our purposes – and that the Committee will approve it in good time before the BiH Constitution is likely to enter into force.

Strasbourg, 7 January 1993

DRAFT RESOLUTION

The Committee of Ministers of the Council of Europe,

By virtue of the Statute of the Council of Europe, done in London on 5 May 1949,

Having regard to the Convention for the Protection of Human Rights and Fundamental Freedoms signed on 4 November 1950,

Considering that all European States are called upon to accede to the Convention in due time,

Anxious to enable European States not members of the Council of Europe to provide, on a transitional basis, in their constitutional order for a control of compliance with Human Rights,

Having ascertained that all the States parties to the European Convention of Human Rights have expressed their consent to the creation of such a control drawing from the irreplaceable competence and experience of the control bodies instituted under the Convention,

Having consulted the European Court and Commission of Human Rights which have both given their agreement;

DECIDES

Article 1

Upon request by European States not members of the Council of Europe, the Committee of Ministers may decide to make a contribution to the setting up and functionning of a judicial control of the compliance with Human Rights in the territory of such States.

Article 2

To that effect, judges of the European Court of Human Rights and members of the European Commission of Human Rights will be nominated, under a procedure decided upon within the Council of Europe, to sit in the bodies established by those States in their constitutional order.

Article 3

The jurisdiction of those constitutional bodies will be determined by the legislation of the State concerned; however, it shall cover the substantive provisions of the European Convention of Human Rights.

Article 4

The Secretary General of the Council of Europe shall be entitled to conclude an agreement on the administrative and budgetary modalities for the participation of the judges of the Court and the members of the Commission with any State designed to benefit from the contribution provided for in this resolution.

Article 5

The participation of the Council of Europe will come to an end when the State will have become a member of the Council of Europe and a party to the European Convention of Human Rights.

INTERNATIONAL CONFERENCE ON THE FORMER YUGOSLAVIA

HIGHLIGHTS OF AN INFORMAL MEETING ON HUMAN RIGHTS MONITORING IN BOSNIA AND HERZEGOVINA

11 March 1993

Introduction

The Co-Chairmen of the International Conference on the former Yugoslavia, Cyrus Vance and Lord Owen, convened on Thursday, 11 March 1993, an informal meeting on future human rights monitoring in Bosnia and Herzegovina. The purpose of the meeting was to bring together representatives of non-governmental organizations working on human rights issues with United Nations human rights officials and ICFY representatives - in order to explore and develop new ideas to make human rights monitoring as effective as possible in Bosnia and Herzegovina.

Ambassador Okun, Mr. Ahtisaari and Mr. Ramcharan co-chaired the meeting, on behalf of Mr. Vance and Lord Owen. The agenda and a list of the documentation distributed is reproduced in Annex I. A list of the participants is reproduced in Annex II.

The following is a summary of the main points that arose at the meeting:

I. The Need for Human Rights Monitoring in Bosnia and Herzegovina

Participants identified the following needs to be borne in mind in the establishment of future human rights monitoring mission:

- Observe and report on the human rights situation in all parts of Bosnia and Herzegovina immediately.
- Provide access for existing monitors, including non-governmental organizations.
- Provide protection for current and future human rights monitors.
- Obtain the agreement of the parties to the conflict for human rights monitoring.
- Support local human rights groups.
- Support and reinforce the functioning of the local judicial establishment.
- Be more victim-oriented.
- Publicize human rights violations.
- Monitor the treatment of refugees, including those who wish to return.
- Deal with human rights violations, war crimes and crimes against humanity.
- Address the issue of accountability for human rights violations, war crimes and crimes against humanity.

II. Functions to be Performed by an International Human Rights Monitoring Mission

- Collect the information and get it out.
- Contribute to effective prosecution of those guilty of crimes.

- Monitor the entire country.
- Address medical and public health aspects. (See Annex III)
- Draw upon the United Nations experiences in El Salvador, Cambodia, Haiti, and South Africa.
- Address the question of immunity.

III. Organization of a Future Human Rights Monitoring Mission
- Keep it an independent entity; independence is important.
- Include women in its leadership and its monitors.
- Plan for a large number of human rights monitors (300 to 1,000).
- Coordinate efforts with the Special Rapporteur of the UN Commission on Human Rights.
- Coordinate with non-governmental organizations.
- Pay particular attention to publicity and the broadcasting of news; have a "publicity arm".
- Deploy field officers throughout the country.
- Designate as the head someone with great prestige worldwide.

IV. Timing of the Establishment of a Human Rights Monitoring Mission

There were two schools of thought: One argued forcefully that the Security Council should act now, before a peaceful settlement has been achieved, and that an international human rights monitoring mission should be deployed immediately. The second school of thought was that without the cooperation of the parties, a monitoring mission could not function; hence, one should look to the deployment of a human rights monitoring mission after a peace agreement has been signed.

V. Resources

There was little discussion on how to obtain resources for a future international human rights monitoring mission. Some non-governmental organizations indicated that they would be prepared to provide assistance.

Conclusion

It was suggested that the most fruitful way to proceed would be to send a small (3–5 persons) team of independent international human rights experts to Bosnia and Herzegovina to assess the feasibility of a human rights monitoring mission (a) before a peace settlement is concluded, and (b) as part of an overall peace settlement. The team would also be expected to provide concrete proposals on the mandate, structure and operations of any mission to be established. The recent three-person mission to Haiti was a useful precedent. Such a team could be selected, visit the region, and report back to the Secretary-General, within a very short space of time, such as three weeks.

BGR
15 March 1993

ANNEX 1

United Nations
THE INTERNATIONAL CONFERENCE ON THE FORMER YUGOSLAVIA
OFFICE OF THE CO-CHAIRMEN
New York, New York 10017
FAX No. (212) 963-1992

INFORMAL MEETING ON HUMAN RIGHTS MONITORING IN BOSNIA AND HERZEGOVINA

Thursday, 11 March 1993
Room S-3327B
3:30 p.m.– 6:00 p.m.

AGENDA

1. Welcome by Ambassador Okun
2. Discussion of elements that should be borne in mind in the establishment of a human rights monitoring mission
   - A. Needs to be addressed
   - B. Functions to be performed
   - C. Organization of mission
   - D. Timing
   - E. Resource requirements and how to be provided

Documentation

1. San Jose Agreement on Human rights
2. Human rights parts of Agreements on Cambodia
3. Announcement on the International Civil Mission in Haiti
4. Information on the activities of the United Nations Observer Mission in South Africa
5. Commission on Human Rights resolution on Former Yugoslavia, 1993
6. Extracts from Mazowiecki report to 1993 session of Commission on Human Rights
7. Extracts from Secretary-General's report on Human Rights mission in Cambodia to Commission on Human Rights (E/CN.4/1993/50)
8. Extract from Report of the Secretary-General to Security Council: "The Co-Chairmen and Human Rights Issues" (S/25221)

ANNEX 2

United Nations
THE INTERNATIONAL CONFERENCE ON THE FORMER YUGOSLAVIA
OFFICE OF THE CO-CHAIRMEN
New York, New York 10017
FAX No. (212) 963-1992

INFORMAL MEETING ON HUMAN RIGHTS MONITORING IN BOSNIA AND HERZEGOVINA

Thursday, 11 March 1993
Room S-3327B
3:30 p.m.– 6:00 p.m.

NAME	ORGANIZATION	ADDRESS	TEL. #
Andrew Clapham Meg Henry	Amnesty International	777 U.N. Plaza New York, NY 10017	(212) 867-8878
Jeri Laber	Helsinki Watch	485 Fifth Avenue New York, N.Y.	(212) 972-8400
Aryeh Neier	Human Rights Watch	485 Fifth Avenue New York, N.Y. 10017	(212) 972-8400
Donna Sullivan Director, Women in the Law Project	International Human Rights and Law Group	1601 Connecticut Av NW Suite 700 Washington, DC 20009	(202) 232-8500
Michael Posner Candy Whittone	Lawyers Committee for Human Rights	330 Seventh Avenue New York, N.Y. 10001	(212) 629-6170
H. Jack Geiger, M.D. Susannah Sirkin, Deputy Director	Physicians for Human Rights	100 Boylaton Street Boston, MA 02116	617-695-0041 (PHR) 212-650-6860 (O)
Ed Luck, President Russell M. Dallen, Jr., Esq.	UNA-USA	485 Fifth Avenue New York, NY 10017	(212) 697-3232
(Rev.) Dwain C. Epps	World Council of Churches	777 U.N. Plaza New York, NY 10017	(212) 867-5890 (212) 867-7462 (F)
Ms. Elizabeth Salter	CCIA/WCC	150, route de Ferney 1211 Geneva 2	41-22-791-6221 41-22-791-6305 (F)

NAME	ORGANIZATION	ADDRESS	TEL. #
G. Mautner-Markhov Anne-Marie Bernadel	Centre for Human Rights	Geneva UN Headquarters	41-22-917-3356 (212) 963-5931
Alexander Borg Olivier Principal Officer	Dept. of Humanitarian Affairs	Room S-3600H UN Headquarters	(212) 963-0226 (212) 963-1312 (F)
Gustave Feissel Director, Europe Divison	Dept. of Politcal Affairs	Room S-3577 UN Headquarters	(212) 963-5058
John Ressinger	Dept. for Polital Affairs	Room S-3760A UN Headquarters	(212) 963-3071
Iqbal Riza Assistant Secretary-General Shashi Tharoor Peter Schmitz	Dept. of Peace-keeping Operations	Room S-3630A Room S-3727D Room S-3650J UN Headquarters	(212) 963-3446 (212) 963-3446 (212) 963-3650J
Daphna Shraga	Office of Legal Affairs	UN Headquarters	(212) 963-2250
Wilbert van Hovell	UNHCR	Geneva	41-22-776-7022

ANNEX 3

PHYSICIANS FOR HUMAN RIGHTS
AN ORGANIZATION OF HEALTH PROFESSIONALS

NOTES ON HUMAN RIGHTS MONITORS

A. General Issues
1. Monitoring will be useless without a real prospect of effective prosecution. The most striking characteristic of current human rights violation is the widespread belief that no one will ever be held accountable. What will be the relationship between monitors and a War Crimes Commission? Given the delays and complexities inherent in a WCC,

will there be some other neutral judicial system? Some mechanism of enforcement?

2. Will monitors be responsible for evidence of past (pre-treaty) violations, or only for those subsequent to the political settlement? After the return of populations to the sites of previous conflict, it seems likely that victims will turn to monitors with complaints of grave violations that occurred during the conflict.
3. Will there be protection for human rights monitors? What will be their system of communication? What will be the process of citing violations?
4. Will the number of monitors be adequate both to do the job and to convey the message that this is a serious effort?

B. The Role of Medicine in Human Rights Monitoring
The issues include:
1. Protection of medical neutrality and sanctuary
   a. Non-invasion/interference with hospitals, clinics, and ambulances, and with the delivery of medical care at these and other sites.
   b. Non-interference with the delivery of medical supplies and equipment.
   c. Protection of physicians, nurses and other health personnel from attack or harassment, limitations on mobility and communication, or denial of licenses or staff positions on the basis of ethnicity.
   d. Freedom of access to medical care by all patients, and protection of patients from torture, abuse or neglect.
   e. Assurance of equitable and appropriate treatment regardless of ethnicity.
2. Prevention of torture and protection of the rights and health care of civilian and military prisoners; investigation of torture allegations; closure of illegal/informal "prisons."
3. Investigation of suspicious deaths.
4. Investigation of allegations of rape.
5. Protection of the rights and access to care of pregnant women, children and the elderly, especially during travel/population movements following a settlement. Protection of patients with mental illness.
6. Investigation of interference with public health measures: immunization, protection of water supplies, etc.

C. Personnel Required for Medical Human Rights Monitoring
1. Physicians, nurses or other health personnel with previous human rights monitoring experience or training.
2. Pathologists and forensic pathologists from neutral nations, in the field and/or on call as consultants.
3. Physicians with experience in the diagnosis and treatment of torture victims, including psychiatrists and gynecologists.
4. On call as consultants: epidemiologists and toxicologists.
5. It is essential that the human rights monitoring force includes women.

D. Organizational Structure
1. Relationship to other UN agencies: UNHCR, WHO, etc.?
2. Relationship to NGOs: ICRC, MSF, IRC, etc.?

FOR INFORMATION OF UNITED NATIONS SECRETARIAT ONLY
Not for Distribution or Dissemination

17 March 1993

PRESS BRIEFING ON HUMAN RIGHTS ASPECTS OF VANCE-OWEN PLAN FOR BOSNIA AND HERZEGOVINA

The future constitution of Bosnia and Herzegovina would establish a number of important human rights institutions to assist the country in its reconstruction process, Bertie Ramcharan, a United Nations expert on human rights, told correspondents at a press briefing Tuesday afternoon. Those institutions would consist of a constitutional court, an interim human rights court, four ombudsmen's offices and an interim human rights monitoring mission.

Introducing Mr. Ramcharan to correspondents, Fred Eckhard, spokesman for the Co-Chairmen of the Steering Committee of the International Conference on the Former Yugoslavia, said he had been an original member of the Geneva negotiating team headed by Cyrus Vance and Lord Owen. The human rights component of the Vance-Owen plan had been built into the constitutional framework and plans for the interim period, when the entire country would be undergoing "a painful transition from a war to a period of reconciliation", Mr. Eckhard said.

Mr. Ramcharan, who had specialized in human rights for 14 years, before moving to the Office of the Secretary-General and then the Department of Political Affairs, was Special Assistant to the Head of the Centre for Human Rights and had written 10 books on the subject, Mr. Eckhard continued. He was also an Adjunct Professor at Columbia University. As political adviser to the negotiators, Mr. Ramcharan had worked on preparing the human rights component of the Bosnian constitution, together with Paul Szasz, legal adviser to the Co-Chairmen, and Martti Ahtisaari, the Co-Chairmen's chief negotiatior on Bosnia.

Mr. Ramcharan had also worked on the proposals for human rights monitoring which were described in the Secretary-General's most recent report on the Conference, Mr. Eckhard went on to say. Each of the Secretary-General's reports on the Conference contained a substantive section on human rights. He referred correspondents to two previous reports that were particularly detailed on the issue (documents S/24795 of 11 November 1992 and S/25221 of 2 February).

When the negotiators arrived in Geneva last September, Mr. Ramcharan said, they found that Lord Owen had already been very active in advocating that the Council of Europe's human rights machinery be made available to the States of the former Yugoslavia, particularly Bosnia and Herzegovina. That process had culminated about 10 days ago, when the Council had adopted a special resolution making its human rights machinery available to those States.

The parties to the conflict in Bosnia had to be taken through a process of education on human rights norms, he continued. Mr. Szasz had put before them a long list of all international human rights conventions and had distilled from that a detailed set of norms which he suggested might be incorporated into the future constitution of Bosnia and Herzegovina. (Copies of a document dated 27 October 1992, detailing those norms, had been distributed to the Security Council; it could be made available to interested correspondents.)

The Bosnian constitution would contain a commitment that the country should ratify and apply a lengthy list of human rights conventions, Mr. Ramcharan continued. In addition, as part of the human rights machinery to be provided by the constitution, there would, first, be a constitutional court to interpret the constitution and pronounce on human rights issues. Second, the constitution would provide for an interim human rights court with a majority of judges nominated from the outside by the Co-Chairmen.

Third, he went on to say, the constitution would provide for the establishment of four ombudsmen, who would initially be appointed by the Co-Chairmen. After conditions had normalized, the lower house of Parliament would make those appointments. The ombudsmen would be vested with the competence to monitor the rights of each of the country's three communities – the Croats, Muslims and Serbs – as well as of a fourth community of "others" – the Yugoslavs.

The Co-Chairmen had also proposed an idea, still on the negotiating table, to establish an international human rights commission for Bosnia, Mr. Ramcharan reported. However, the Co-Chairmen were sensitive to the need to impact on the situation in Bosnia now, regardless of what a future constitution would establish. The Secretary-General's most recent report on the negotiations (document S/25403) dated 12 March, reflected the Co-Chairmen's discussion with the parties on the establishment of an international human rights monitoring mission.

Such a mission would be headed by an interim human rights commissioner of international standing, he said. Deputies would be located in sensitive areas of Bosnia, particularly where "ethnic cleansing" had occurred. There would be a back-up staff of international human rights monitors – estimates ranged from 100 to 500 to 1,000 people. Consultations on a human rights monitoring mission to Bosnia had been held last week with non-governmental organizations, and a summary of that meeting was contained in the report circulated to correspondents.

The concept behind the monitoring mission was to establish a United Nations presence on the ground, he stressed. The mission would also submit regular reports to the Secretary-General, who would in turn brief the Security Council and the Commission on Human Rights. The purpose was to bring international pressure to bear on the situation. Human rights officials and monitors could also intercede vis à vis the local authorities, the Government and the United Nations Protection Force (UNPROFOR) in order to protect a group that seemed to be in danger.

Comparing the proposed human rights monitoring mission for Bosnia with such missions to El Salvador, Cambodia and Haiti, he said there was a qualitative difference in the intensity of violence in Bosnia. If a monitoring mission were put on the ground there now, it would be a novel operation since war was still going on in the country.

Mr. Eckhard pointed out that the ombudsmen provided for in the constitution were not just individuals but institutions, represented by offices with staffs.

Did the human rights institutions have to be agreed upon by the Bosnians? a correspondent asked. Also, how long would it take for them to be put into effect? And were the Co-Chairmen appointing foreigners to the interim human rights court? The constitutional court and the interim human rights court would come into force when the constitution did, Mr. Ramcharan replied. The ombudsmen were provided for by the constitution, but the Co-Chairmen were already moving ahead with establishing that office, and considering qualified individuals for the posts.

The interim human rights court, he continued, would be composed of a majority of foreigners. However, in the case of the ombudsmen, the Co-Chairmen were not bound to choose foreigners. They could consider qualified, impartial individuals from among the communities of Bosnia and Herzegovina. Further, the Co-Chairmen had explored the idea of a monitoring mission with the parties, and there had been "a meeting of minds on this idea". The establishment of such a mission would depend on Security Council action; there was a school of thinking that advocated acting on the issue as soon as possible.

A correspondent inquired how the interim human rights court would differ from the international criminal court that was being established by the Security Council. Mr. Ramcharan replied that Bosnia would ratify a number of international human rights conventions; problems that arose in their application would go through the constitutional court and, if necessary, the interim human rights court. The tribunal to be established by the Council had a different, specialized purpose: it would try persons accused of war crimes and crimes against humanity. To further questions, Mr. Ramcharan said the two courts in Bosnia to which he referred would deal with day to day human rights issues in the country.

A correspondent said he understood that the issue of power-sharing between the provinces and central Government in Bosnia was still very fluid. What jurisdiction would a centralized human rights court have? The parties to the negotiations had signed onto a set of constitutional principles, Mr. Ramcharan replied. In addition to considering normal human rights issues, the constitutional court would deal with differences that arose between the provincial and central Government.

The four ombudsmen, he continued, would operate at the national level to protect all four communities in the country. The human rights court would be a supplementary arrangement. In so far as the reign of human rights is concerned, there will be an important role for the constitutional court, he said. The ombudsman and the human rights court would also have primacy at the national level. To a further question, he replied that if he was being asked whether the future human right regimes would stand up, he said that one would have to wait and see.

Would the human rights monitoring mission be dispatched prior to a cease-fire? a correspondent asked. It could be, Mr. Ramcharan replied. He proceeded to read out the following paragraph from the report, distributed to correspondents, on an informal meeting with non-governmental organizations on the human rights situation in Bosnia and Herzegovina:

On the timing of the establishment of a human rights nonitoring mission, Mr. Ramcharan went on, there were two schools of thought. One argued forcefully that the Security Council should act now, before a peaceful settlement has been achieved, and that an international human rights monitoring mission should be deployed immediately. The second school of thought was that without the cooperation of the parties, a monitoring mission could not function; hence, one should look to the deployment of a human rights monitoring mission after a peace agreement has been signed.

Mr. Ramcharan reported that Co-Chairman Vance's feeling on the issue was to act as soon as possible to establish a monitoring mission. The Co-Chairmen favoured putting the issue before the Council, if necessary, before a cease-fire was reached.

Mr. Ramcharan was asked how practical it was to send a mission to monitor human rights in Bosnia when UNPROFOR could not even guarantee food deliveries there. In all bad situations, Mr. Ramcharan replied, the role of the international community was to identify forms of action that could ameliorate the problem. There were no magic wands. While an international presence might not transform a problematic situation, it could have a mitigating effect. It was also important to have regular reports on what was going on throughout the country.

In response to further questions on the interim human rights court, he said the role of the court was connected with the vindication of human rights in Bosnia. That court was not meant to try people accused of human rights violations. The international war crimes court, to be set up by the Council, was different in concept. To other questions, he replied that the court would "pronounce on human rights issues that are brought to it under the constitution" or referred to it by institutions such as the offices of the ombudsmen. The court had a future-oriented character.

Further clarifying the function of the human rights court, he said the court might deal with violations of rights such as those contained in article 27 of the International Covenant on Civil and Political Rights, which says that persons belonging to minorities shall not be denied the right to practise their religion, enjoy their culture or use their language. The Co-Chairmen's intention had been to weave into the future legal and constitutional fabric of Bosnia an intricate and elaborate range of protective devices to guarantee the rights of all communities.

A correspondent said that if the human rights regimes went into effect with the entry into force of the constitution, it would take two years. Which mechanisms would first be put into effect after the signing of a peace agreement? Mr. Ramcharan said the constitutional court, the human rights court and the ombudsmen would come into being when the constitution entered into force. However, the Co-Chairmen were examining the idea of accelerating the establishment of ombudsmen. They also favoured immediate action on the international human rights monitoring mission. If the remaining two parties signed to the map, any subsequent resolution adopted by the Council was expected to provide for the monitoring mission. The two regimes that would come into place first were the ombudsmen and the monitoring mission.

Would the human rights court have any power? Was there a government behind it? a correspondent asked. The constitutional proposals provided that policing functions would belong to the provinces, Mr. Ramcharan answered. However, the thinking was that since all parties were committed to constitutional order, they would respect the decisions of the court.

A correspondent observed that Mr. Ramcharan had said the human rights courts would be forward-looking. Did he mean they would not address such violations as ethnic cleansing because they had occurred in the past? Mr. Ramcharan said the reversal of ethnic cleansing had been "an article of faith" for the Co-Chairmen. They had thus included in the constitutional framework a doctrine declaring the invalidity of any document signed under duress, including one surrendering property. The reversal of ethnic cleansing would also require an expanded UNPROFOR presence and human rights monitors. The presence of monitors on the ground was intended to make it easier for people to return to their homes. He stressed that the human rights institutions could act on past violations.

Mr. Ramcharan was asked if the future human rights court would replace courts already in place. Would it have the power to order executions? The country would have a constitution as well as regular courts and criminal courts, Mr. Ramcharan replied. The human rights court would not try people guilty of human rights violations. Asked if it would be a court of appeals, Mr. Ramcharan said yes.

A correspondent said there seemed to be no provisions to enforce the decisions of the court. "One is trying to stitch a country together", Mr. Ramcharan replied, "one is trying to take a country from war into peace". The Co-Chairmen's plan was to devise a fabric of institutions that would be respected in good faith in the future. The Co-Chairmen's scheme was to "walk the parties to the conflict down a path leading to human rights institutions, in the hopes that they would respect their commitments".

Mr. Ramcharan was asked if the Co-Chairmen had found support in the Council and from the parties to the conflict on sending human rights monitors to Bosnia before a peace agreement was signed. He said the Co-Chairmen had been alerting Council members that it would be important to move ahead quickly on the issue. The Co-Chairmen's preference was for a map to be signed and for a monitoring mission to then be established by a Council resolution that would follow the signing. However, the Co-Chairmen had firmly indicated that if it were necessary to move ahead more quickly on the monitors – even if a map were not signed by the other two parties – the Council must be prepared to act.

COUNCIL ON FOREIGN RELATIONS

Symposium on International Responses to Alleged War Crimes in Former Yugoslavia

Harold Pratt House, NYC, 24 March 1993

The International Conference on the Former Yugoslavia and the War Crimes Issue

Paul C. Szasz

A. The International Conference on the Former Yugoslavia

Before entering on the issue of alleged war crimes in former Yugoslavia and their connection with the work of the International Conference on the Former Yugoslavia, it may be useful if I gave a brief explanation about the nature of the Conference itself. This ad hoc institution, which instead of being known by its long formal name has recently become almost notorious as the Geneva Conference on Yugoslavia, or the Yugoslav Peace Conference, and still more popularly as the Vance-Owen Negotiations, is – unsurprisingly – not generally understood. Perhaps this is so because the initials of the Conference, ICFY, do not lend themselves to a catchy acronym – a serious media crime in this age of sound-bites.

One confusing element is that the International Conference on the Former Yugoslavia is the direct successor of a somewhat similar earlier institution: the EC Conference on Yugoslavia, or the Carrington Negotiations, which functioned from September 1991 until August 1992. At that time its sponsor, the European Communities, and the United Nations, which had already since March 1992 deployed a growing peace-keeping force, the UN Protection Force, or UNPROFOR, in Croatia and later in Bosnia and Herzegovina, decided to join forces. They convened the London Conference on August 26th and 27th, which in effect perpetuated itself in the form of the present International Conference on the Former Yugoslavia.

The second confusing factor is that this Conference is not a "conference" at all, in the normal sense of that term. Except for the founding 2-day London plenary session, ICFY is really a medium-scale floating set of multiple negotiations, largely centered on Geneva, but manifesting itself in diverse places such as New York, Brussels, Belgrade, Zagreb, Skjope – or any other place where one can assemble representatives of one or more of the entities that have an interest in all or parts of the former Yugoslavia. The participants in the London Conference were a diverse lot – indeed, for that no definitive list of participants was released. Under the Co-Chairmanship of the UN Secretary-General and the President of the Council of Ministers of the European Community, there were assembled representatives of:

- all member states of the Community
- the permanent members of the UN Security Council
- certain European states occupying leadership positions in the CSCE

- neighboring states of the former Yugoslavia
- two international organizations, the European Community itself, and the Organization of the Islamic Conference
- the six so-called "successor states" of the former Yugoslavia, as well as the newly formed union of just two of them, the Federal Republic of Yugoslavia, which was unsuccessfully asserting prime successor status, and, finally
- some dubious entities, such as the Serb and Croat states of Bosnia and Herzegovina and the equally unrecognized Krajina Serb state.

The London Conference adopted a series of Statements, Decisions, Conclusions and Programmes, by one of which it set out the scheme by which it would continue to function as long as the Yugoslav crisis so demanded. It established a Steering Committee of the most important of its participating states and organizations – but not including any of the Yugoslav successor states or entities – and it appointed as the Co-Chairmen of that Committee Cyrus Vance and Lord David Owen. The Co-Chairmen were charged with supervising a number of Working Groups, including ones on Bosnia and Herzegovina, on Humanitarian Issues, on Ethnic and National Communities, on Succession Issues, etc. There is also a small Secretariat, as well as the Arbitration Commission – carried over from the former EC Conference, at whose request it had issued a series of important Advisory Opinions.

The work of ICFY involves constant negotiations: within the Working Groups, within subsidiary or ad hoc fora or directly conducted by one or both of the Co-Chairmen. The participants in these negotiations may, as appropriate, be representatives and often the heads of one, more or all of the ex-Yugoslav states, interested neighboring states (such as Albania), unrecognized entities claiming statehood such as the Bosnian Serbs and Croats, and non-independent ethnic groups such as the Kosovo Albanians and the Vojvodina Hungarians. Some of these high officials have, more or less authoritatively, been accused of war crimes and crimes against humanity.

B. The Co-Chairmen and an International Criminal Court

One of the "Specific Decisions" of the London Conference was that, in connection with "Violations of International Humanitarian Law", the Co-Chairmen should "carry forward a study of the creation of an international criminal court" – a somewhat inartful way of authorizing them to establish a war crimes tribunal for ex-Yugoslavia.

Consequent on that assignment, the Co-Chairmen, almost as soon as they had settled in Geneva last September, looked into the question of establishing such a tribunal. They thereupon rather rapidly reached the following conclusions, which have guided them ever since:

1. They very much encouraged the international community to establish such a tribunal; however,
2. They concluded that, for both political and legal reasons, such a tribunal should not be established under the aegis of the Conference, nor should the prosecution or investigation of war crimes take place there.

Now, before you all conclude that this is just a classic case of "letting George – or rather Boutros do it", let me illustrate and explain the various aspects of these conclusions.

First of all, the Co-Chairmen have both publicly and privately often conveyed their firm view that the alleged war criminals in ex-Yugoslavia should be prosecuted in an effective international forum. In particular, they so declared at a meeting of the expanded Steering Committee – in effect, all the states and organizations participating in the Conference, with the exception of the ex-Yugoslav ones – meeting on December 16th at the Foreign Minister level – which was the meeting at which Secretary of State Eagleburger read out his list of Yugoslav war criminals. They also so declared in a recent report to the Security Council – a report that the Council cited in taking its decision that a War Crimes Tribunal for Yugoslavia should be established. This position is in line with the deeply held conviction of the Co-Chairmen that the solution to the Yugoslav crises must be sought at the highest moral level, requiring not only the insertion of effective human rights protective mechanisms into the agreements and other legal instruments being negotiated with their assistance, and the designing of devices for the reversal of ethnic cleansing, but also the conviction and punishment of those who have inflicted the recent horrors in Yugoslavia.

Why, then the effort to hold war crimes prosecutions away from the Conference? As I have said, the reasons therefor are both political and legal.

Let me address the latter first. Even though the London Conference in effect encouraged the Co-Chairmen to establish a war crimes court under the aegis of ICFY, and thus appears to have authorized them to do so, they realized that the Conference was itself not really in a position to take such a step effectively. In the first place there is the difficulty that the Conference, under its rules, must take its decisions by consensus – and it hardly appears likely that all these participating states, which include all the ex-Yugoslavian ones, would consent to such a decision. But even if this obstacle could be overcome, and the Conference by a resolution established a tribunal of the type here contemplated, such a body would be completely impotent in the face of the refusal by any non-consenting state to make available accused persons, as well as witnesses and other forms of evidence. Indeed, the Chairmen saw this as a potential weakness of any tribunal created by resolution of any international organ – with the sole exception of the Security Council, to which I will revert. Thus they also discouraged other organs, such as the Council of Europe, from taking such a step.

In the long-run it would be best if an international criminal tribunal would be set up by a treaty, i.e. not by a mere resolution of an international organ, such as the UN General Assembly, and that it have a global mandate, i.e. one not limited to a particular state or region, and also a wide substantive mandate, i.e. one not limited to war crimes. However, such a treaty, in spite of the recent progress made by the International Law Commission in that area, would still take years to negotiate and then years to enter into force for a substantial number of states. Even a treaty limited to war crimes in former Yugoslavia would take some time to negotiate and enter into force – and it appears likely that at least some of the ex-Yugoslav states principally implicated would not become parties to it and therefore would have no obligations to cooperate with such a tribunal, by subjecting defendants to its jurisdiction and by obliging witnesses to appear before it, etc.

Although non-cooperation by states with such a tribunal could, in principle, be overcome by a Security Council order adopted under Chapter 7 of the UN Charter, if one must resort to that route anyway it would seem simpler and more direct to have the Security Council itself establish the Tribunal and equip it with sufficient authority vis-a-vis uncooperative states. That approach – which in effect is the one that is now in the course of implementation as a consequence of Council resolution 808 – simplifies the negotiation of the necessarily complicated texts of the Statute of the proposed Tribunal and of the required ancillary arrangements, such as those concerning the prosecutorial organ. Instead of a negotiation among an undefined number of states, most of which are at best mediately concerned, and some of which may – either for reasons of direct interest or on some abstract issue of principle – be fundamentally opposed to the project – the negotiations would instead take place among just the 15 members of the Security Council.

Thus, the Co-Chairmen concluded that for dealing with the current outrages within the former territory of Yugoslavia, the Security Council option is the only viable one. It is also hoped that such an initiative will have a stimulating effect on the advancement of a long-term solution, that is the establishment of a general international criminal court on the basis of a global treaty negotiated under the aegis of the General Assembly. Contrariwise, not to initiate any international prosecutions of those responsible for the Yugoslav outrages might well inhibit the establishment of any tribunal to deal primarily with lesser offenses. It should, however, be recognized that if the world community should falter or fail in the current enterprise addressed to the Yugoslav crisis, such failure is likely to constitute a major setback to any more general and long-term project.

As I indicated earlier, the Co-Chairmen also had important political reasons for declining to have a War Crimes Court established directly under their aegis or generally within ICFY. As I explained in the very beginning, the Conference is a continuing negotiating forum, in which some of the negotiators are leaders accused of major command responsibility for many of the alleged war crimes. In addition, it is fashionable for the leaders of different parties in these negotiations to accuse one another of war crimes.

It is clear that serious peace negotiations cannot be conducted in an atmosphere of mutual or unilateral accusations of criminal conduct. The Co-Chairmen couldn't seriously say: "Please sign this agreement, Mr. X, and as soon as you do so and fighting has ceased we expect you to answer the following criminal charges in our war crimes court." Therefore they must keep their distance from the establishment or operation of such a tribunal, from the prosecution of alleged offenses within it or even from the investigation of charges. However, they need not take an attitude of indifference towards war crimes as such, and they have definitely not done so. Aside from encouraging the creation of a suitable and effective tribunal – i.e. one established by the

Security Council – they have also encouraged the Special Rapporteur of the UN Human Rights Commission, as well as various inter- and non-governmental organizations to conduct the most thorough investigations of war crimes allegations and to publicize their findings as widely and loudly as possible – if only to impress on the parties a healthy sense of urgency and even of fear. Similarly, they have encouraged the work of the Commission of Experts – also located in Geneva – that is already examining the extensive charges and evidence that have been submitted to the Secretary-General.

The question has been raised: How can the Co-Chairmen talk to or negotiate with accused war criminals? – As if there were a choice!

The facile answer to this question, or rather charge, which has been expressed from time to time, is to say that everyone must be presumed innocent until proven guilty – and we are still a long way from that.

More seriously, peace negotiations must evidently be conducted with the persons who control the warring forces. It is no use seeking to talk to persons who are uncompromised by the struggle, for most likely they could not cause its termination. To insist that one will not talk to accused war criminals would bring the negotiations to a halt, with all that that implies. Incidentally, that response also applies to the occasional well-meant suggestion that the Co-Chairmen keep receiving, that they should refuse to negotiate at all as long as fighting or the violation of human rights continues. A doctor who insists on seeing only healthy patients or a fireman who avoids smoky buildings would be just as ineffective as a peace negotiator who insists on dealing only with persons of good will and proven probity.

There is, of course, another possible course. During the Second World War the allies – i.e., the United Nations, as they called themselves – insisted on the unconditional surrender of the Axis forces and governments; they refused to negotiate with Hitler or his colleagues, or his homologues in Italy and Japan. But that meant that the Allies were willing to conduct a long and bloody war – and we all know that this has – at least until now and probably also in the future – not been true in respect of the current Bosnian and Croat wars. Well, if one is unwilling to conduct a war leading to unconditional surrender, and does not wish to see the conflict continue indefinitely or until one or more peoples are utterly destroyed, then one must negotiate with those are carrying the smoking guns and bloody knives.

C. Amnesty

This now brings me logically to the final question that is constantly raised in connection with the subject we are considering. Is not an over-all peace settlement negotiated within the framework of our Conference necessarily going to include an amnesty provision under which all the accused war criminals will escape responsibility for their acts? This question is an entirely natural one in light of what has just happened in El Salvador over the past weekend, and in light of the experience with the conclusion of other long-lasting armed struggles or periods of dictatorial government.

The answer is really quite simple. The parties can, indivi-dually or collectively, only grant each other and themselves immunity from prosecution under their own laws and within their own courts. War crimes, and crimes against humanity, such as the ones that would be prosecuted in an international war crimes tribunal, are, however, not primarily national crimes, but rather are crimes against the world community. And just as no US State Governor or combination of Governors or even of State legislatures could grant amnesty to their citizens from any federal crimes, just so national organs cannot not, whether by domestic actions or by regional treaties, exculpate their citizens from crimes these may have committed against the world community.

It might be noted that at least some of the ex-Yugoslav states are quite aware of this differentiation, and have, in their national amnesty legislation relating to the current conflict, specifically excepted "war crimes".

If the world community, through the Security Council, decides that particular offenses should be prosecuted in a war crimes tribunal, then it is only the world community – presumably, but not necessarily, acting through the same organ – that could grant amnesty or respite from prosecution. Whether such a possibility should even be contemplated – perhaps within a negotiated Security Council resolution endorsing a Yugoslav peace package, is not something I can speculate on. All I can say is that the Co-Chairmen have at no time made any suggestion or even hint in that direction.

Let me close on a note of caution and of warning. If the world community decides – as I personally believe it should decide – that the outrages committed in former Yugoslavia cannot and must not go unpunished, and establishes a war crimes tribunal and a prosecutorial mechanism to ensure such punishment – then it would be disastrous if at some point the process would be stopped or permitted to slowly fade out, whether for political or for bureaucratic reasons. If that is considered a real possibility, then it would be better not to start the process at all. For once the world community puts its hand to this particular plough, it can only look back at the peril of surrendering all moral authority to those who have committed unspeakable acts in the cynical expectation that they would never have to answer for these. I trust they will be proved wrong!

ECMM RESTRICTED

HQ ECMM
Zagreb

Mr Stoltenberg
1 June 1993

HUMAN RIGHTS MONITORING IN FORMER YUGOSLAVIA

BACKGROUND

1. The conflicts in the former Yugoslavia have resulted in the worst abuses of human rights in Europe since the Second World War. The news media have brought vivid pictures of atrocities to the attention of the civilised world, but so far the best attempts of the international community have failed to prevent all parties in the conflict from continuing to violate human rights on a large scale as they pursue their political agendas.

REQUIREMENT

2. Positive Action. There is a very clear requirement for the international community to take positive action to halt the continuing violations of human rights in former Yugoslavia. This is to save the people who will otherwise become victims in the future, and to give a very clear signal to leaders in other potential areas of inter-ethnic conflict that the international community will not tolerate such behavior.
3. Cost of Inaction. Failure to meet this requirement means that the parties in former Yugoslavia will continue to ignore the observance of human rights as a factor in their political and military planning. It also means that the international community will have to pick up the pieces on a far larger scale in the near future as this problem spreads to other areas of mixed ethnic groups.

CURRENT HUMAN RIGHTS MONITORING

4. Currently there are a number of international organisations operating within former Yugoslavia which have an interest in the monitoring of the human rights situation, and are attempting to promote correct observance of human rights by the parties to the conflict. The main organisations and their characteristics are listed below:
   a. UNHCR. UNHCR has been designated as the lead agency for humanitarian activities in former Yugoslavia. It has a mandate to protect refugees, through the provision of relief and through the activities of Protection Officers. In practice this mandate has been stretched to include the protection of minorities and displaced people.
   b. UNICEF. UNICEF has a mandate to protect the special interests of children in the conflict area.
   c. UNPROFOR. UNPROFOR is present in Croatia with a mandate to implement the Vance Plan. UNPROFOR is present in Bosnia-

Hercegovina with a mandate to support the international humanitarian agencies. UNPROFOR is not allowed to use force to prevent abuses of human rights.

d. UNMO. UNMOs are present throughout the conflict area and in addition to monitoring ceasefires they monitor the observance of human rights. Being unarmed, they can only protest if they see abuses of human rights occurring.
e. UN CIVIL AFFAIRS. The civil arm of UNPROFOR is responsible for the political side of UNPROFOR activities. They will have a large role in the political elements of the implementation of the Vance Owen Peace Plan (VOPP), and direct the work of UNCIVPOL.
f. UNCIVPOL. UNCIVPOL are present in Croatia and Bosnia-Hercegovina. They work with the indigenous civil police to ensure that correct police methods are employed, and have a direct impact on the monitoring of human rights and investigation of violations of human rights.
g. UN CENTRE FOR HUMAN RIGHTS. Represented in Zagreb, the UN Centre for Human rights investigates and reports on specific allegations of violations of human rights. There have been no prosecutions following their investigations.
h. MAZOWIECKI. Represented in Zagreb, the Special Rapporteur also investigates and reports on specific allegations of violations of human rights. The Special Rapporteur is not established with prosecutions in mind.
i. ICRC. ICRC have a mandate to protect the rights of prisoners under the Geneva Conventions. They operate largely in Bosnia-Hercegovina, and protect minorities and refugees in emergency situations.
j. CSCE. CSCE has long term missions in Vojvodina, Sandzak, Kosovo and FYROM. These missions have a mandate to monitor the observance of human rights, with particular emphasis on ethnic minorities in those areas.
k. ECMM. ECMM operates throughout former Yugoslavia and in the neighboring states of Hungary, Bulgaria and Albania. ECMM observes and reports in detail on the observance of human rights. ECMM monitors actively promote human rights through their work with the warring parties.

PROPOSED HUMAN RIGHTS MONITOR MISSION

5. Organisation. The formation of a Human Rights Monitor Mission (HRMM) is proposed in the VOPP. It will be lead by an interim Human Rights Commissioner of international standing. Deputies will be located in sensitive areas of Bosnia-Hercegovina, particularly where ethnic cleansing has occurred.
6. Concept. The concept behind the HRMM is to establish a United Nations presence on the ground. The HRMM will submit regular reports to the Secretary General of the UN, who will in turn brief the UN Security

Council and Commission on Human Rights. While the HRMM may not transform the situation, it may have a mitigating effect.

7. Role. HRMM will bring international pressure to bear on the situation, and officials and monitors will be able to intercede with the local authorities, government and UNPROFOR in order to protect a group that seems to be in danger. They will also make it easier for people to return to their homes.

CONCLUSIONS

8. Background. Human rights continue to be abused on a massive scale in former Yugoslavia. The international community needs to take rapid action to halt this, both for the benefit of the indigenous population and within the wider context of international stability.
9. Current Position. Currently there are a large number of United Nations and other international organisations working in former Yugoslavia, many of whom have a direct mandate to protect the rights of individuals. They report what they see, and take action to promote observance of human rights.
10. HRMM. Because so many other organisations monitor human rights from different perspectives and deal with the political and military leaders of the warring parties at all levels, there is a need for coordination and a focus of effort. There are many monitors, very few investigators and no international prosecutors. There is clearly a role for HRMM in this field.
12. Effective Deterrence. One of the major reasons why the warring parties continue to ignore observance of human rights as an issue, in reality as opposed to rhetoric, is that they are confident that nothing will be done to stop them. The visible investigation and prosecution of war criminals would be an effective deterrent and would protect minorities more effectively than soldiers with no mandate to use force.
13. Security. The complete, conscious, disregard for human rights also means that investigators will be unwelcome, and will be at personal risk once their role is widely understood. After the Second World War investigators were armed and had bodyguards for exactly this reason.

RECOMMENDATIONS

14. Mandate. The HRMM should be established as soon as possible, with a clear mandate to investigate violations of human rights with a view to prosecution. The legal mechanisms must be established to allow them to do this. HRMM must have the ability to task UNCIVPOL. The HRMM should be present in all areas of former Yugoslavia where abuses of human rights have taken place.
15. The HRMM should provide the focus of expertise for investigating and prosecuting violations of human rights, using its own investigators, UNCIVPOL and by calling in teams of experts. It should use the extensive networks of monitors already present in former Yugoslavia (UNHCR, ICRC, UNCIVPOL, ECMM) to monitor and report on observance of human rights.

16. Reporting. HRMM teams should liaise with the monitoring agencies to collect and collate their information on observance of human rights. As well as being passed back to the Secretary General, this information should be used to direct the efforts of the various monitoring agencies onto problem areas as they are identified and to direct investigators.
17. ECMM Assistance. HRMM teams will have instant access to the knowledge gained by ECMM monitors chairing the joint commissions, currently the most productive forum for addressing allegations of abuses of human rights. When appropriate, HRMM should advise ECMM and others to act immediately to defuse a situation through reconciliation, rather than taking it to prosecution.
18. Judicial Support. In order to be effective, the HRMM must be backed up by a judicial system that is seen to be actually prosecuting individuals for human rights violations, although this does not have to be directly linked to the HRMM. They would be greatly assisted if UNPROFOR were given powers to step in and prevent abuses of human rights when they occur.
19. Immediate Action. A Human Rights Commissioner should be appointed and HRMM teams should be established at the level of provincial government within the VOPP, with the first three located in Mostar, Travnik and Zenica, the capitals of Provinces 8, 9 and 10, as soon as possible.
20. Composition. HRMM teams should be lead by investigating magistrates and include criminal lawyers, human rights lawyers, police criminal investigators and collators. With the addition of driver&backslash;body guards and administrators, a team could be 15 people and would also need several interpreters. With a team in each proposed Province, three teams in each of Croatia and Serbia, and a headquarters staff including forensic experts, the HRMM could be about 300 strong.
21. Security. Security for the HRMM teams, if they are going to have a worthwhile role as the link between the existing monitors and the prosecutors, will be a key issue. Security should be considered at every stage of the establishment and running of the HRMM, and teams should be co-located with the existing UN infrastructure.

Ole Brix Andersen
Deputy Head of Mission

José Cutileiro
Special Representative of the Commission on Human Rights on the Situation in Bosnia and Herzegovina and Serbia and Montenegro

Address to the Commission on Human Rights, 27 March 2003*

* *Check against delivery.*

In the interests of time, I will not rehearse in detail the issues that are addressed in my formal Report which was completed in December 2002, and in the Addendum that has been distributed. Instead, I will highlight those matters of greater significance, referring first to *Serbia and Montenegro*. Here, I must draw the Commission's attention to two new and significant developments: the adoption of the Constitutional Charter forming the "new" State Union of Serbia and Montenegro on 4 February 2003, and the tragic assassination of the Serbian Prime Minister, Zoran Djindjic, on March 12, which was followed by the Declaration of a State of Emergency in Serbia. At the time I expressed the view that the reforms, which the late Prime Minister had so vigorously and courageously pursued, should be maintained and even accelerated. I am convinced that if organized crime - with its links to past human rights violations and war crimes - is to be successfully rooted out of Serbian society, then the reformist government must be given full political, financial and other support from the international community.

The *proclamation, on 12 March 2003, of a State of Emergency within Serbia* has involved very substantial derogations from the State's human rights obligations under Article 4 of the International Covenant on Civil and Political Rights (ICCPR).

I understand fully the threat posed by organized crime to the institutions of democracy on the path of reform and I am completely supportive of the Government's efforts to deal decisively with this threat through exceptional measures. I am also satisfied that the authorities promptly informed the Secretary-General of the derogations in accordance with the ICCPR and that some suspension of normal rights will be necessary for a period of limited duration.

However, I must report also my concern that the derogations have been stated in insufficiently precise terms to admit clear application and appear to permit measures that go beyond those strictly required to meet the exigencies of the present situation. In view of indications from the authorities that the state of emergency is likely to remain until at least the end of April, I would like to see established some objective mechanisms by which the various measures taken in derogation of the ICCPR can be monitored and measured.

I am also concerned that these tragic events and the present state of emergency not be used as justification for actions that are not strictly required by the exigencies of the situation. For example, in my Report I express concern that the independence of the judiciary is being undermined by media reports implying the guilt of suspects; reports which often originate in statements from politicians or the police. I am deeply worried that this phenomenon is even more evident under the state of emergency. In addition, the measures undertaken by the authorities in the past two weeks have included the summary removal of judges and prosecutors. While judicial reform must clearly be a priority, extreme care must be exercised in the way this is executed so as not to undermine judicial independence.[†]

[†] I am grateful to the Minister of Justice of the Republic of Serbia for his prompt and substantive reply to my written enquires about the urgent changes within the judiciary of 17 March 2003.

I would like next to draw the Commission's attention to one matter - on which I have commented in earlier Reports - but warrants special mention today:

I am deeply concerned by the *lack of progress and real commitment to investigate the mass graves discovered in Serbia.* For example, the bodies of more been 700 ethnic Albanians killed in Kosovo in 1999 have been exhumed at a military/police compound in a suburb of Belgrade (Batajnica). The evidence discloses a large scale, clandestine and criminal operation and yet, during my last mission, I was again informed that not one single criminal prosecution has been initiated in almost 2 years. Various conflicting and unsatisfactory explanations were given to me and I concluded that the real problem is a lack of genuine cooperation between the institutions involved - particularly the police and the state prosecutor's office - and a lack of genuine commitment on the part of some persons in key positions, to make progress on these issues.

Turning to *Kosovo*, I must state that it is crucial that the different views on the timing and nature of Kosovo's final status should not interfere with current efforts to ensure the proper development of the protection of human rights. In my Report, I therefore welcome the "benchmarks" that the Secretary-General's Special Representative (SRSG), Michael Steiner, introduced in May 2002 (commonly called *"standards before status"*). Six (6) of the eight (8) standards are related to important human rights guarantees. Although the question of Kosovo's "final status" lies beyond my mandate, I believe, firmly, that these standards will be fundamental in defining the quality of the Rule of Law and democracy in Kosovo, whatever that final outcome may be.

Since my Report was finalized, the SRSG has introduced a further policy that will accelerate the transfer of many of his powers to the Provisional Institutions of Self-Government (PISG) by the end of 2003. I welcome the process to encourage greater responsibility and accountability of PISG but I am concerned that the "benchmarks" should remain as a credible and objective measure of the quality of the devolution process - particularly the capacity and political commitment of the Albanian majority. Although the transfer of powers implies sustainability, an injudicious application of these policies and neglect of human rights standards may lead to devolution that is premature and unsustainable.

The *human rights situation for ethnic minorities* living in Kosovo and for those displaced to other parts of Serbia and Montenegro (IDPs) is still cause for very serious concern. There have been some improvements in some areas but overall, the security situation for minority populations in Kosovo is poor, despite the presence of a large international police and a peacekeeping force. There are frequent incidents of violence, harassment and intimidation; most ethnic minorities do not enjoy freedom of movement, and encounter severe discrimination in access to public services, healthcare, employment opportunities and the enjoyment of basic property rights. For as long as this deeply unsatisfactory situation exists, displaced persons are unlikely to be able or willing to return in any significant numbers. Continued monitoring of their human rights situation is essential.

I welcome the efforts of UNMIK to increase the representation of ethnic minorities as judges and prosecutors. The process of recruitment has been extremely slow and there are still unacceptable delays within the Kosovo Assembly in the consultation process. UNMIK must intensify its efforts and the Kosovo Assembly must refrain from politicising and delaying the implementation of this crucial initiative. In the meantime the international community must continue to "second" judges from their national legal systems until such time as local judges and prosecutors have proved their ability and genuine commitment to dispense justice professionally and without discrimination. Independent monitoring and analysis will be essential in assessing compliance with the SRSG's standards in this area.

I am also concerned that due to the complexities in the applicable law, victims of human rights violations may not have adequate remedies available to them. This lack of effective legal remedies cuts across all legal and administrative activities under UNMIK and PISG jurisdiction. There is a need for continued law reform in terms of remedies, in particular measures to address discrimination on ethnic grounds that, regrettably, is systemic and systematic in Kosovo.

To sum up: for some time to come Kosovo will require permanent and detailed attention from the international community, if we want human rights to be properly upheld by the different entities currently exercising authority there.

I will turn now to *Bosnia and Herzegovina*: the problems which it faces today are direct consequences of the internal conflicts of the 1990s. To be able to progress, Bosnia and Herzegovina must deal with the legacy of the war: returnees and internally displaced persons; the question of war criminals; persons who remain unaccounted for after the war; a damaged economy; and organized crime which to a certain extent is an offshoot of war profiteering.

Implementation of property laws has progressed; Bosnia and Herzegovina has now achieved a rate of 72% repossession of pre-war property. I observe, however, that repossessions are largely technical, with property owners not actually returning to their pre-war residences. The climate of security has not been assured for returnees; 8 years after Dayton, those that choose to return to their pre-war homes face problems of threats or outright violence as well as discrimination in obtaining documentation, finding employment in a generally depressed economy, accessing health care, and access to education for their children. In some areas, separate schools for different nationalities exist despite efforts by the international community and government to come up with a joint curriculum for all schools.

Current *economic conditions* are also problematic. Unemployment rates continue to rise. The Government is in the process of drafting a development strategy, which stresses the issue of poverty and its relation to human rights, but I observe that the whole process seems woolly and unfocused.

A considerable amount of legislation, which is not always internally coherent, has gone into the statute books. Implementation, however, lags far behind.

I believe that *national war crimes prosecutions, and cases of missing and enforced "disappearances"* are a microcosm of the general situation of rule of law in the country. To date, there have been few national prosecutions in

Bosnian courts. Government officials agree that there is a lack of qualified judges to deal with domestic war crimes cases. Individuals are afraid to come forward and testify, as there is no operational system of witness protection in the country. I am particularly concerned that relatives of the missing and enforced disappeared have reported that their repeated requests for information from local authorities on the whereabouts of their loved ones have remained unanswered, and they are now reluctant to rely on national institutions. These problems also affect the prosecution of other crimes, such as trafficking in women, corruption and organized crime.

I cannot say that the Bosnian Government is entirely to blame for this situation. The country continues to be very heavily influenced and in some circumstances, controlled, by the various international organisations. There are often competing interests within the international community that inevitably cause difficulties for Bosnia and Herzegovina. This increases the inherent weaknesses of the State level government and prevents the growth of a truly representative identity. I believe that the climate has not yet been reached in which the government would be able to make fully independent decisions on vital issues of policy and for which it would have to take responsibility. In truth, it cannot yet be said that Bosnia and Herzegovina functions as an independent sovereign State.

EU CONFERENCE ON YUGOSLAVIA

Treaty Provisions for the Convention

CHAPTER 1

1. GENERAL

Article 1

1. The new relations between the republics will be based on the following:
   (a) Sovereign and independent republics with an international personality for those that wish it;
   (b) A free association of the republics with an international personality as envisaged in this Convention;
   (c) Comprehensive arrangements, including supervisory mechanisms for the protection of human rights and special status for certain groups and areas;
   (d) European involvement, where appropriate;
   (e) In the framework of a general settlement, recognition of the independence, within the existing borders, unless otherwise agreed, of those republics wishing it.
2. The republics recognize that cooperation between them and the creation of this association is part of the process of building a new Europe envisaged in the Paris Charter of November 1990, and will improve the prospects for cooperation and closer relations with the European Community. They will cooperate in the fields for which these arrangements provide and other agreed fields, without thereby precluding closer forms of cooperation in such areas between republics that so wish.

CHAPTER 2

HUMAN RIGHTS AND RIGHTS OF ETHNIC AND NATIONAL GROUPS

Article 2

A. Human Rights

1. The Republics guarantee the following human rights:
   (a) The right to life;
   (b) The right not to be subjected to torture or to inhuman or degrading treatment;
   (c) The right not to be subjected to slavery or compulsory labour;
   (d) The right to liberty;
   (e) The right to a fair and public hearing by an impartial tribunal and not to be subject to retrospective criminal proceedings;

(f) The right to respect for private and family life, the home and correspondence;
(g) The right to freedom of thought, conscience and religion;
(h) The right to freedom of expression;
(i) The right of freedom of peaceful assembly and freedom of association;
(j) The right to marry and form a family; and
(k) All the other rights envisaged in the instruments listed below,

subject only to the exceptions and restrictions set out in those instruments, and without discrimination on any ground such as sex, race, colour, language, religion, political or other opinion, national or social origin, association with a national minority, property, birth or other status.

The instruments referred to above are:

- The Universal Declaration of Human Rights, the International Covenant on Civil and Political Rights, the International Covenant on Economic, Social and Cultural Rights of the United Nations;
- The Final Act of the Conference on Security and Cooperation in Europe, the Charter of Paris for a New Europe, and the other CSCE documents relating to the human dimension, in particular the document of the Copenhagen Meeting of the Conference on the Human Dimension of the CSCE and the document of the Moscow meeting of the Conference on the Human Dimension of the CSCE;
- The Council of Europe Convention for the Protection of Human Rights and Fundamental Freedoms and the Protocols to that Convention.

B. Rights of Members of National and Ethnic Groups

2. The republics guarantee human rights as applied to national or ethnic groups, in particular, and embodied in:

- The instruments of the United Nations, CSCE and the Council of Europe referred to in paragraph 1 of this article;
- The Convention on the Elimination of Racial Discrimination, the Convention on the Prevention and Punishment of the Crime of Genocide and the Convention on the Rights of the Child of the United Nations;
- The report of the CSCE meeting of experts on national minorities held at Geneva.

In giving effect to this Convention, they shall also take appropriate account of:

- Proposals for a United Nations declaration of the rights of persons of national, ethnic and linguistic minorities;
- The proposal for a convention for the protection of minorities of the European commission for democracy and law in the framework of the Council of Europe.

3. The republics shall guarantee to persons belonging to a national or ethnic group, not forming a majority in the area where they live, the following rights:

- The principle of non-discrimination as set out in the legal instruments mentioned in paragraph 2 of this article;
- All cultural rights as set out in the instruments mentioned in paragraph 2 of this article, in particular the right to identity, culture, religion, use of language and alphabet both in public and private, and education;
- Protection of equal participation in public affairs such as the exercise of political and economic freedoms, in the social sphere, in access to the media and in the field of education and cultural affairs generally;
- The right to decide to which national or ethnic group he or she wishes to belong, and to exercise any rights pertaining to this choice as an individual or in association with others. This will particularly apply in the case of marriage between persons of different national or ethnic groups. Those persons of the same national or ethnic group living distant from others of the same origin, for example, in isolated villages, shall be granted self-administration, to the extent that it is practicable.

The above principles shall also apply in areas where members of the main national or ethnic group of a republic are numerically inferior to one or more other national or ethnic groups in that area.

4. The republics shall guarantee to persons belonging to a national or ethnic group forming a substantial part of the population in the area where they live but not forming a majority, in addition to the rights set out in paragraph 3 of this article, a general right of participation of members of this group in public affairs. On the level of the government of the republic, they must be able to participate in decision-making by the central government concerning their affairs.

C. Special Status

5. In addition, areas in which persons belonging to a national or ethnic group form a majority, shall enjoy a special status of autonomy.
   Such a status will provide for:

   (a) The right to have and show the national emblems of that group;
   (b) The right to a second nationality for members of that group in addition to the nationality of the republic;
   (c) An educational system which respects the values and needs of that group;
   (d) (i) A legislative body,
   (ii) An administrative structure, including a regional police force,
   (iii) And a judiciary

responsible for matters concerning the area, which reflects the composition of the population of the area;

   (e) Provisions for appropriate international monitoring.

   These areas are listed in annex …

5A Such areas, unless they are defined in part by an international frontier with a State not party to this Convention, shall be permanently demilitarized and no military forces, exercises or activities on land or in the air shall be permitted in those areas.

5B (a) The republics shall provide for international monitoring of the implementation of the special status of autonomy. To this end, they shall conclude agreements which would provide for a permanent international body to monitor implementation of this paragraph.

(b) The monitoring missions thus established shall:

- Report to the republics in question as well as to the other parties to the agreement, and
- As appropriate formulate recommendations on the implementation of the special status.

(c) The republics shall give effect to such recommendations through legislation or otherwise. In case of dispute, the Court of Human Rights shall be requested to give its decision.

6. Without prejudice to the implementation of the arrangements set forth in this paragraph, the republics shall apply fully and in good faith the provisions existing prior to 1990 for autonomous provinces.

D. General Provisions

7. Persons belonging to a national or ethnic group, in exercising their rights, respect the rights of the majority and of persons belonging to other groups.
8. The republics should jointly or individually as the case may be, become parties to international instruments in the field of human rights, including related complaint procedures.
9. The republics shall provide, by legislation and through national institutions, in respect of the rights referred to in this article, full implementation of the rights and an effective remedy for breaches of any of those rights.
10. As none of the republics will have an ethnically homogeneous population, they shall cooperate and consult one another directly or through a mixed commission in respect of matters dealt with in paragraphs 3 to 5 of this article.

CHAPTER 3

OTHER AREAS OF COOPERATION

Article 3

A. Economic Relations

1. The republics recognize their interest in establishing appropriate measures for economic cooperation among themselves.
2. The republics shall base their policies on the principles of market economy, private property and free enterprise, and openness to world trade.
3. The republics hereby establish between themselves a customs union, in order to maintain a common internal market, within which goods shall

move without either tariff barriers or quantitative restrictions. The customs union shall have a common external tariff, a common external trade policy and arrangements for sharing customs receipts. Subject to any decision by the Council of Ministers for Economic Cooperation (in this part A referred to as "the Council") the common external tariff shall be that applied for imports into Yugoslavia at 1 July 1991, and the external trade policy shall include the continued implementation of external regimes and external agreements as applied by Yugoslavia at 1 July 1991. Customs receipt shall be shared in accordance with the provisions of annex ...

4. The republics shall cooperate through the Council to limit the adverse effects of other obstacles impeding the free movement of goods, such as technical standards, subsidies and regulations affecting trade, by taking flanking measures, such as sharing information, concerting policy objectives and, if necessary, harmonizing rules and regulations which distort competition.
5. The republics shall cooperate and, subject to any decision of the Council or the Council for Transport, shall maintain existing arrangements, in the fields of transport and infrastructure. The Council shall take measures to maintain competition, especially for the protection of the common internal market, and the freedom to supply services.
6. Rights of establishment and freedom to provide services shall be maintained in particular for the professions, where they exist at present.
7. The republics shall cooperate, through the Council for the Environment, for the protection of the environment.
8. The republics shall cooperate in monetary matters with a view to maintaining or achieving monetary stability and the highest possible degree of currency convertibility. As a minimum, in the absence of a common currency and currency convertibility, they shall consider, for their mutual transactions, the establishment of a common payments system, based upon a clearing mechanism and a reserve fund.
9. This article shall be reviewed by the republics at the end of a period of five years from the entry into force of this Convention.

Article 4

B. Foreign Affairs and Security

1. The republics shall consult on all matters of common interest in the areas of foreign affairs and security, and shall cooperate where they can agree on common positions, including the possibility of common representation in specific areas agreed between them.
2. Relations between the republics, individually or jointly, shall be based on CSCE commitments. They may decide to apply between themselves the practices and procedures agreed in the CSCE, among others.
3. The republics shall decide for themselves what armed forces to have or allow on their territory and what cooperative defence arrangements to have among themselves.

Article 5

C. Legal Cooperation

1. The republics shall consult and cooperate in the field of legal cooperation, such as control of international crime, terrorism and drug trafficking, in accordance with European and international standards, such as those developed in the Council of Europe and the United Nations, and shall seek, individually or jointly, to become parties to international conventions in these matters.
2. In the field of international crime, terrorism and drug trafficking, the law enforcement authorities of the republics, including the police forces shall estabish and maintain close links and cooperation with a view to the effective prevention and punishment of these crimes.

CHAPTER 4

INSTITUTIONS

Article 6

The Republics establish hereby the institutions for which this chapter provides in order to give effect to their cooperation under this Convention. They may establish additional institutions to the extent that they agree to further cooperation in these or other fields.

Article 7

A. Human Rights

1. A Court of Human Rights is established by this Convention. It shall have jurisdiction within the republics to consider appeals from courts in the republics involving questions dealt with in articles 2.1 to 2.5 of this Convention. The Court shall include members from all the republics. The Statute of the Court is set set out in annex …
2. Mixed commissions shall be established under this Convention by any republic that jointly decides to do so, for the purpose of making recommendations or taking decisions on matters entrusted to them by the republics concerned, where such mixed commissions might assist in avoiding or dealing with disputes concerning human rights and the rights of ethnic or national groups and areas having special status. Subject to the decision by which they are established, annex … shall apply to the mixed commissions.
3. The Court of Human Rights and, if the decision establishing them so provides, the Mixed Commissions for which this part provides, shall include the participation of persons drawn from European States other than the republics, and the republics hereby request the States members of the European Community to nominate distinguished jurists or other appropriately qualified persons to participate in the work of these institutions.

Article 8

B. Economic Relations

1. The republics hereby establish a Council for Economic Cooperation, which shall meet every month, unless otherwise agreed.
2. Meetings of the Council shall be prepared by a Committee of Senior Officials from each republic, meeting weekly. Specialized standing committees will be established to prepare proposals to the Council.
3. An Executive Committee, headed by a Secretary General appointed for four years and assisted by a permanent secretariat, shall make recommendations, monitor decisions and service meetings.
4. In external relations on matters covered by agreed arrangements or policies in the internal market, customs union or economic and monetary cooperation, the Council shall, where necessary, agree on common positions for the conduct of negotiations with third countries including the making of international agreements with States and international organizations. In such negotiations it shall decide whether to be represented by the Presidency or the Secretary General of the Executive Committee.
5. The republics hereby establish:

   (a) A Council for Transport, which shall consider transport questions and which shall meet once every three months unless otherwise agreed;
   (b) A Board for Transport consisting of one member and one alternate from each republic which shall be responsible, under the Council for Transport, for the proper functioning from day to day of railways, roads and other transport operations between the republics.

6. The republics hereby establish:

   (a) A Council for Energy which shall consider energy questions and which shall meet once every three months, unless otherwise agreed;
   (b) A Board for Energy consisting of one member and one alternate from each republic which shall be responsible, under the Council for Energy, for the proper functioning from day to day of pipelines, electricity grids and other arrangements concerning energy between the republics.

7. The republics hereby establish a Council for the Environment which shall consider questions of the environment and which shall meet once every three months unless otherwise agreed.
8. The Councils established under this article shall consist of one Minister from each republic and shall take decisions by consensus, unless otherwise agreed.

Article 9

C. Political and Security Cooperation

1. The republics hereby establish a Council for Political and Security Cooperation of Foreign Ministers for the purpose of the cooperation

envisaged in articles 4.1 to 3. It shall take decisions by consensus. It shall meet monthly, unless otherwise agreed.
2. When agreement on a common approach can be reached by all or some republics, those republics shall be guided by it.
3. When common positions can be reached by consensus, a decision shall be taken whether to invite the President of one of the republics to speak or act for the association.
4. The Council may discuss any security matters raised by any republic. The Concil may decide by consensus on defence cooperation.
5. Meetings of the Council shall be prepared by senior officials from Foreign Ministries.

Article 10

D. Legal Cooperation

1. The republics shall establish a Council for Legal Cooperation for the purpose of cooperation as envisaged in article 5. It shall take decisions by consensus. It will meet every six months, unless otherwise agreed.
2. The Council may discuss any matters raised by any republic within the specific fields expressly mentioned in article 5 and it may discuss any other topic to which it decides to extend its discussion.
3. Meetings of the Council shall be prepared by senior officials from appropriate Ministries.

Article 10A

The Presidency of the Councils for which Chapter 3 provides shall be held for a term of six months by each member of the Council in turn.

Article 11

E. Parliamentary Body

The republics shall consider the establishment of a parliamentary body to discuss matters arising out of these arrangements.

Article 12

F. Arbitration

Any dispute between republics concerning the implementation or application of this Convention shall be subject to binding arbitration under procedures which ensure that it shall not be obstructed. Arbitration may be initiated at the request of any Republic which considers that another republic is in breach of any of its obligations. Annex … shall apply to such arbitrations.

Article 13

G. Location of Institutions

The seat of the institutions for which provision is made by this Convention shall be located in different republics.

HUMAN RIGHTS CHAMBER
FOR BOSNIA AND HERZEGOVINA

DOM ZA LJUDSKA PRAVA
ZA BOSNU I HERCEGOVINU

Opinion of the Human Rights Chamber for Bosnia and Herzegovina on the Proposal of the International Community to Close the Human Rights Chamber on 31 December 2003

The Office of the High Representative (OHR) will present to the Peace Implementation Council (PIC) meeting on Thursday, 12 June 2003 in Brussels a proposed "Agreement on Annex 6 to the General Framework Agreement for Peace in Bosnia and Herzegovina" accompanied by a "transfer" document setting forth a way to implement the Agreement. The PIC will be invited to endorse the proposal. The Agreement in essence provides for the Human Rights Chamber for Bosnia and Herzegovina to stop receiving new applications on 31 July 2003, to cease functioning on 31 December 2003 and for its remaining pending cases at that time to be transferred to the Constitutional Court of Bosnia and Herzegovina.

The Chamber has been requested by OHR to give its opinion on this proposal. For the reasons set forth in the following paragraphs, the Chamber is of the opinion that the adoption of this proposal will violate the Constitution of Bosnia and Herzegovina (BiH), contradicts basic principles of the Dayton Peace Agreement (DPA), is based on false assumptions, is legally unsound and also shortsighted.

1. The Human Rights Commission for Bosnia and Herzegovina, provided for in Article II(1) of the Constitution of BiH and in Article II of Annex 6 of the DPA ("Agreement on Human Rights") in order to "ensure the highest level of internationally recognised human rights and fundamental freedoms", was established in early 1996 as a permanent institution. One of the basic aims of the DPA is to assist the people of BiH in achieving a sustainable peace by establishing and maintaining professional institutions for the protection of human rights. Contrary to a view held by the present US administration and the EC delegation in BiH, the mandate of the Commission is not of a transitional nature, but only its international component. Five years after the DPA entered into force, i.e. on 14 December 2000, "the responsibility for the continued operation of the Commission" should have been transferred from the Parties of Annex 6 (the State of BiH and its two Entities) to the institutions of BiH (Article XIV of Annex 6). Members appointed to the Chamber after the transfer should, as provided in Article VII(4) of Annex 6, be appointed by the Presidency of BiH. The transfer was achieved for one part of the Commission, the Human Rights Ombudsman for BiH, whereas the transitional period of the other part of the Commission, the Human Rights Chamber for BiH, as a quasi-international court with 8 international and 6 national judges, was extended until the end of 2003. The transfer of the Chamber to a permanent domestic human rights court as an institution of the State of BiH, whether in its present composition or restructured, should therefore take place as of 1

January 2004. The proposal to be placed before the PIC, notwithstanding the word "transfer" in its title, does not constitute a transfer as envisioned in Article XIV of Annex 6 because the jurisdiction and the competencies of the Chamber are not transferred to the institutions of BiH but just eliminated. This solution, i.e. the simple abolition of the Chamber, violates not only Article XIV of Annex 6, but also Articles II(1) and X(2) of the Constitution of BiH.

2. The DPA provides a perfect model for the preparation of states in transition towards future membership in the Council of Europe. First of all, the European Convention on Human Rights (ECHR) was made directly applicable under domestic law with priority over all other law (Article II(2) of the Constitution) some 7 years before BiH ratified the ECHR. Secondly, a special human rights court with the participation of international judges, appointed by the Committee of Ministers of the Council of Europe, was established in order to apply the ECHR and to develop a specific Bosnian case-law based on the jurisprudence of the European Court of Human Rights. This had the effect of not only ensuring a high standard of human rights protection in a post-conflict society, but also of familiarising judges, lawyers and other members of the legal community in BiH with European (and international) human rights standards. It was envisaged that the "nationalisation" of the Chamber would take place about the same time as the ratification of the ECHR, which made BiH subject to the jurisdiction of the European Court of Human Rights. As from this time, the Chamber would function as the highest domestic court for the protection of human rights and, consequently, as the final domestic remedy to be exhausted before lodging an application to the Strasbourg Court. The existence of such a special and experienced human rights court would be the best guarantee for screening human rights cases at the domestic level and, thereby, preventing the European Court of Human Rights to be flooded with individual complaints from new member States.
3. The recent experience of the European Court of Human Rights proves that such an effective screening body has not been established in most of the other new member States. As a consequence, the Strasbourg Court has in recent years been overburdened by large numbers of applications from Poland, the Russian Federation and other Central and Eastern European States. Only five years after the major reform brought about by the 11th Additional Protocol to the ECHR, which established a full-time professional Court in 1998, this Court is in fact unable to deal with its rapidly growing case-load. The Committee of Ministers of the Council of Europe, therefore, is presently contemplating far-reaching reform proposals to reduce the workload of the Court, which include the recommendation to member States, among them Western European countries where the judiciary is highly developed, to improve the national mechanisms for the protection of ECHR rights (see the Interim Report of the Steering Committee for Human Rights to the Committee of Ministers of the Council of Europe entitled "Guaranteeing the long-term effectiveness of the European Court of Human Rights", CM(2002) 146 of 18 October 2002). At exactly the same

time, the International Community in BiH proposes to abolish the only effective and specialised judicial body for the protection of human rights in BiH. This makes no sense. Thanks to the Chamber, only very few cases from BiH have so far reached the Strasbourg Court. With the abolition of the Chamber, the individual complaints to Strasbourg will no doubt drastically increase, which cannot be in the interest of human rights protection in BiH or of the member States of the Council of Europe.

4. The decision of the International Community to abolish the Chamber is based on the assumption that the Constitutional Court of BiH (CC) can take over most of the present and future cases of the Chamber. This assumption is legally incorrect and practically unrealistic. The competencies of the CC are defined in Article VI(3) of the Constitution and cannot be extended without an amendment of the Constitution. The main competencies of the CC are to decide on constitutional disputes between the entities or between the political institutions of BiH. In addition, it has appellate jurisdiction over constitutional issues (including human rights as defined in the Constitution) arising out of a judgment of any other court in BiH. The competence of the Chamber is defined in Annex 6 in totally different terms. It has a general competence to decide on violations of the ECHR by the State of BiH, the RS, the Federation of BiH or any of their organs, not just the courts. Some of the human rights violations in BiH arise out of a judgment of a court, and the CC has in the past decided in a few cases about a violation of the ECHR by the courts. Similarly, the Chamber is only competent to decide cases in which the applicants have exhausted effective domestic remedies. But in many cases a violation is found because the courts, e.g., do not decide a case or cannot decide because the human rights violation arises from an action or omission of a political, administrative or legislative body in this country which cannot be appealed to the courts. Furthermore, in addition to finding violations of the ECHR, the Chamber has a special mandate to decide about alleged or apparent discrimination in the enjoyment of any of the rights (including economic, social and cultural rights or rights of minorities) provided for in the ECHR and 15 additional European and international treaties listed in the Appendix to Annex 6. In view of the national, religious and social tensions in BiH, this competence is particularly important, and the Chamber has in many cases found systematic discrimination in the enjoyment of the rights to work, housing, property, religion, social security, access to justice and other fields. Finally, the Chamber has very broad powers, in case it finds a violation of the ECHR or discrimination, to order the respondent Parties to take appropriate steps to remedy such violation. The Chamber has issued a wide variety of orders, including compensation, which the CC could not take, as its judgments in individual cases (appellate jurisdiction) are not directed at the State of BiH or its Entities.
5. In addition to these legal obstacles, the CC, which until now has only met on a part-time basis and which has to decide about many other highly complex constitutional disputes, is simply not in a position to take over the present or future case-load of the Chamber. At present, there are more

than 10,000 cases pending before the Chamber, and it currently receives around 200 new applications each month. With the gradual improvement of the quality of the ordinary courts, the police and the rule of law in general, the number of new applications will hopefully decrease in the future. But the high number of individual complaints, many of which turn out to be justified, is the best indicator for the continuing need for an effective specialised human rights court. Realistically speaking, only a very small percentage of the cases presently brought before the Chamber will be taken care of by other courts, above all the CC and the European Court of Human Rights. As a consequence, the comparatively high level of human rights protection in BiH, one of the major achievements of the DPA, will seriously suffer with the dissolution of the Chamber.

6. Sound legal reasoning and due consideration of the practical aspects should be the basis on which a decision should be made about the future of the Human Rights Chamber. Should the Agreement be adopted, however, and the "transfer" take place in accordance with the current proposal, the Chamber will cooperate to the extent appropriate with its status as an independent and impartial tribunal. The Chamber will endeavour to solve as many cases as possible within the time remaining in its mandate. At the same time it will concentrate on ensuring that the remaining cases it resolves will have the greatest impact on the protection of human rights in Bosnia and Herzegovina.

Adopted by the Human Rights Chamber for Bosnia and Herzegovina in Sarajevo on 5 June 2003 by Mme. Picard, Messrs. Tadi}, Rauschning, Bali}, Aybay, Juka, Möller, Dekovi}, Grasso, Paji}, Nowak, Popovi}, Masenko-Mavi and Grotrian.

WORKING GROUP ON HUMAN RIGHTS ISSUES, ZAGREB, 31 JANUARY 1995 MAIN CONCLUSIONS OF THE MEETING

The Head of Civil Affairs chaired a meeting of the Working Group on Human Rights Issues in Zagreb on 31 January 1995. Participants included the Centre for Human Rights, ICRC, UNHCR and CIVPOL.

Mr. Moussalli gave a brief account of the consultations held in Geneva on 23 and 24 January 1995 with the High Commissioner for Human Rights and his colleagues, and UNHCR. He explained that Mr. Ayala Lasso took a personal interest in the monitoring of human rights in the former Yugoslavia, and expressed a desire to be particularly active in Bosnia and Herzegovina. He further explained that the Centre for Human Rights was unfortunately constrained by its lack of resources. Among the ideas discussed in Geneva was the appointment in Zagreb of a senior representative of the High Commissioner for Human Rights. A high-level meeting will be held in Geneva on 3 February 1995 to discuss further those issues.

The discussion which followed focused on methods of redress available to enhance a human rights monitoring. HCA noted the already existing field operation of the Centre for Human Rights, serving the Special Rapporteur, and the International Tribunal on War Crimes. Both organizations will be represented at the next Geneva meeting.

The UNHCR representative recalled the recent nomination by the OSCE of the three Ombudsmen in Sarajevo. It was noted, however, that they would have no impact in Bosnian Serb-held territories, as the Ombudsmen are appointed in the frame-work of the Federation Constitution. UNHCR suggested that the JCPC (Joint Commission Policy Committee), might serve as a useful mechanism for seeking redress, however, noted that its influence would also be limited.

It was noted that the Central Joint Commission and its four Regional Joint Commissions (Bihac, Gorni Vakuf, Tuzla and Sarajevo), established pursuant to the Cessation of Hostilities Agreement, could offer a forum in which to raise human rights concerns with the parties. It was also noted that a consultative committee had been established by the protocol of 23 January 1995 to arbitrate between the parties in the event of dispute.

UNHCR suggested promotion of local human rights organisations, especially in Bosnian Serb-held territory and that judges and courts could be helped by international jurists groups like the International Commission of Jurists in Geneva.

The HCA welcomed the contributions of the ICRC, UNHCR, and the Centre for Human Rights to the guidelines for field staff and suggested that a thorough review of the various agencies mandates be undertaken to identify areas of overlap or omission.

28 February 1995 was chosen as the date for a training session on human rights, to be organized by UNPROFOR with the assistance of the agencies.

Participants would include 10 Civil Affairs Officers, 10 CIVPOL monitors, 5 staff members of UNHCR and 5 ICRC staff members.

It was decided that the booklets "Human Rights:Questions and Answers" and the "Universal Declaration of Human Rights" should be widely disseminated throughout the mission area, in both English and the local languages.

Marc Van Wynsberghe
Civil Affairs Officer

31 January 1995

INTERAGENCY TRAINING SESSION

Human Rights Monitoring in the Former Yugoslavia

Participants:	Field staff of UNPROFOR, UNHCR, ICRC with the assistance of the UN Centre for Human Rights
Venue:	Building N, UNPROFOR THQ, Zagreb
Date:	Tuesday, 28 February 1995

Tentative Programme

08:45	Welcoming of participants – HCA
09:00	"Overview on International Humanitarian law and Human Rights" – UN Centre for Human Rights
09:30	"Human Rights & Protection of Minorities" – Case Study, UNHCR
10:00	Group Discussion
11:00	Coffee Break
11:15	"Human Rights & Police Monitoring" – Case Study, UNPROFOR
11:45	Group Discussion
13:00	Lunch
14:00	"Working obligations & Arbitrary detention" – Case Study, ICRC
14:30	Group Discussion
15:30	"Mechanism for redress of HR abuses" – Case Study, UN Centre for Human Rights
16:00	Group Discussion
17:00	Concluding Remarks – HCA
17:30	END

BIBLIOGRAPHY

Martti Ahtisaari, by F.P. Miller et.al., 2010.

Anonymous, Human Rights in Peace Negotiations, 18 Human Rights Quarterly, 1996, 249.

C. Bell, Peace Agreements and Human Rights. Cambridge, Cambridge University Press, 2004.

——, On the Law of Peace: Peace Agreements and the Lex Pacificatoria. Cambridge, Cambridge University Press, 2008.

C. Bildt, Peace Journey. The Struggle for Peace in Bosnia. London, Weidenfeld and Nicolson, 1998.

R. Caplan, Europe and the Recognition of New States in Yugoslavia, 2005.

J. Cutileiro, Vida e Morte dos Outros - A communidade internacional e o fin da Jugoslavia. Lisboa, Imprensa de Ciencias Sociais, 2003. (Life and death of others. The International Community and the end of Yugoslavia. - English version available at the Princeton University Library.)

F. Gaer, UN-Anonymous, Reflection on Human Rights in Peace Negotiations, 19 Human Rights Quarterly, 1997, 1.

M. Goulding, Peacemonger, London, John Murray, 2002.

R. Holbrook, To End a War. New York, Random House, 1998.

Human Rights Chamber of Bosnia and Herzegovina. Digest. Decisions on Admissibility and Merits, 1996 - 2002. With an Introduction by Manfred Nowak. Kehl/Strasbourg, Engel Publisher, 2003.

K. Kenny, Formal and Informal Innovations in the United Nations Protection of Human Rights: The Special Rapporteur on the Former Yugoslavia, 48 Austrian Journal of Public International Law, 1995, p. 19.

Lawyers Committee for Human Rights, Refugee Project. Discussion Paper: Protection by Presence. The Limits of United Nations Peacekeeping Activities in Croatia, 1993.

T. Mazowiecki, Reports to the UN Commission on Human Rights and the UN General Assembly, 1992 - 1995.

G. Nystuen, Achieving Peace or Protecting Human Rights? Conflict between Norms Regarding Ethnic Discrimination in the Dayton Peace Accords. Nijhoffs, 2005.

M. O'Flaherty and G. Gisvold (Eds.), Post-War Protection of Human Rights in Bosnia and Herzegovina. The Hague, Martinus Nijhoff, 1998.

S. Ogata, The Turbulent Decade. Confronting the Refugee Crises of the 1990s. New York, W.W. Norton (2005).

D. Owen, Balkan Odyssey. Victor Gollancz, 1995.

J. Pettifer and M. Vickers, The Albanian Question. Reshaping the Balkans. London, I.B. Tauris, 2007.

J. Phillips, Macedonia. Warlords and Rebels in the Balkans. London, I.B. Tauris, 2004.

B.G. Ramcharan (Ed.), The International Conference on the Former Yugoslavia. Official Papers. Martinus Nijhoff, 1997. 2 Vols.

Refugee Policy Group, Humanitarian Action in the Former Yugoslavia.The UN's Role, 1991–1993. RPG, Washington, DC.

B. de Rossanet, Peacemaking and Peacekeeping in Yugoslavia. Nijhoffs, 1995.

——, War and Peace in the Former Yugoslavia. Nijhoffs, 1997.

J.R. Schindler, Unholy Terror. St Paul, Minnesota, Zenith Press, 2007.

M. Rose, Fighting for Peace. London, The Harvill Press, 1998.

G. Salvesen, Thorvald's Verden. Chr. Schibsteda Forlag A/S, Oslo, 1996.

R. Smith, The Utility of Force: The Art of War in the Modern World, 2008.

H. Sokalski, An Ounce of Prevention: Macedonia and the UN Experience in Preventive Diplomacy. Washington, D.C. US Institute for Peace, 2003.

T. Stoltenberg, De tusen dagen: Fredsmedlere pa Balkan, 1996. (Memoirs on his efforts as a peacemaker and peacekeeper in the Balkans).

P.C. Szasz, The Protection of Human Rights Through the Dayton/Paris Peace Agreement on Bosnia, 90 AJIL (1996), 301.

——, Protecting Human and Minority Rights in Bosnia: A Documentary Survewy of International Proposals. 25 California Western International Law Journal, No. 2, Spring, 1995, pp. 237 – 310.

S. Touval, Mediation in the Yugoslav Wars. The Critical Years, 1990 – 1995. London, Palgrave, 2002.

C. Vance, Hard Choices. Critical Years in American Foreign Policy, 1983.

R. Wieruszewski, International Response to Human Rights Violations in the Territory of the Former Yugoslavia, Polish Yearbook of International Law, 1992.

A. William, Preventing War: The UN and Macedonia. (Lanham, MD: Rowman &Littlefield, 2000).

S. Woodward, Balkan Tragedy, Washington DC, Brookings, 1995.

A. de Zayas, "The Kalshoven Commission", Leiden Journal of International Law, vol. 6, April 1993, pp. 131-134.

INDEX

www.ingramcontent.com/pod-product-compliance
Lightning Source LLC
LaVergne TN
LVHW081514300926
849161LV00006B/1178